# THE QUEST FOR LE CARRÉ

# THE QUEST
# FOR LE CARRÉ

edited by
## Alan Bold

VISION PRESS · LONDON
ST. MARTIN'S PRESS · NEW YORK

Vision Press Ltd.
Fulham Wharf
Townmead Road
London SW6 2SB

and

St. Martin's Press, Inc.
175 Fifth Avenue
New York, N.Y. 10010

ISBN (UK) 0 85478 266 9
ISBN (US) 0 312 02419 3

Library of Congress Cataloging-in-Publication Data

The Quest for le Carré.
  (Critical studies)
    1. Le Carré, John, 1931–     —Criticism and
interpretation.   2. Spy stories, English—History
and criticism.   I. Bold, Alan Norman, 1943–
II. Series: Critical Studies series.
PR6062. E33Z83     1988     823'.914          88-18208
ISBN 0-312-02419-3 (St. Martin's Press)

Printed and bound in Great Britain at
The University Printing House, Oxford.
Phototypeset by Galleon Photosetting,
Ipswich, Suffolk.
MCMLXXXVIII

# Contents

|  |  | page |
|---|---|---|
| | Acknowledgements | 7 |
| | Introduction by *Alan Bold* | 9 |
| *1* | A Perfect Spy: A Personal Reminiscence by *Vivian Green* | 25 |
| *2* | The Clues of the Great Tradition by *Owen Dudley Edwards* | 41 |
| *3* | Women's Place in John le Carré's Man's World by *Margaret Moan Rowe* | 69 |
| *4* | Le Carré and the Idea of Espionage by *Trevor Royle* | 87 |
| *5* | Information, Power and the Reader: Textual Strategies in le Carré by *Stewart Crehan* | 103 |
| *6* | *The Little Drummer Girl*: An Interview with John le Carré by *Melvyn Bragg* | 129 |
| *7* | The Hippocratic Smile: Le Carré and Detection by *Glenn W. Most* | 144 |
| *8* | Le Carré: Faith and Dreams by *Philip O'Neill* | 169 |
| *9* | The Writing on the Igloo Walls: Narrative Technique in *The Spy Who Came in from the Cold* by *Robert Giddings* | 188 |
| | Notes on Contributors | 211 |
| | Index | 215 |

# Acknowledgements

Quotations from the works of John le Carré are reprinted by permission of John Farquharson Ltd., on behalf of John le Carré: the kind co-operation of George Greenfield, director of John Farquharson Ltd., is acknowledged.

The edited extract from Melvyn Bragg's interview with John le Carré—first transmitted on the I.T.V. network on 27 March 1983—is published by permission of The South Bank Show, London Weekend Television plc.

'The Hippocratic Smile', which originally appeared in *The Poetics of Murder* (New York: Harcourt Brace Jovanovich, 1983), edited by Glenn W. Most and William W. Stowe, is reprinted by permission of Glenn W. Most.

# Introduction

## by ALAN BOLD

John le Carré is that rarity, a bestselling novelist who has also won acclaim for the aesthetic quality of his writing: television and film versions of his novels have made him a household name; literary critics have seen in his work a profound analysis of the moral relativism of the western world. Graham Greene and Hemingway, both influences on le Carré's prose style, enjoyed comparable commercial and critical success but the combination eluded, to his chagrin, Somerset Maugham. Significantly, le Carré feels that Maugham, involved with the Secret Service during the First World War, was a 'feeble [agent], which did not prevent him from dramatizing himself as the seen-it-all observer of the great game'.[1] Le Carré himself referees the great game with immense skill in his writing, always alert to the foul play attempted by both sides—but then, circumstantial and internal textual evidence suggests, he has been a player in his time, and not a feeble one. Just possibly, like his fictional counterpart Magnus Pym, in *A Perfect Spy* (1986), he was once 'king-pin of the Czecho operation and of several other little shows in Eastern Europe besides'.[2] Le Carré is not saying; apart from a few hints he lets his fiction speak for itself and it deals in dissimulation.

To the general public le Carré is synonymous with spying though his work is more varied than his popular reputation, as the creator of George Smiley, indicates. His eleven novels include a brilliant work of detection (*A Murder of Quality*), a melancholy account of the cynical standards of cold warriors (*The Spy Who Came in from the Cold*), an experimental portrait of an artist (*The Naïve and Sentimental Lover*), a chilling portrayal of political rôle-playing (*The Little Drummer Girl*), an autobiographical fiction (*A Perfect Spy*). Though the atmospheric world of

9

le Carré is often bleak, his books are suffused with a subtle sense of humour. In *Smiley's People* (1980) the ritual of making oneself inconspicuous is made ridiculous by its ostentatious routine:

> Inside the main cabin of the steamer, the boy looked a nobody. He kept his eyes lowered; *avoid eye contact*, the General had ordered. . . . He waited awkwardly, trying to look calm. . . . Clumsily, the boy groped his way between the seats, making for the stern. . . . They suspect me of being a terrorist, thought the boy. There was engine oil on his hands and he wished he'd washed it off. Perhaps it's on my face as well. *Be blank*, the General had said. *Efface yourself. Neither smile nor frown. Be normal.* . . . He felt a fool. The oranges were too conspicuous by far. Why on earth should an unshaven young man in a track suit be carrying a basket of oranges and yesterday's newspaper? The whole boat must have noticed him![3]

Le Carré is acutely conscious of the absurd behaviour that passes as normal in the secret world. Later in the same novel, Smiley has a large whisky in a pub called—wait for it—the Sherlock Holmes.[4]

By any standards, secret or otherwise, le Carré has had a spectacular career. Not only is he one of the most marketable novelists of his, or any other, time, but, for a man who shuns personal publicity almost as much as Graham Greene, he has become an obsession of the media. Four of his novels have been turned into feature films—*The Spy Who Came in from the Cold* in 1965, *Call for the Dead* (as *The Deadly Affair*) in 1966, *The Looking-Glass War* in 1969, *The Little Drummer Girl* in 1984—and two (*Tinker Tailor* in 1979 and *Smiley's People* in 1981) have been screened as series by B.B.C. Television. He has been interviewed in the popular and quality press, pilloried by *Private Eye* (who disapproved of the reverential reviews of *The Little Drummer Girl*), parodied by Tom Stoppard (whose radio play *The Dog It Was That Died* hilariously recreates the intellectual confusion of double agents), patronized by some unlikely people. Kim Philby, the most celebrated of Soviet agents, found *The Spy Who Came in from the Cold* (1963) sophisticated, if basically implausible. Margaret Thatcher, possibly unaware that le Carré is a professed socialist, thinks le Carré compulsive reading and names *The Little Drummer Girl* (1983) as her favourite spy novel.

One of the reasons for le Carré's unshakeable status as the

literary master of espionage is his apparent ability to anticipate the headlines. *Tinker Tailor* was serialized by the B.B.C. in the same year that Andrew Boyle's *The Climate of Treason* (1979) drew attention to a Fourth Man in the Burgess–Maclean–Philby spy ring. While Smiley (played to perfection by Alec Guinness) unmasked the fictional mole 'Gerald' as Bill Haydon, Boyle provided details about the real mole he code-named 'Maurice'. *Private Eye* drew the obvious conclusion and identified 'Maurice' as Sir Anthony Blunt, former Surveyor of the Royal Pictures and still Adviser of the Queen's Pictures and Drawings. On 15 November 1979 Prime Minister Thatcher made a statement in the House of Commons, naming Blunt as a man who had recruited for the Russians in the 1930s and passed information to them during the Second World War. The expanded edition of *The Climate of Treason* declared that 'the real-life Blunt story put into the shade John le Carré's television fiction *Tinker Tailor Soldier Spy*.'[5] Not so: the public were even more convinced that le Carré was a novelist who made fiction from fact, who had impeccable inside information about espionage.

There is an amusing confirmation of the public perception of le Carré as the supreme authority on spies and spying. In 1987 *Spycatcher*, a book banned by the British government, was published in the U.S.A. Written by Peter Wright, a former Assistant Director of MI5, it told of covert plans to assassinate Nasser and to overthrow the Wilson government. As soon as the book was available in the U.S.A. transatlantic travellers bought copies and brought them back to Britain with impunity, thus increasing the embarrassment of a government that had taken legal steps to prevent newspapers from carrying extracts of Wright's book. Both the B.B.C. and I.T.N. reporters were on hand to record the responses of those who might have enjoyed an in-flight perusal of *Spycatcher*. The best comment came from the individual who, when asked about *Spycatcher*, enquired 'Is it the latest le Carré?' Say the word 'spy' and the public will connect it with the name of le Carré.


Born David John Moore Cornwell in Poole, Dorset, in 1931, he had a difficult, not to say painfully complicated, childhood. When he was 6 his mother abandoned the family—'just sort of vanished'[6]—leaving him with deep feelings of guilt. The preparatory schoolboy Bill Roach, in *Tinker Tailor*, is partly made in the image of young David Cornwell:

> Coming from a broken home Roach was also a natural watcher. . . . In work and play he considered himself seriously inadequate. . . . He blamed himself very much for these shortcomings but most of all he blamed himself for the break-up of his parents' marriage, which he should have seen coming and taken steps to prevent. He even wondered whether he was more directly responsible, whether for instance he was abnormally wicked or divisive or slothful, and that his bad character had wrought the rift.[7]

Seeking a refuge from his domestic predicament, le Carré retreated into a fantasy world in which he was an agent and his father was in the Secret Service. What he did not know, as he passed through various preparatory schools then Sherborne Public School, was that his father Ronnie Cornwell—the Rick Pym of *A Perfect Spy*—was a consummate conman who had served a term in prison for his sins. Le Carré was 18 when he discovered what his father had been up to in the past and by then he was studying German at Berne University. Betrayal and deception, his central themes, have an obvious biographical basis in the agonizing absence of his mother and the painful presence of his father.

While at Berne, le Carré immersed himself in German literature, language and philosophy. Perhaps—again the mysterious le Carré attracts speculation—he was recruited into the Secret Service in Berne because, like Magnus Pym, he was the right type:

> Short back and sides, speaks the King's English, decent linguist, good country public school. A games player, understands discipline. Not an arty chap, certainly not one of your over-intellectual types. Level-headed, one of us. Comfortably off but not too grand—how typical that you [Jack Brotherhood] never bothered to check Rick [= Ronnie Cornwell] out.[8]

After Berne, le Carré did his National Service with the Intelligence Corps in Austria from 1949–51, a period that witnessed the defection of Burgess and Maclean to the Soviet Union and made the security service suspicious, for the first time, of

Anthony Blunt, then publicly established as Director of the Courtauld Institute but privately engaged in his work as a mole who had burrowed deep into the foundations of the British establishment. In Austria le Carré's intelligence work was, he insists, limited to helping an interrogation unit persuade individuals to cross the Czechoslovakian border so they could be tapped as sources of information.

In 1952 le Carré went to Lincoln College, Oxford, to study German but had to leave at the end of his second year when his father was declared bankrupt. He did a year's teaching, returned to Lincoln College on a scholarship, married Ann Sharp, and graduated, in 1956, with a first-class degree. He taught German for two years at Eton, the favourite public school of the British establishment, and left to enter the Foreign Office. At this time, so the consensus of rumour goes, le Carré served in MI5 under Maxwell Knight. Whatever the precise details are, le Carré has emphasized the chaotic condition of Britain's security services:

> It is an irony I shall enjoy for the rest of my life that I, who was looking for the impossible, should have entered the intelligence community at a time when it was so wracked with self-doubt that it was practically inert. Of all the vintage years of betrayal the spies have given us since the war, mine, I like to think, will be relished longest. The director general of MI5, Sir Roger Hollis, was under suspicion of espionage inside his own house. . . . Its sister service, MI6, was still stretched out on the psychiatrist's couch trying to admit what MI5, and other friends as well, had been telling it for so long: that Kim Philby, once an heir apparent to its post of chief, was now and always had been a Russian spy.[9]

In 1961, the year he was posted to the British Embassy in Bonn as second secretary, le Carré published his first novel, *Call for the Dead*, featuring George Smiley of the security service—the Circus (because based in Cambridge Circus). In 1963, the year Philby was exposed as Third Man in the Soviet spy ring, le Carré published *The Spy Who Came in from the Cold*, one of his finest works and popular enough to enable him to resign from the Foreign Office. About this time le Carré met another successful writer, the Scot, James Kennaway, whose first novel, *Tunes of Glory*, had been published in 1956 and who had written stylish screenplays for *Tunes* (1960) and *The Mind Benders* (1963).

Le Carré was impressed by Kennaway and attracted to his wife Susan.

Susan Kennaway has discussed the relationship between herself, Kennaway and le Carré in *The Kennaway Papers* (1981) in which she tells how her husband met a writer called David who had recently published a very successful novel; when *The Kennaway Papers* was published journalists were not slow to identify David as David Cornwell. Writing to Susan, Kennaway recorded his opinion of le Carré's character: 'I'm truly amazed by David. Believe me, he didn't get there by luck. The head is strong and the heart a much hunted one.'[10] The two men went to Paris, in August 1964, for discussions on a film based on *The Looking-Glass War* (dedicated to Kennaway and scheduled for publication in 1965). There were some problems with director Karel Reisz who resented Kennaway's presence; there was also, as Kennaway admitted, a good deal of late-night drinking. In November, le Carré came to stay with the Kennaways in London and Susan fell in love with him, as she acknowledges in *The Kennaway Papers*:

> James [did not anticipate] that I would actually fall in love with David. To complicate matters further I still loved James. I believe also that David fell in love with me and I know now that James and David loved each other in the way that David and Jonathan were brothers. . . . [David and I] had arrived at the same point at the same time and what followed was inevitable. I never considered the rights or wrongs, it was just like coming home.[11]

Kennaway reacted hysterically to the affair, creating a scene that ended with him in tears at the Haus am Berg, a villa at Zell-am-See, the skiing resort south of Salzburg. Susan knew then that the affair was over. Kennaway recreated the triangular relationship in *Some Gorgeous Accident* (1967) in which he appears as James Link, a scheming Irish-American war photographer who falls in love with Susie Steinberg, a fashion editor with a successful magazine. Susie is, of course, Susan Kennaway whose affair is recreated as the character comes into contact with Richard David Fiddes, a doctor modelled on le Carré. Link's self-destructive personality is contrasted with the positive appeal of his rival, for Fiddes is sleek, charming and assured.

Kennaway died in a car crash in 1968, at the age of 40, but survived through his books and the verbal portrait le Carré created in *The Naïve and Sentimental Lover*. After *A Small Town in Germany* (1968) le Carré temporarily deserted Smiley and the Circus to write his portrait of an erratic artist. Published in 1971, the year of le Carré's divorce from Ann (he subsequently married Jane Eustace, an editor with Hodder & Stoughton), *The Naïve and Sentimental Lover* was savaged by the critics who expected another spy novel. Drawing on Schiller's distinction between 'naïve' (spontaneous) and 'sentimental' (contemplative), le Carré arranges his novel contrapuntally, initially contrasting the respectable businessman Aldo Cassidy with the outrageous, boozy novelist Shamus. Shamus is evidently modelled on Kennaway: he has written a brilliant first novel, *The Moon by Day*, which has been filmed, and he has an attractive wife, Helen, with whom Cassidy falls in love. The Kennaways liked to think of themselves as the Scott and Zelda Fitzgerald of the British literary scene and le Carré vividly shows them playing games designed to make them the focus of any gathering.

Aldo Cassidy is a satirical self-portrait of le Carré. He has been to Sherborne and Oxford, like his creator; however, he has no gift for writing though he does attempt a spy novel since 'The spy vogue was high at that time, and he thought he might get in on the market.'[12] Le Carré describes Cassidy thus:

> In both build and looks he might have served as an architectural prototype for the middle-class Englishman privately educated between the wars; one who had felt the wind of battle but never the fire of it. Heavy at the waist, short in the leg, a squire always in the making, he possessed those doggedly boyish features, at once mature and retarded, which still convey a dying hope that his pleasures may be paid for by his parents.[13]

Ironically, le Carré gradually reverses the rôles of the protagonists in the novel. Shamus, insistently artistic, is actually dependent on the domesticity he claims to despise. Cassidy, who earns his living by manufacturing accessories for prams, is genuinely romantic by nature. For him, Helen is not so much a woman as the embodiment of a romantic ideal:

> Her breasts, which despite his simulated myopia he could not help remarking, were unsupported, and trembled delicately as

15

she moved. Her hips were similarly unbound, and with each balanced stride a white knee, smooth as marble, peeped demurely through the division of her robe.[14]

The novel has been neglected mainly because so few have appreciated its comic qualities, its use of parody and reversal: Cassidy is a frustrated writer of romantic novels, while Shamus is a 'failed businessman'[15]; the eternal triangle is reduced to the confusion of three individuals pushed into a tight corner together. Le Carré uses modernist techniques complete with streams of consciousness and interior monologues to dissolve reality into dreams. Shamus, the literary lion, even misquotes Joyce:

> 'The heaventree of stars,' said Shamus. 'Hung with humid nightree fruit.'
> 'That's beautiful,' said Cassidy reverently.
> 'Joyce. Old girl friend. Can't get her out of my hair. Hey lover. Watch out for frostbite for God's sake. Nip it off in a jiffy, I warn you.'[16]

That exchange takes place while the two men are having a 'pee-break' at the edge of a moat, so perhaps Shamus can be forgiven for forgetting that what Joyce actually wrote was 'The heaventree of stars hung with humid nightblue fruit.'[17]

*The Naïve and Sentimental Lover* is not so drastically different from the classic le Carré works as has been supposed. In human terms it implies that opposites not only attract: they interact. Cassidy and Shamus see in each other attributes they have suppressed for practical purposes. Similarly in *The Quest for Karla* trilogy—*Tinker Tailor*, *The Honourable Schoolboy* (1977), *Smiley's People*—the two antagonists, Smiley and Karla, are two sides of the same coin even if one is burnished, the other tarnished. Smiley undoubtedly has the nobler motives, but he sadly accepts a system that uses atrocious means for a supposedly idealistic end. Early on, in *A Murder of Quality* (1962), 'It was a peculiarity of Smiley's character that throughout the whole of his clandestine work he had never managed to reconcile the means to the end.'[18] However, at the end of *The Honourable Schoolboy*, Peter Guillam quotes Smiley as saying (admittedly in his blue period):

> So far as I can ever remember of my youth, I chose the secret road because it seemed to lead straightest and furthest toward

my country's goal. . . . Today, all I know is that I have learned to interpret the whole of life in terms of conspiracy. That is the sword I have lived by, and as I look round me now I see it is the sword I shall die by as well. These people terrify me but I am one of them. If they stab me in the back, then at least that is the judgement of my peers.[19]

If judged by their actions, the agents for liberal humanism and communism are interchangeable; Smiley's Circus, like Karla's Centre, does the dirty work for a government that publicly preaches commitment to a great cause. Smiley is involved with an organization that defends liberal humanism through 'scalp-hunters' and 'lamplighters': respectively, hired assassins and skilled liars. Before *The Quest for Karla*, le Carré had forcefully undermined the idealism of the west in *The Spy Who Came in from the Cold*. Control tells Leamas 'our methods—ours and those of the opposition—have become much the same',[20] then says it is essential to get rid of Mundt since he is 'A practitioner of the cold war'.[21] Leamas drily comments, 'Like us.'[22] Behind the acerbity of the exchange is the irony that Mundt, ostensibly head of operations for the Abteilung, is actually a British spy, though Leamas is ignorant of this information.

Leamas is deceived by those who employ him. Likewise, in *The Looking-Glass War*, the British agent Leiser is sent to East Germany and abandoned. The plot prompted a former colleague of le Carré's to castigate the author as a traitor:

> 'You *bastard*!' yells a middle-aged intelligence officer, once my colleague, down the room at me as we assemble for a diplomatic dinner at a British embassy . . . 'You utter bastard.' . . . He is not suggesting I have revealed secrets. What makes him furious is that my books are a distortion of the truth. The book that particularly enrages him is called *The Looking-Glass War* and tells the story of a British agent sent into East Germany and left to rot. 'Heartless, aren't we? Heartless incompetents.'[23]

A distortion of the truth? Le Carré's supremacy as a writer of spy stories is based on his authoritative manner, the persuasive way he builds up entirely convincing scenarios. A mole, according to Irina's diary in *Tinker Tailor*, is 'a deep penetration agent so called because he burrows into the fabric of Western imperialism'.[24] Le Carré is a literary mole, burrowing deep into the consciousness of the reader, stealthily releasing information. He convinces the readers of his novels that he is infallible on the subject of spying but elsewhere points out that his admired authenticity is an illusion, like so much else in the world of espionage:

> The world of intelligence that I described never existed. It is nice of people to say it did, but it didn't. No lamplighters, scalp-hunters, babysitters or pavement artists graced the secret corri-dors, though I am proud to learn on the grapevine that some of the absurd jargon has been adopted.[25]

Le Carré could not make it clearer—Smiley, Karla, the Circus, the Centre, all are illusions. Le Carré's world is a fiction.

It could be argued, of course, that le Carré's disclosure that his work is entirely fictional is itself a fiction. That would be in keeping with the great game where actuality is illusory, where disbelief is perpetually suspended, where lies are told to preserve a truth—or an ideological abstraction. Since the life of an effective agent is a creative, or destructive, fiction we can credit le Carré with the evidence of his own ingenuity. If his realism is mainly a virtuoso literary performance we can also assume that it has some basis in his own experience, that his fiction has a factual foundation subsequently transformed into art by the exercise of a hyperactive imagination. His realism in dealing with the intricacies of espionage is surely rooted in reality just as some of his most memorable characters are only one remove from their originals: Smiley was modelled on Vivian Green, tutor at his Oxford college; Shamus on Kennaway; Charlie on his sister Charlotte Cornwell; Rick Pym on his father Ronnie. Le Carré's own training in intelligence has equipped him to manipulate the truth inventively. In *The Little Drummer Girl*, Joseph calls the apparatus of deception 'the fiction'.[26] Le Carré may not have been a perfect spy but, as a novelist, he is a master plotter.

'One day,' the baroness tells Rick Pym in *A Perfect Spy*, '[Magnus will] be a great actor.'[27] Le Carré is a superb reader of his own novels, as witness his recordings of them, and he made a brief Hitchcockian personal appearance in the film of *The Little Drummer Girl*. More than that, though, he knows how enthusiastically individuals assume rôles, how readily they play games, how willingly life imitates art. Agents take their parts in an ideological drama much as actors perform in plays. In Smiley's Circus, Control is like a theatrical director, organizing the action, establishing the approach, supervising texts and subtexts, casting the main characters. In *The Little Drummer Girl* Charlie is easily transported from the stage to the theatre of the real. Mary Pym, in *A Perfect Spy*, reflects on the rôle-playing of agents when observing Jack Brotherhood: 'He lit one of his fat yellow cigarettes and watched her theatrically through the flame. There's a poseur in all of them, she thought.'[28] Espionage, in le Carré's books, is drama with farcical undertones and tragic consequences. To convey this drama through fictional realism he has lifted the spy story from the level of genre to the status of art. His formal artistry (the use of monologue and flashback is assured), his development of plot through dialogue, his depth of characterization (with the major characters), his tonal repertoire (Smiley's black moods are crucial to the books), his structural strength, his narrative tension (including the switching of tenses)—these qualities confirm le Carré's status as a serious novelist. His position as a bestseller is largely irrelevant to his artistic achievement, a consequence of the coincidence that the public are fascinated by spying, the subject le Carré happens to know best.

Spying—fiction masquerading as fact and vice versa—has not only given le Carré precedents for his elaborate plots. It has also reinforced his style. His narrative tone is conspiratorial. Secrets are being revealed and the reader assumes that, through the text of a le Carré novel, he is being put in possession of privileged information. Le Carré self-consciously puts conspiracy theory to artistic use. Interviewed by Melvyn Bragg on London Weekend Television's *The South Bank Show*, on 27 March 1983, he said:

> I think that the conspiracy alone is some kind of solace to the reader or to the audience: people want to interpret their lives in terms of conspiracy, they know that it's around them, they know that we live in an increasingly secretive society in many ways, where they're cut off from the decisions of power. . . .

One artistic device that le Carré uses to implant the conspiratorial emotion in the reader is his use of specialized jargon—scalphunters, lamplighters, the workname, the safe house, the dead-letter drop, the running and turning of agents. A typical le Carréan sentence combines jargon with esoteric information: 'In Spain a year later, acting on a tip-off supplied by Bill Haydon, Tarr blackmailed—or burned, as the scalphunters would say—a Polish diplomat who had lost his heart to a dancer.'[29]

Supporting his conspiratorial tone is the narrative affectation of omniscience. Le Carré may withhold essential information from the reader until the plot demands its revelation, but he always writes with immense authority. Two examples of this will suffice, the first from *A Small Town in Germany* (1968), the second from *The Little Drummer Girl*:

> Bonn had never seen such faces. The old and the young, the lost and the found, the fed and the hungry, the clever, the dull, the governed and the ungoverned, all the children of the Republic, it seemed, had risen in a single legion to march upon her little bastions. Some were hillsmen, dark-haired, straddle-legged and scrubbed for the outing; some were clerks, Bob Cratchits nipped by the quick air, some were Sunday men, the slow infantry of the German promenade, in grey gabardine and grey Homburg hats.[30]

> Somewhere in every bomb explosion there is a miracle, and in this case it was supplied by the American School bus, which had just come and gone again with most of the community's younger children who congregated every schoolday in the turning-circle not fifty metres from the epicentre. . . . The rear windows shattered, the driver went side-winding into the verge, a French girl lost an eye, but essentially the children escaped scot-free, which was afterwards held to be a deliverance. For that is also a feature of such explosions, or at least of their immediate aftermath: a communal, wild urge to celebrate the living, rather than to waste time mourning the dead.[31]

The general catalogue of information in the first passage gives the reader a sense of security, persuades him that the author's display of knowledge is a guarantee of truth. The second passage gives a speculative scenario the solidity of certainty. On both occasions le Carré provides a pictorial clarity so sharp that the reader is drawn into the action. Experience alone could not account for such literary power; le Carré has imposed on his raw material technical lessons he has learned from his reading of Balzac, Dickens, Mann and Greene.

While his style demonstrates the artistic intelligence and ingenuity of the man, his themes reveal an obsessive interest in deception and betrayal; the insights of his youth have been honed by his professional contact with British intelligence. As a microcosm of the larger world, the sphere of the spy is circumscribed by deceit. Not only is Leamas deceived by the Circus, he is compelled to betray Liz Gold in an attempt to save her, describing the woman he loves, in court, as 'a frustrated little girl from a crackpot library'.[32] Leiser is betrayed by the Department. Bill Haydon betrays the Circus. Charlie, the little drummer girl, betrays Khalil. Magnus Pym betrays Axel, his friend. Individual integrity is shattered by ideology; almost every calculated act compromises somebody. This is why Smiley, in perhaps the best-known exchange from *The Quest for Karla*, realizes there are no winners in this sordid system:

> From long habit, Smiley had taken off his spectacles and was absently polishing them on the fat end of his tie, even though he had to delve for it among the folds of his tweed coat.
> 'George, you won,' said Guillam as they walked slowly towards the car.
> 'Did I?' said Smiley. 'Yes. Yes, well I suppose I did.'[33]

Though the quest for Karla is over, Smiley remains a vulnerable man in a vicious world.

Smiley is one of the great creations of modern literature, a character who seems to be larger than life, though he is contained within the covers of books. He is, from the early novels on, a dependable creature utterly unlike the spies of pulp fiction. Indeed le Carré carefully distinguishes between Smiley and stereotypes in novels: 'Obscurity was his nature, as well as his profession. The byways of espionage are not populated by the brash and colourful adventurers of fiction.'[34] Smiley is as much at the mercy of the system as the spies he pursues. His home—in Bywater Street, Chelsea, just behind Sloane Square—is easily penetrated by the Circus, for Peter Guillam enters it with ease at the beginning of *Tinker Tailor*, despite Smiley's precautions. His wife, Lady Ann, is faithless, thus constantly reminding him of the lack of faith in his profession. He has scholarly tastes (his fondness for Grimmelshausen) and odd habits (polishing his glasses on the fat end of his tie). Though contaminated by the deception that surrounds him, he is not entirely destroyed by it. He retains his essential decency. For all his faults, he seems genuine though that is another illusion, for he is a fiction, albeit an immortal one and one made in the image of a real man.

Smiley's humanity corresponds to le Carré's own. He has no blind faith in the establishment, no dogmatic belief in the moral superiority of the western world. In *A Murder of Quality* Smiley is especially vulnerable as an outsider encroaching on the closed world of a snob school. Fielding, the murderer, is motivated by a desire to avoid blackmail but also operates as a chorus of complaint against 'a ruling class which is distinguished by neither talent, culture, nor wit'.[35] Le Carré's own view of a privileged education is expressed in *A Perfect Spy* when Magnus Pym looks back on his country academy and concludes that 'the British hierarchical system provided a natural order for the exercise of sadism.'[36] Throughout *The Quest for Karla* le Carré is sceptical of the methods of the Secret Service, and in *The Little Drummer Girl* he sympathizes with the Palestinian victims of Israeli oppression. Taken as a whole, the argumentative thrust of his work is subversive of institutional arrogance. His troubled vision of the world puts him on the side of the victims of the great game.

As far as the general public are concerned there is really no way of knowing how accurate le Carré's evocation of espionage is; spying is something that the majority understands vicariously, through news or novels. Le Carré persuades the reader that his version of spying is truthful, less fanciful than Ian Fleming's, but he does so by literary expertise rather than the regurgitation of inside information. The documentary texture of le Carré's work is an artistic accomplishment, though it is probably informed by an operational past. What makes le Carré a major modern novelist is not that he has been involved in intelligence work, but that he has rearranged a particular experience as art accessible to outsiders. He does not merely transcribe actual situations naturalistically; he uses all the resources of realism—selection, juxtaposition, imagery, invention, characterization—with aplomb.

Le Carré knows how the great game is played and, paradoxically, owes his fame and fortune to a system he despises.

Perhaps this is why his vision is troubled. He has dreamed the idealistic dreams of youth, and he has observed the nightmare of the great game as played by hardened and cynical professionals. The means have obscured the end and so le Carré has allowed the dreams to fade and the nightmare to predominate. He has exposed the claustrophobically closed world that lies at the centre of a supposedly open society. That in doing so he has revitalized the finest traditions of realism is the key to the mystery of le Carré. The quest for le Carré begins and ends with his creativity.

## NOTES

1. John le Carré, 'Don't Be Beastly to Your Secret Service', *Sunday Times*, 23 March 1986, 41.
2. John le Carré, *A Perfect Spy* (London: Hodder & Stoughton, 1986), p. 108.
3. John le Carré, *Smiley's People* (1980; rept. London: Pan Books, 1980), pp. 29–30.
4. Ibid., p. 123.
5. Andrew Boyle, *The Climate of Treason* (1979; revd. London: Coronet, 1980), p. 494. On the back of this paperback edition there is a quotation from the *Oxford Mail* praising Boyle's book as 'The natural and marvellous follow-up to le Carré'.
6. *A Perfect Spy*, p. 144.
7. John le Carré, *Tinker Tailor Soldier Spy* (1974; rept. London: Pan Books, 1975), p. 10 and p. 15.
8. *A Perfect Spy*, p. 206.
9. *Sunday Times*, 23 March 1986, 42.
10. James and Susan Kennaway, *The Kennaway Papers* (London: Jonathan Cape, 1981), p. 17.
11. Ibid., p. 24.
12. John le Carré, *The Naïve and Sentimental Lover* (1971; rept. London: Pan Books, 1972), p. 429.
13. Ibid., p. 10.
14. Ibid., p. 36.
15. Ibid., p. 189.
16. Ibid., p. 45.
17. James Joyce, *Ulysses* (1922; rept. London: Bodley Head, 1960), p. 819.
18. John le Carré, *A Murder of Quality* (1962; rept. Harmondsworth: Penguin Books, 1962), p. 79.
19. John le Carré, *The Honourable Schoolboy* (1977; rept. London: Pan Books, 1978), p. 543.

20. John le Carré, *The Spy Who Came in from the Cold* (1963; rept. London: Pan Books, 1964), p. 20.
21. Ibid., p. 22.
22. Ibid.
23. *Sunday Times*, 23 March 1986, 41.
24. *Tinker Tailor*, p. 56.
25. *Sunday Times*, 23 March 1986, 42.
26. John le Carré, *The Little Drummer Girl* (London: Hodder & Stoughton, 1983), p. 155.
27. *A Perfect Spy*, p. 155.
28. Ibid., p. 58.
29. *Tinker Tailor*, p. 37.
30. John le Carré, *A Small Town in Germany* (1968; rept. London: Pan Books, 1969), p. 305.
31. *The Little Drummer Girl*, pp. 4–5.
32. *The Spy Who Came in from the Cold*, p. 212.
33. *Smiley's People*, p. 335.
34. *A Murder of Quality*, p. 83.
35. Ibid., p. 14.
36. *A Perfect Spy*, p. 94.

# 1

# A Perfect Spy: A Personal Reminiscence

by VIVIAN GREEN

It was the end of the Summer Term, 1948, at Sherborne School in Dorset. After assembly in the Big School the masters gathered in the gravelled quad, under the shadow of Sherborne's fine medieval abbey, to shake the hands of the boys who were leaving. Among them was David Cornwell, a fair-haired, attractive boy from Westcott House who was leaving to study at Berne University. I had myself never taught him, for I was a historian and he was a modern linguist with a special interest in German. Recently he had been awarded the school prize for English verse, perhaps a presage of things to come. Yet though I hardly knew him nor anything of his background, for reasons impalpable he made an impression so vivid that it did not fade from the memory.

John le Carré's attitude towards his old school has been ambivalent. He resented the inflexibility of its moral code, its seeming blind adherence to traditional values, its basic inegalitarianism, amply illustrated in the clashes and crises which were an endemic feature of its history in the late nineteenth and early twentieth centuries.[1] Yet there is an instinctive nostalgia which, as his novel *A Perfect Spy* so clearly demonstrates, sends him back to his roots, among them the school which nestles in the green flurries of down and woodland in Dorset. Sherborne, together with Eton where he was to teach after leaving Oxford, provides in part the background for Carne School in *A Murder of Quality* (1962).

In *A Perfect Spy* the schools seem in part a recall to his preparatory school, St. Andrew's Pangbourne, as well as to Sherborne. In the naïve figure of Father Murgo[2] there seems some recollection of Sherborne's connection with the Anglican Franciscans who had a house at Hilfield near Cerne Abbas, more especially their then Minister-General, Father Algy Robertson.

Moreover it was at Sherborne that there appeared that clash of loyalty, the contrasting values, which in a sense were to thread his own life, and which form the dramatic basis of *A Perfect Spy*. 'His housemaster', John le Carré wrote of Cassidy in *The Naïve and Sentimental Lover*, 'at Sherborne had told him that Grandpa Cassidy was the devil, and . . . Grandpa Cassidy had said very much the same about his housemaster, and how Daddy had found it very hard to know whom, if either, to believe.'[3] 'The boy', le Carré's housemaster had actually written,

> found a disturbing contrast between his very material home background and what he experienced at school. He was afraid that he would 'lose' his family. . . . So he thought that the only thing to do was to leave the place which was causing the conflict within him.

'It was', he added, 'the case of a miniature Faustus story.' John le Carré has not told us his version of the episode of his leaving school which might well be different in its emphasis, for the relationship between housemaster and boy did not end on a very happy note, but that there was already a clash between the values of school and home seems evident.

Home meant the dominating yet charismatic figure of his father, Ronnie Cornwell, Rick Pym of *A Perfect Spy*. Although Ronnie Cornwell was rarely without a succession of female companions, the 'lovelies' or surrogate mothers of the novel,[4] David's early life was motherless, for his mother parted from Ronnie while David was still a child; nor was it until his Oxford days that he rediscovered her, and even then the relationship remained tenuous rather than deep. 'Not long ago he talked to me about his mother for the first time . . . he said he had taken to visiting her again. He unearthed her somewhere and put her in a house.'[5] Of his father David Cornwell wrote recently:

Ronnie's life accomplishments, if unorthodox, were dazzling: a string of bankruptcies spread over nearly 50 years and accounting for several millions of pounds: literally hundreds of companies with grandiose letter paper and scarcely a speck of capital: a host of faithful friends who smiled on his business ventures even when they were themselves the victims of them: four healthy and successful children: seven grandsons: an undimmed faith in his creator: spells of imprisonment on two continents which had left no discernible mark upon everything: spectacular acts of individual charity that would be remembered by the beneficiaries for as long as they had breath: and a sexual virility which, as he had assured me only a few months earlier, could still surprise the most optimistic.[6]

The tensions to which the relationship between father and son gave rise, more especially in adolescence, left behind a train of memories which needed in some sense to be exorcized. It was also true, to use a cliché, that the story of Ronnie Cornwell's life was stranger than fiction. On personal as well as professional grounds the subject continued to haunt the novelist's mind. Ronnie had made already some fleeting appearances.

Cassidy's feelings about his father varied. He lived in a penthouse in Maida Vale, a property listed among the assets of the Company and let to him rent free in exchange for unspecified consultative services. From its many large windows, it seemed to Cassidy, he followed his son's progress through the world as once the eye of God had followed Cain across the desert. There was no hiding from him; his intelligence system was vast, and where it failed, intuition served him in its place. In bad times Cassidy regarded him as undesirable and made elaborate plots to kill him. In good times he admired him very much, particularly his flair.[7]

In *The Honourable Schoolboy* we are told that Jeremy Westerby's father, recently deceased, had left a complex will:

my son to manage all the newspapers of the group according to the style and codes of practice established in my lifetime. . . . The only trouble was: the cupboard was bare. The figures on the account sheet wasted steadily away from the day the great man's empire tottered into liquidation. 'Can't go chasing the dolly birds where *he* is, can he Pet?' . . . 'Wouldn't put it past him, mind. Wouldn't be for want of trying, I dare say.'[8]

The tangles and drama of such relationships have in the past evoked outstanding books: Edmund Gosse in his classic *Father and Son* (1907); J. R. Ackerley in his marvellously evocative *My Father and Myself* (1968); Susan Campion painted a caustic yet amusing portrait of her father, the historian G. G. Coulton, in *Father* (1948); and, more recently, in a sad but sympathetic book Susan Cheever wrote about her father, the American novelist John Cheever, *Home before Dark* (1984). John le Carré tells us that at first he thought of writing simply a straight narrative.

> Should my book about Ronnie be fact or fiction? As lately as 1980 I was still considering hiring a researcher and tracing Ronnie through the years of foreign exile. . . . Perhaps one day I will, though from where I sit now I doubt it. . . . The truth, it seemed to me, was more likely to emerge through fiction than through the specious arrangement of documentary information. Moreover Ronnie himself was never certain which of the two categories he belonged to. Was he art, was he life? Like a novelist, his fictions were his reality.[9]

So *A Perfect Spy* is a fictional portrait rooted in a historical relationship, a glorious intermingling of the real and the fallacious. Le Carré drew an astonishingly rich, vital, yet vigorous portrait in which the bitterness and anger which that relationship evoked in earlier days are ultimately mellowed, even exorcized, by an emotional catharsis which seeks to understand, even to forgive. Rick's rise is painted in bold strokes. In fact this son of a Poole building contractor in real life managed to combine chicanary and, invoked at the same time, high moral principle, very likely drawn from his Baptist background. Although he had his ups and downs, outward success cantered in his wake. Here is John le Carré describing Rick Pym:

> Rick, meanwhile, in his immense maturity, acquired a twenty-acre mansion in Ascot with white fencing down the drive and a row of tweed suits louder than the Admiral's, and a pair of red setters, and a pair of two-toned country shoes for walking them, and a pair of 12-bore Purdey shotguns for his portrait with them, and a mile-long bar to while away his rustic evenings over bubbly and roulette. . . . A platoon of displaced Poles was hauled in to staff the place, a new and classy mother wore high heels on the lawn, bawled at the servants. . . . A Bentley appeared. . . . Up in London the court commandeered a pillared Reichskanzlei in Chester Street staffed by a troupe of Lovelies who were changed as often as they wore out. A stuffed jockey in the Pym sporting

colours waving his little whip at them, photographs of Rick's neverwozzers and a Tablet of Honour commemorating the unfallen companions of the latest Rick T. Pym & Son empire completed the Wall of Fame. . . . The best celebrate the victory at arms that Rick by now was convinced he had obtained for us single-handed: the Alamein Sickness & Health Company, the Military & Permanent Pensions Fund, Dunkirk Mutual & General, the TP Veteran Alliance Company—all seemingly unlimited, yet all satellites of the great Rick T. Pym & Son holding company, whose legal limitations as a receptacle of widows' mites were only gradually revealed.[10]

That there is some element of exaggeration in the portrait is likely, but truth still remained larger than life. His existence at Tunmers in Chalfont St. Giles where Ronnie entertained the Australian test team, patronized Arsenal, bought racehorses, dressed in dapper fashion and lived lavishly was not so different, nor did his business empire, run from No. 51 Mount Street, follow such very dissimilar lines. There were high-spending trips to the winter sports at the Kulm Hotel, St. Moritz.

> Paradise was also St. Moritz where Swiss army penknives came from. . . . Even today I have only to sniff the leather interior of a grand car and I am wafted willingly away to the great hotel drawing rooms of St. Moritz in the wake of Rick's riotous love of festival.[11]

Then back to the never-never land of floating companies and speculative ventures:

> Then home again to London with the bills all taken care of, which meant signed, and the concierges and head waiters seen right, which meant tipped lavishly with the last of our cash, to resume the ever-mounting cares of Pym & Son empire. . . . No income is so sacrosanct that expenditure cannot exceed it; no expenditure is so great that more loans cannot be raised to hold the dam from breaking altogether.[12]

But if Ronnie or Rick, for the two seem interchangeable personalities, saw himself as the man of property, a Forsyte of Mayfair, his empire was founded on shifting sand. Liquidity might become as arid as the proverbial desert.

From early days, the wheels of fortune turned in spectacular fashion. Even when his son was at Sherborne, he was reduced to living in a caravan and making spurious patent medicines to thwart his creditors. There was a brief spell in which he tasted the pleasure of Her Majesty's hospitality. 'All his life Daddy had camped in places and never lived in them, fleeing before the wrath of Grandpa Cassidy's creditors.'[13] Yet he never lost confidence in his capability and in the darkest days retained his optimism about the future, a master of self-deception. His posture as a Liberal candidate espousing moral causes, which in his own life he implicitly rejected but to which he paid serious lip-service, is itself a measure of the illusory world he inhabited. Le Carré's description of the Gulworth by-election is as rich in invention and as comic as Charles Dickens's account of the goings on at Eatanswill. Rick/Ronnie was defeated and yet continued to ride high until he was confronted by a major crisis in 1953 when the Skipton Building Society collapsed and he was declared a bankrupt.

Although he was to bounce back with amazing aplomb, he never fully recovered. He survived, for survival was of the essence of his life. Indeed, for a time he continued to enjoy a life-style not so very different from that of palmier days, sending David's half-brother to Winchester and maintaining a penthouse, with an appropriate 'lovely', in Mayfair. He had, however, in practice reached the great climacteric of his existence. The descent was to be long and in latter years humiliating, though he appears never to have seen it in that light. As an undischarged bankrupt he became a wanderer over the continents, returning to Britain only under an assumed name. Yet his business trips were still festooned with grandiose schemes reminiscent of the prospectus of many a bogus company in the famous year of the South Sea Bubble. He would buy the hair of Korean girls for wigs, endeavour to sell football pools to the Chinese; 'My dearest Father . . . Unfortunately I am not yet in a position to persuade Pandit Nehru to grant you an audience so that you can put your football pool scheme to him.'[14] Rick/Ron seemed to see his son's growing reputation as an extension of his own genius. With an imagination and a braggadocio which reminds one of how George IV wrongly came to believe that he had fought at the battle of Waterloo, so Ronnie Cornwell saw himself as the responsible agent in the propagation of his son's highly successful novels. 'Never forget', his father remarked

> . . . the sacrifices I made for you. . . . You've got assets no man can put a price on, least of all you. Where do they come from? They come from your old man. And when I'm judged as judged I shall one day surely be . . . I shall be judged *solely and exclusively* on the many wonderful talents and attributes I have passed on to you. . . . Your education, your brilliance, your inventiveness, the lot. . . . Where would *they* be if I hadn't done you right?[15]

He felt that it was his right to have a time-share in his son's handsome royalties by ordering goods in his name, and even, on at least one occasion, according to David Cornwell, assuming his son's identity.[16]

Like the Wizard of Oz, he could not maintain his imposture for ever. Though he seldom lost his bonhomie, his dignity had been challenged. He was goose-stepped to the Swiss frontier as an undesirable alien. So he had with the years grown smaller. 'Rick shrank. He abandoned monstrosity as a way of life, and came weeping and cringing to me like a whipped animal.'[17] Then, suddenly at the age of 70, he died, leaving a windfall of debts and dishonoured paper as well as a whirlpool of memories.

It is with Rick's death, Ronnie's death, that *A Perfect Spy* begins. What follows is a perfect lesson in recall. The portrait of Ronnie as Rick bears signs of exaggeration, yet what strikes the reader is its adherence to the original. But what of the author, Rick's son, Magnus? Le Carré's future biographers will have a field day in disentangling truth from fiction, and the plot of the novel requires artifice if we are to see in the powers of deception which Magnus inherited from his father the makings of *A Perfect Spy*.

> Like Rick he [Magnus] was learning to live on several planes at once. The art of it was to forget everything except the ground you stood on and the face you spoke from at that moment.[18]

'All his life he's been inventing versions of himself that are untrue.'

What then vestigially in Magnus may be seen of the author? There were, as the books make evident, conflicting loyalties, a clash of private and public values, to which John le Carré's own experience at Sherborne testified. From Sherborne the scene moves in the novel to Berne where he meets the Czech Axel Ollinger, creating a personal relationship that, in spite of elements of betrayal, is both deep and touching, far more so than his relationship with his wives. 'We betray to be loyal. Betrayal is like imagining when the reality isn't good enough. . . . Betrayal is love.'[19] Magnus was, like David Cornwell, to do national service in Austria where among other things the author represented the army at skiing. How much, how little of what happened at Berne where he was drawn into the secret service hardly allows room for speculation; but almost self-evidently the skill of the professional novelist is at work.

Then came Oxford where by a series of accidents our own paths crossed, and the boy whose hands I had shaken at Sherborne became the man whom I interviewed for admission at Oxford. And, at this stage, Rick or Ronnie characteristically appears again, not indeed in the novel but in real life. The entrance examination for admissions in the Michaelmas term 1952 had already taken place; so a special plea had to be advanced if Ronnie's son was to get a place. Ronnie found a go-between in the person of Sir James Barnes, K.C.B., K.B.E. both with interests in the Arsenal football club. Barnes had a colleague in the civil servant, Folliott, later Sir, Sandford, who was to become a much respected registrar of the university (he died in October 1986), whom he approached on Cornwell's behalf. Sandford too had a friend in the energetic and capable rector of Lincoln College, Oxford, Keith, later Lord, Murray. Murray had had a distinguished career in the war years as Director of Food and Agriculture for the Middle East. Folliott wrote to Murray (on 8 March 1952) to enquire whether there was likely to be a vacancy at Lincoln for 'the son of an old friend, who is anxious to read Modern Languages with a view to entering the Foreign Service'. 'On paper', he added

> the young man looks distinctly promising and, as I believe, Lincoln is a College with a Modern Languages tutor, I have been wondering whether there is any chance of your having a vacancy next October.

In fact Lincoln did not then have a modern language tutor, relying, until Donald Whitton's appointment in 1955, on the services as lecturers of Richard Sayce in French and Gilbert Mackay in German. Murray consulted me as a former member of the staff of Sherborne. 'He recalls him', Murray told Sandford 'as a very intelligent person. . . . The prospects are, I am afraid, not very good at this late date as we have got a full quota of freshmen.' David Cornwell did, however, come for interview from the Intelligence Corps depot at Maresfield in Sussex, displayed the charismatic qualities which at later dates have enchanted his interviewers and submitted to a somewhat perfunctory examination. Not unexpectedly he passed this with flying colours. Richard Sayce, who marked his Unseen, giving him an alpha mark, commented that 'it does not mean that I believe him to be potentially first-class' but 'I should regard him as an exceptionally promising commoner'. The authorities at Sherborne doubted whether an exception ought to be made to allow him to take a place as early as Michaelmas 1952. 'The Cornwells tend to assume what they want they get. . . . Mr. Cornwell is an enigma—very charming and persuasive but wholly without principle.' But the College did make an exception and David Cornwell came into residence in October 1952. There could not be the slightest possible doubt that he had deserved his entry on academic grounds, but his father had acted once more as the grand manipulator.

Throughout his career the figure of his father hovered continuously in the background, as Rick did over Magnus's.

> The college porter said staircase five, across the Chapel Quad. He climbed the winding wooden stairs until he saw his name written on an old oak door, M. R. Pym. He pushed the second door and closed the first. He found the switch and closed the second door on his whole life till now. I am safe inside the city walls. Nobody will find me, nobody will recruit me. He tripped over a case of legal tomes. A vaseful of orchids wished him 'Godspeed, son, from your best pal.' A Harrods invoice debited them to the newest Pym consortium.[20]

There was in fact to be no real escape from his father's consuming affection and pervasive influence.

Oxford plays an inconspicuous part in *A Perfect Spy*. 'University', Magnus tells his own son,

> was a conventional sort of place in those days, Tom. You would have a good laugh at the way we dressed and talked and the things we put up with, though we were the blessed of the earth. They shut us up at night and let us out in the morning. They gave us

girls for tea but not for dinner and God knows not for breakfast. . . . Once more Pym embraced everything, stretched every
sinew to excel. He joined the societies, paid more subscriptions
than there were clubs, became college secretary of everything from
the Philatelists to the Euthanasians.[21]

Outwardly John le Carré's life was indeed full and enjoyable. In
spite of a busy social life he had an exemplary academic record.
All his tutors paid tribute to his high intelligence and pene-
trating intellect, though his German was of a higher standard
than his French. 'Civilized and urbane', as one report phrased
it, 'strong intelligence and perception, but lacking somewhat in
imagination and enthusiasm.' Strangely the writer added that
'he seems to need something explosive behind him.' He developed an interest in seventeenth-century German literature,
more especially that classic of the Thirty Years War, Grimmelshausen's *Simplicissimus*, references to which are sprinkled
through the novels. In *A Perfect Spy* his Czech friend Axel gives
him

> a much-used copy of Grimmelshausen's *Simplicissimus*, bound in
> old brown buckram, which Pym had heard of but could not wait
> to read since it would give him an excuse to bang on Axel's door.
> He opened it and read the German inscription, 'For Sir Magnus,
> who will never be my enemy.'[22]

'He threw himself afresh', he wrote of Magnus's time at Oxford,

> upon the German muse and scarcely faltered when he discovered
> that at Oxford she was about five hundred years older than she
> had been in Bern. . . . By the end of his first term he was an
> enthusiastic student of Middle and Old High German. By the
> end of his second he could recite the *Hildebrandslied* and intone
> Bishop Ulfila's Gothic translation of the Bible in his college
> bar. . . . And when he found himself briefly transported into the
> perilous modernisms of the seventeenth century, he was pleased
> to be able to report, in a twenty-page assault on the upstart
> Grimmelshausen, that the poet had marred his work with
> popular moralising and undermined his validity by fighting on
> both sides in the Thirty Years War.[23]

Life, was however, vastly social.

> He wrote sensitive articles for university journals, lobbied
> distinguished speakers, met them at the railway station, dined

them at the society's expense and brought them safely to empty lecture halls. He played college rugger, college cricket, rowed in his college eight, got drunk in college bar and was by turn rootlessly cynical towards society and stalwartly British and protective of it, depending on whom he happened to be with.[24]

If David Cornwell was less ceaselessly active than Magnus Pym, yet he was socially energetic, contributing cartoons and drawings to the college magazine, interesting himself in college dramatics, tentatively proposing a production of *Androcles and the Lion* until the college authorities poured cold water. And all the time there was the admiring and acquisitive figure of Ron/Rick who could not understand why his overtures were greeted first with coldness and eventually with hostility.

His father's bankruptcy constituted a watershed in his Oxford existence. It threw into high relief the inner conflict between his father's life-style and his own liberal idealism. To escape the embarrassment and publicity I suggested a trip to the Swiss Alps. So we travelled by couchette, an experience made memorable by female members of the Oxford group or Moral Rearmament who seemed to spend a restless night searching for the loo, and left the train at Sion where we caught a bus to Evolène in the Val d'Herens in the shadow of the Dent Blanche, walking to the little hamlet of Le Goulet near Arolla where a shepherd enquired naïvely whether we knew Winston Churchill and whether it was true that the Second World War had ended. We walked over the neighbouring pass to the next valley, the Val d'Anniviers, and in the process were nearly blown to smithereens by workmen mining to create a dam in the neighbourhood of Grimentz. In the leisurely surroundings of the Hotel Bella Tola at St. Luc we engaged in putting together a children's story which David illustrated with brilliant cartoons which I rather regret I later returned to him. The story, written under the impact of recent experience, told of the determined efforts of Alpine bears, assisted by an assortment of other animals, to foil the exploiting capitalist M. Pampelmousse who planned a dam which would desecrate the valley's natural beauties, an objective which they were eventually able to achieve by successfully melting a glacier which destroyed the workmen's huts and all their tools. It was a simple story which not unexpectedly failed to find a publisher and since the plot was my own it lacked the finesse which the later le Carré could have contributed. His drawings were superb and showed that had he not become a writer he could well have earned his living as a cartoonist of the highest order.

Strangely enough the modern world seemed then to have a habit of intruding into the Alpine fastness. After we had climbed over the Bella Tola to the Turtmantal, so remote and beautiful that it lacked a road, consisting only of a hotel and a few chalets at Gruben, we spent the noisiest of nights, for Swiss soldiers on manoeuvres made the darkness horrid with the clatter of machine guns and the throwing of grenades. No sooner had the hideous din which precluded all sleep died away, than the valley rang to the continuous clangor of thousands of cow bells as the herds made their way from the valley below to their summer pastures on the high Alps.

As unspoiled as the Turtmantal was the Lotschental where we walked to Falferalp, though the hotel in which we stayed at Kippel could only offer us bacon and eggs. As the rain descended we made for Berne, visiting David's landlady, Frau Schreuers, who regaled us with salami and herb tea for breakfast. The final goal was the little inn at Stechelberg at the end of the Lauterbrunnen valley, now modernized, at the foot of one of the loveliest of all Alpine walks to Trachsellauenan and the steep fortress of the Obersteinberg, with its enchanted Oberhornsee, a lake of wondrous clarity embowered by mountain flowers. David took the opportunity to renew his acquaintance with his fellow student at Berne, Caspar von Almen, who regaled us with strawberry tarts at his Trummelbach hotel before he drove us at speed in his Jaguar to Interlaken to catch the train to Calais.

The Swiss trip was a hiatus in a sea of troubles. His father's bankruptcy obliged David to go out of residence. He took a job at Edgarley Hall, near Glastonbury, the prep school for Millfield, and married Ann Sharp. By the summer of 1955 things had somewhat improved, and with some support from the Buckinghamshire County Council, he returned into residence, living in a flat in Polstead Road owned by a spritely 90-year-old. His social activities were severely restricted as he concentrated on his academic studies, so that he was deservedly placed in the first class in the summer of 1956.

## A Perfect Spy: A Personal Reminiscence

In *A Perfect Spy* Magnus Pym tells how he was first involved in the British Secret Service, having been lured into the net at Berne, a connection consolidated while he was at Oxford by a meeting with an agent at the Monmouth Arms, though there is no such hotel of that name, at Burford. It is a relationship to which John le Carré has from time to time alluded,[25] but the interstices of which remain still elusive. When we were at St. Luc he had taken a keen interest in the fascinating Visitors' Book at the Hotel Bella Tola, which went back to the 1870s, in the signature of a visitor there, Professor Pontecorvo, who had defected to the Soviet Union recently. It may be taken for granted that a connection established earlier was to be furthered and promoted in the coming years. Indeed, a college report from an outside tutor, the destination of which remains unclear, may help to clarify the Oxford connection. It begins with a deserved tribute to le Carré's academic and personal qualities:

'he has a discriminating mind with some power and subtlety and a good deal of imagination. As far as his character and general suitability to represent this country abroad is concerned, I would rate him alpha. He speaks faultless English and has charm and poise; he is a thoroughly likeable person.' Then there came a qualification. 'There is, though, one point which perhaps should be borne in mind. He is of a somewhat unstable disposition, very much inclined to be swept off his feet for a time by some passing enthusiasm, inclined to let generous and idealistic impulses cloud the clarity of his thinking. He had, some time ago, considerable difficulty with his father when the latter learnt that he was associating with undergraduates of left-wing political views, and he eventually undertook to give up all activity on behalf of socialist groups. He is a man of integrity and has kept his undertaking, I think. Nor do I think that there is much damage of his succumbing to the blandishments of Communism on the Continent, but he might be impelled to some equally silly course of action.

The powers that be were then in some sense forewarned. They did not take then or later kindly to his novels which seemed to show the British Secret Service in a grey light. They sought so far as they were able to infiltrate criticism and even to prevent the series from being televized, but with a noticeable lack of success. A sense of grievance was left behind in the established

37

order, betrayed in the comments of a retired diplomat of very high rank who recently observed to me that le Carré was not a very good spy.

All this in 1956 remained very much in the future. His father had designed him for the Foreign Service; but immediately he was attracted by the possibility of teaching, more especially if this involved art. Sir Walter Oakeshott, who had replaced Murray as Rector of Lincoln, wrote round to a number of schools, including St. Edward's, Oxford, and Eton, both of which offered him a job. Attracted by Robert Birley, the Headmaster of Eton, he opted for the latter, but did not find the traditional atmosphere of Eton entirely sympathetic. He joined the War Office in 1958 and subsequently moved to the Foreign Office where he served in Germany until the success of *The Spy Who Came in from the Cold* led to his resignation. He had begun to write after leaving Eton, and I remember well how after placing the manuscript in my hands which I read between Paddington and Oxford I realized what ability and talent lay latent in *Call for the Dead*, the first of his novels, published in 1961, in which George Smiley made his first appearance. The last quarter of a century has seen the florescence in a series of novels which has established his reputation as one of the world's greatest writers of spy stories.

Yet the intriguing feature of these spy stories has been that their intrinsic dramatic content appears to reflect even deeper strains. Remarkable as a story as well as an entertainment *A Perfect Spy* seems somehow a culmination of unresolved conflicts, the tension between the search for idealism in a world of competing materialism and of other loyalties to false gods which are no less demanding, between Magnus's father Rick, and Magnus's own allusive standards. In his earlier novels le Carré had created a father figure in George Smiley, a man of impeccable integrity, shrewd, silent, at times sad, cuckolded by the world but loyal to his ideals. Yet le Carré seems to have been unable to put out of his mind the real father for whom George Smiley was merely a substitute, and basically the legacy of his inheritance from Rick, in its moral subjectivism, its stress on material wealth and comfort, its egocentric objectivity. Magnus discovers in himself reflections as in a distorting mirror of Rick, not of George Smiley, and so became the Perfect Spy. *A*

*Perfect Spy* is a triumphant exercise in the exorcize of a demon. By its close if Rick is dead, so too is Magnus. Only le Carré lives to tell the tale. Whatever else he may write, I doubt whether he may ever come as close to the bone as in *A Perfect Spy*.

Yet the issue is still enigmatic. Are we not tempted to read too much into a novel which is above all a fine piece of entertainment, theatrical, dramatic and moving, only waiting to be filmed? It would be too sophisticated to advance the theory that le Carré is a moralizer without a message. Yet moral his novels are. The world which they portray, whether of the east or the west, stands self-condemned by its hypocritical materialism, its pursuit of selfish ends screened as they often are by high-flown diction. Institutions and corporations seem to steam-roller individuals in the name of patriotism or religion or both. Espionage becomes ultimately, whatever side is involved, a banal, discomforting and even ludicrous pursuit. It hardly matters who spies for whom. It does not much matter whether Magnus sells his country to Axel or not. What does matter is that Magnus's only loyalty is itself so frail, that even in the act of love there is a forewarning of betrayal. Le Carré does not seem to look hopefully, as Lord Annan suggests,[26] at a simplified solution to human ills. A deep note of pessimism pervades the scene. The redemptive quality which redeems the darkness lies less in individuals than in the fluctuating span of human relationship, in Magnus's own relationship with his father, and perhaps above all in his symbolic friendship with Axel. Whether le Carré would have agreed with E. M. Forster that affection should take precedence of patriotism I do not know; but the novel's argument points in that direction. Axel's relations with Magnus as Cassidy's relationship with Shaun (and Helen) seem somehow to penetrate to the deeper realities of human existence. Interestingly love is sexually ambivalent, as if to suggest that physical attraction is less important than spiritual affinity. In *A Perfect Spy* le Carré has brought together not merely many of the outstanding ingredients of his earlier novels, but has interfused his own personal problems with fiction of a high order. Rick Pym stands boldly, full square, against the sky-line, but Magnus, doubtless of set purpose, stands still in the shadow.

## NOTES

1. See, for example, A. B. Gourlay's *Sherborne School* (1951, pp. 162–70).
2. John le Carré, *A Perfect Spy* (London: Hodder & Stoughton, 1986), pp. 146–47.
3. John le Carré, *The Naïve and Sentimental Lover* (London: Hodder & Stoughton, 1971), p. 121.
4. *A Perfect Spy*, p. 75 and p. 87.
5. Ibid., p. 382.
6. John le Carré, 'Spying on my Father', *Sunday Times*, 6 March 1986.
7. *The Naïve and Sentimental Lover*, pp. 97–8.
8. John le Carré, *The Honourable Schoolboy* (London: Hodder & Stoughton, 1977), pp. 103–4.
9. 'Spying on my Father'.
10. *A Perfect Spy*, pp. 129–30.
11. Ibid., pp. 74–5.
12. Ibid., p. 136.
13. *The Naïve and Sentimental Lover*, p. 121.
14. *A Perfect Spy*, p. 425.
15. *The Naïve and Sentimental Lover*, p. 99.
16. 'Spying on my Father'.
17. *A Perfect Spy*, p. 450.
18. Ibid., p. 99.
19. Ibid., p. 121–22.
20. Ibid., p. 257.
21. Ibid., pp. 257–58.
22. Ibid., p. 199. Cf. 'His old buckram-bound copy of *Simplicissimus* occupies pride of place as usual. His mascot' (p. 118).
23. Ibid., p. 258–59.
24. Ibid., p. 258.
25. John le Carré, 'Don't be Beastly to Your Secret Service', *Sunday Times*, 23 March 1986.
26. *London Review of Books*, 29 May 1986.

# 2

# The Clues of the Great Tradition

by OWEN DUDLEY EDWARDS

The instructions of my editor—the cry that went out from the Bold—were that his volume was to be entitled *The Quest for le Carré*, that I was to discuss John le Carré's relationship to the great traditions of thriller fiction, and that a starting-point for my investigation would be le Carré interviews in the *Sunday Times* (23 March 1986), and the *Observer* (3 February 1980). Mr. Bold stressed that the latter acknowledged literary obligations by le Carré to Arthur Conan Doyle and P. G. Wodehouse; this last was a gracious compliment with a faint aroma of menace, of the kind that might be firmly, if regretfully, proffered by George Smiley in tightening his hold on a potentially wayward recruit, for I have written books on both writers and any avenues of escape were thereby closed.

Still, the prospect was pleasing: I had looked on John le Carré as the greatest spy novelist of my time since reading *The Spy Who Came in from the Cold* in 1964, assuming (an assumption that later proved important) that Graham Greene was too great to be classified as simply a spy novelist. Subsequent reading had only deepened this impression. Of course, there remained more reading to do: interviews, reviews of the works, reading or re-reading the works themselves, and I was not at all looking forward to what critics so widely united in terming the unrewarding slog of getting through *The Naïve and Sentimental Lover*. My chief unease lay in the fact that my previous pursuit

of clues to the unexamined sources of such writers as George
Orwell and Scott Fitzgerald, Conan Doyle and Wodehouse,
possessed that great solace for the reader, the critic, the
historian, captured so well in Macaulay's essay on Bacon:

> Time glides on; fortune is inconstant; tempers are soured; bonds
> which seemed indissoluble are daily sundered by interest, by
> emulation, or by caprice. But no such cause can affect the silent
> converse which we hold with the highest of human intellects.
> That placid intercourse is disturbed by no jealousies or resent-
> ments. These are the old friends who are never seen with new
> faces, who are the same in wealth and in poverty, in glory and in
> obscurity. With the dead there is no rivalry. In the dead there is
> no change. Plato is never sullen. Cervantes is never petulant.
> Demosthenes never comes unseasonably. Dante never stays too
> long. No difference of political opinion can alienate Cicero. No
> heresy can excite the horror of Bossuet.

And Macaulay never talks too much, whatever the complaints
of his contemporaries. It seemed unfair, indeed anti-social, that
my chief grievance against Mr. le Carré at the outset should be
that he was alive: unfair all the more in that a much stronger
emotion was (and is) my passionate anxiety to read many more
books by him.

But it was a problem. To employ a Wodehousean term
beloved of Mr. le Carré, the 'stuffed eelskin' I feared might
descend on my neck was my subject answering the ascription of
this or that literary influence with a roar of 'April Fool! I never
read a line of the blighter in my puff!', or some crushingly
graver and less Wodehousean equivalent. More, the evidence in
my earlier quests had certainly been that of the writers' works,
but fortified and supplemented by their private correspondence
and their acquaintances' posthumous revelations. Wodehouse,
whom I investigated just after his death, is something of an
exception here; but having lived for almost a century he had
scattered a reasonable number of clues, including his invaluable
publication of letters on his work as a writer, *Performing Flea*.
Mr. le Carré has not imitated this aspect of his output, nor that
of editing an anthology of favourite writers. Not only was he not
dead; he also needed to live for at least another forty years to
satisfy my optimum requirements. (The least the man can do is
to fall in with this last request.)

At all events there were the two tangible clues when he answered the *Observer*'s inquiry about 'writers who mean the most to you': 'P. G. Wodehouse for rhythm and timing. Conan Doyle for thrust and instant atmosphere.'

The first deduction to be made from these is that if Mr. le Carré ever does get down to publishing something like *Performing Flea*, it should be pretty good. This is very nice succinct working criticism, as straight from the craftsman's bench as Wodehouse in his letters reprinted in *Performing Flea* and as Conan Doyle, more formally, in *Through the Magic Door*. Unlike customary forms of academic criticism, they are perceptions of a reading writer's needs rather than the noting of literary qualities acceptable to some vaguely agreed yardstick. I like Mr. le Carré's generous response to authors whose popularity had apparently inhibited their appreciation by most of the critical Establishment. I could see signs in these interviews, and found many others later, that Mr. le Carré could show a rigour as harsh as that Establishment's own in his dealing with other popular figures: here, there was a debt, and he had pleasure in owning to it. And the argument was emphatically his own: there was little in common here, apart from the salute to good stylists, with other illustrious encomia. Edmund Wilson's admiration for Conan Doyle, and Evelyn Waugh's apotheosis of Wodehouse, have their ultimate emphases in nostalgia. To Mr. le Carré they have an immediate and present significance.

My immediate work thus placed before me by Mr. le Carré was obvious enough. We might expect such influence to be most noticeable in the first book, *Call for the Dead*. A writer of distinctive originality such as Mr. le Carré might be expected to show his greatest dependence on an admired literary forebear in his first book, unlike an Ian Fleming forever trapped in the derivative, his borrowings peering, mole-like, outward at every stage of his output (e.g. *Dr. No*, and *You Only Live Twice*, the best caged of all prisoners of Sax Rohmer's Dr. Fu Manchu, as clear an instance as one could find of the crude leading the lewd). Sherlock Holmes is closest to his several human originals at the beginning of *A Study in Scarlet*. And Mr. le Carré virtually signals the major point of obligation to Conan Doyle by his chapter-title 'Echoes in the Fog'. Fogs suggest Baker Street, although their presence in that location is popularly exaggerated. The climax of Smiley's first adventure is on the London waterfront, although stationary where Conan Doyle's great use of it is in a fevered riverborne chase in *The Sign of Four*. But it is the Dartmoor fog whence bursts the hound of the Baskervilles that supplies the origin of this passage.

He dropped on his knees and clapped his ear to the ground. 'Thank Heaven, I think that I hear him coming.'

A sound of quick steps broke the silence of the moor. Crouching among the stones we stared intently at the silver-tipped bank in front of us. The steps grew louder, and through the fog, as through a curtain, there stepped the man whom we were awaiting. He looked round him in surprise as he emerged into the clear, star-lit night. Then he came swiftly along the path, passed close to where we lay, and went on up the long slope behind us. As he walked he glanced continually over either shoulder, like a man who is ill at ease.

'Hist!' cried Holmes, and I heard the sharp click of a cocking pistol. 'Look out! It's coming!'

There was a thin, crisp, continuous patter from somewhere in the heart of that crawling bank. The cloud was within fifty yards of where we lay, and we glared at it, all three, uncertain what horror was about to break from the heart of it. I was at Holmes's elbow, and I glanced for an instant at his face. It was pale

Suddenly Mendel stopped, seizing Smiley by the arm in warning. Then Smiley heard it too, the hollow ring of footsteps on a wooden floor irregular like the footsteps of a limping man. They heard the creak of an iron gate, the clang as it was closed, then the footsteps again, firm now upon the pavement, growing louder, coming towards them. Neither moved. Louder, nearer, then they faltered, stopped. Smiley held his breath trying desperately at the same time to see an extra yard into the fog, to glimpse at the waiting figure he knew was there.

Then suddenly he came, rushing like a massive wild beast, bursting through them, knocking them apart like children and running on, lost again, the uneven echo fading in the distance. They turned and chased after him, Mendel in front and Smiley following as best he could, the image vivid in his mind of Dieter, gun in and exultant, his eyes shining brightly in the moonlight. But suddenly they started forward in a rigid, fixed stare, and his lips parted in amazement. At the same time Lestrade gave a yell of terror and threw himself face downwards upon the ground. I sprang to my feet, my inert hand grasping my pistol, my mind paralyzed by the dreadful shape which had sprung out upon us from the shadows of the fog. A hound it was, an enormous coal-black hound, but not such a hound as mortal eyes have ever seen. Fire burst from its open mouth, its eyes glowed with a smouldering glare, its muzzle and hackles and dewlap were outlined in flickering fire. Never in the delirious dream of a disordered brain could anything more savage, more appalling, more hellish be conceived than that dark form and savage face which broke upon us out of the wall of fog.

With long bounds the huge black creature was leaping down the track, following hard upon the footsteps of our friend. So paralyzed were we by the apparition that we allowed him to pass before we had recovered our nerve. Then Holmes and I both fired together, and the creature gave a hideous howl, which showed that one at least had hit him. He did not pause, however, but bounded onwards. Far away on

hand, bursting on them out of the night fog. Ahead, the shadow of Mendel turned abruptly to the right, and Smiley followed blindly. Then suddenly the rhythm had changed to the scuffle of fighting. Smiley ran forward, heard the unmistakable sound of a heavy weapon striking a human skull, and then he was upon them: saw Mendel on the ground, and Dieter stooping over him, raising his arm to hit him again with the heavy butt of an automatic pistol.

Smiley was out of breath. His chest was burning from the bitter, rank fog, his mouth hot and dry, filled with a taste like blood. Somehow he summoned breath, and he shouted desperately:

'Dieter!'

Frey looked at him, nodded and said:

'*Servus*, George', and hit Mendel a hard, brutal blow with the pistol. He got up slowly, holding the pistol downwards and using both hands to cock it.

Smiley ran at him blindly, forgetting what little skill he had ever possessed, swinging with his short arms, striking

45

the path we saw Sir Henry looking back, his face white in the moonlight, his hands raised in horror, glaring helplessly at the frightful thing which was hunting him down.

But that cry of pain from the hound had blown all of our fears to the winds. If he was vulnerable he was mortal, and if we could wound him we could kill him. Never have I seen a man run as Holmes ran that night. I am reckoned fleet of foot, but he outpaced me as much as I outpaced the little professional. In front of us as we flew up the track we heard scream after scream from Sir Henry and the deep roar of the hound. I was in time to see the beast spring upon its victim, hurl him to the ground, and worry at his throat. But the next instant Holmes had emptied five barrels of his revolver into the creature's flank. With a last howl of agony and a vicious snap in the air it rolled upon its back, four feet pawing furiously, and then fell limp upon its side. I stooped, panting, and pressed my pistol to the dreadful, shimmering head, but it was useless to pull the trigger. The giant hound was dead.

with his open hands. His head was against Dieter's chest, and he pushed forward, punching Dieter's back and sides. He was mad, and discovering in himself the energy of madness, pressed Dieter back still further towards the railing of the bridge while Dieter, off balance and hindered by his weak leg, gave way. Smiley knew Dieter was hitting him, but the decisive blow never came. He was shouting at Dieter; 'Swine, swine!' and as Dieter receded still further Smiley found his arms free and once more struck at his face with clumsy, childish blows. Dieter was leaning back and Smiley saw the clean curve of his throat and chin, as with all his strength he thrust his open hand and he pushed further and further. Dieter's hands were at Smiley's throat, then suddenly they were clutching at his collar to save himself as he sank slowly backwards.

It is no crude appropriation of material, but a judicious and economical deployment of atmosphere and imagery. Dieter's footsteps recall those of Sir Henry, Dieter's advent that of the hound, Smiley and Mendel take the place of Holmes, Watson and Lestrade, and then Mendel becomes, like Sir Henry, the victim of the murderous apparition from the fog who has scattered his hunters. The cocking pistol is transferred from the pursuing Holmes to Dieter at bay; Sir Henry's vulnerable throat becomes Dieter's. Dieter's identification with the hound is stressed when he first appears, as the narrator likens him to a massive wild beast, and his reversion to the beast is literally pounded into him by Smiley with his use of the most offensive bestial imagery common in German vituperation. But Dieter shows his humanity in his refusal to give Smiley the *coup de grace*; the hound's abortive final bite is only rendered harmless by death. And then, we are once more invited to see the similarity between Dieter's fate and that of the hound's master, Stapleton, who has set the huge dog on its murderous course and himself afterwards falls to his death:

| | |
|---|---|
| Somewhere in the heart of the great Grimpen Mire, down in the foul slime of the huge morass which had sucked him in, this cold and cruel-hearted man is for ever buried. | He was gone; offered like a human sacrifice to the London fog and the foul black river lying beneath it. <br><br> . . . Somewhere beneath . . . a cripple has dragged himself through the filthy water, lost and exhausted, yielding at last to the stenching blackness till it held him and drew him down. |

But Smiley weeps as Dieter dies below him, for he loved Dieter and Dieter's last action has been to spare his life. There is so forceful a contrast between the epitaph in Smiley's final cry— ' "O dear God what have I done? Oh, Christ, Dieter, why didn't you stop me, why didn't you hit me with the gun, why didn't you shoot?" '—and the eminently fair-minded Watson's grim obituary of Stapleton that the entire passage seems not merely a debt to Conan Doyle, but an act of homage to him, and that by reflecting on Stapleton we can see more clearly Dieter's redemption at his moment of death. I think I found what Mr. le Carré intended to be found, but it seems to have taken a quarter-century to find it. It would not be the last time that Mr. le Carré's allusiveness would lead him to credit his critics with more intelligence than we seem to possess.

There are other points which form a commonplace of all writing of this kind, such as the existence of a Holmes and a

Watson figure. As Dr. Peter Lewis says, 'Mendel is not playing Dr. Watson to Smiley's Sherlock Holmes', nor is he playing Lestrade (although in near-equality of detective talent he may owe something to Inspector Baynes, the very intelligent country detective in 'Wisteria Lodge', first case of *His Last Bow*). But Peter Guillam is surely Watson, in his reactions, and as the reader's focus on Smiley when it is not convenient for Mr. le Carré to have the reader directly explore Smiley's mind; he will be more active than Watson, and it might even be that his place as the handsome, athletic sidekick to the fatter master-mind harks back to Rex Stout's Archie Goodwin and Nero Wolfe, themselves a pleasing variation on Watson and Holmes. But any such origin must be very faint; and the reverence of Guillam's Watsonian fidelity to Smiley has nothing in common with the iconoclasm of Archie's loyalty to Wolfe. The very last sight (in *Smiley's People*) of Guillam and Smiley united, yet with Guillam only dimly aware of Smiley's final doubts, has a faint ring of the final conversation in what in point of fictional chronology is the last 'bow' of Holmes, on the brink of the Great War:

> 'There is an East wind coming, Watson.'
> 'I think not, Holmes. It is very warm.'

On the other hand it is not Guillam, but Leamas, who plays a variant of the rôle of Watson in 'The Dying Detective'. In both that story and *The Spy Who Came in from the Cold* an emissary is dispatched and given instructions as to what he is to say to a certain person who is thereby to be lured into taking certain actions. The emissary knows that he is only telling part of the truth. He is to make much of apparent conditions of decline and destruction on his own side. Watson thinks Holmes is dying, while Leamas knows he himself is not really in disgrace; but Watson is concealing his own future actions from Culverton Smith. What neither Watson nor Leamas is permitted to know is that the figure brought into position is to be thereby destroyed, and the plot succeeds because of the ignorance of the emissary in each case. In this instance there is an even greater contrast between the ultimate victims than we saw between Dieter Frey on the one hand, and Stapleton and his hound on the other. Although Dieter spares Smiley, his intentions towards

Mendel were absolutely homicidal, and he has encompassed the deaths of the Fennans. Fiedler in *The Spy* is ruthless, but he has a decency and integrity contrasting utterly with Mundt's vicious careerism, sadism and anti-Semitism, and thanks to Leamas, Mundt will triumph; Culverton Smith in 'The Dying Detective' is a peculiarly odious physical and mental sadist with one of the nastiest imaginable murders in his recent record— and to Arthur Conan Doyle, M.D., a deliberate employment of medical discovery for purposes of human destruction instead of healing was the action of a 'monster' intent on treason against the human race. Watson, like Leamas, has been befooled in order to win success, and both are befooled in their professional capacities—Watson as a doctor, Leamas as a spy. But Watson has reason to be mollified at the end, whereas Leamas can only embrace death himself when Mundt claims the Jewish Liz as a further victim.

The perils of pursuing literary influences on Mr. le Carré became icily clear when I read *A Perfect Spy*, and Mr. le Carré's comments elsewhere on its portrait of his father. Much of Magnus Pym's father is based on the author's, he tells us: so how much more stems from autobiography? Mr. le Carré does not have obvious variants on Rick Pym in his other work, although there are paternal prototypes (Gerald Westerby's in *The Honourable Schoolboy*, Charlie's in *The Little Drummer Girl*), both of them present only in flashbacks, or reminiscences. But Mr. le Carré's personal account of his father suggests he had previously used him as source-material, not for a person, but an organization. In both *The Spy Who Came in from the Cold* and *The Looking-Glass War* an emissary is sent into hostile territory by a British secret service agency. In the former, the design is worked out efficiently, but it is not what the emissary has been told. In the latter, the design ends in disaster, and was always bound to fail. Apparently the author suffered one or other of these experiences, and possibly both, by his father's contrivances and machinations. The speed with which one book followed the other suggests a twinship of original concept, with the point of departure a memory of gloomy reflection, perhaps thus:

> . . . *either* the old man planned it so that I would ultimately be
> confronted by a set of circumstances he concealed from me, *or* he

loused up the entire miserable scheme by his ineptitude from the first.

Neither Control nor Leclerc suggests any similarity to Rick Pym, but the paternal symbolism of their institutions is both obtrusive and instructive. For these reasons we should be chary of ascribing too much influence in the birth of *The Spy* to either Sherlock Holmes or H.M. Secret Service.

It is also possible, especially after the first two books, to see how Mr. le Carré's sense of the Conan Doyle 'thrust and instant atmosphere' could have expressed itself in subtler ways than those of simple stylistic variation, however sophisticated. The use of Holmes in a spy story does provide the unusual sight of the great man's winning by sheer chance, whatever the general context of scientific deduction, and of his intellectual failure in the precise quest however redeemed by external developments. 'The Second Stain' turns on the coincidence of a blackmailer's murder at the moment of his reception of the critical document— the murder is quite irrelevant, being the contribution of a doubtless justifiably insane wife—although Holmes has earlier belittled Watson's reaction by ' "A coincidence! . . . The odds are enormous against its being a coincidence. . . ." ' And in the Holmes story used most frequently in anthologies of spy fiction, 'The Bruce-Partington Plans', the period of waiting for the victim to enter the trap ends in humiliation as well as triumph: 'Holmes gave a whistle of surprise. "You can write me down an ass this time, Watson," said he. "This is not the bird that I was looking for." ' It is a measure of Mr. le Carré's constructive originality in his use of the source that one of Smiley's clearest debts to Holmes should be in his *humility*, the very last quality the casual observer would ascribe to the sage of Baker Street. But although modesty was condemned by Holmes as unscientific, he is ruthlessly ready to indict himself for failure in the precise context while all around him are indifferent to the intellectual point at issue as they cheer his overall victory. This ironic appraisal of loss and gain dictates the last word Mr. le Carré intends us to have from Smiley: ' "George, you won," said Guillam as they walked slowly towards the car. "Did I?" said Smiley. "Yes. Yes, well I suppose I did." ' Had Holmes ever married, and acquired a wife as faithless as Lady Ann Smiley, one suspects there would be a similarly tortured scientific accounting of emotional loss and gain to end more or less as Smiley ends it, in leaving the symbolic lighter with Ann's inscription to him 'all my love' lying where Karla drops it at the close of *Smiley's People*. Holmes acquired much momentum from Conan Doyle's enjoyment in writing his chivalric romances of the fourteenth century *The White Company* and *Sir Nigel*, and it is the science of chivalric symbolism that a knight may carry and fight to retain or reclaim the token of his faithless lady, only quietly to discard it when the relevant quest is over.

We may offer an additional salute to 'atmosphere' in noticing that both Conan Doyle's Holmes romances and Mr. le Carré's 'Circus' adventures produce some of their finest atmospheric moments in the sheer descriptions of waiting for friend or enemy. It ensures some of the strongest effects in 'The Speckled Band', 'The Empty House', 'Black Peter' and so many others (and it is pointedly avoided in a piece of deliciously satirical contrivance to smoke out the malignant Oldacre in 'The Norwood Builder'); it actually laid the foundation for Mr. le Carré's saga in the melancholy overture to his first great success in attracting mass readership, *The Spy Who Came in from the Cold*, and with a beautiful artistic counterpoint it is waiting at exactly the same place—the Berlin Wall—which heralds our farewell to the Circus. (In theory *Call for the Dead* begins the Circus series, but for all of its satisfactory introduction to Smiley Mr. le Carré regards neither it nor *A Murder of Quality* as more than 'prentice works'; and it is fair to say that in particular Smiley's initial boss Maston is crude to the point of naturalism, and Mr. le Carré was later to show what he could do with such figures in the different dissections of Control, Leclerc, Lumley (in the opening salvos of *A Small Town in Germany*), Bradfield, Percy Alleline, Lacon, Enderby and Brotherhood—these were the Establishment and the blunt instrument Maston was much too quick and too clean an ending for it once Mr. le Carré got down to serious business.)

Conan Doyle himself had been the master synthesist of great literary influence in his creations (Holmes and Watson flow from at least six mighty rivers—Plato, Cervantes, Boswell, Scott, Poe and Stevenson—as well as many brave streams); Mr. le Carré would simply do as his master would urge in looking at some of them. Of Mr. le Carré's novels *The Honourable Schoolboy* is for various reasons the most formally conscious of literary precedents—specifically Greene, Malraux, Maugham, Hemingway and above all Conrad. But Professor Andrew Rutherford, in his most instructive *The Literature of War*, has a valuable meditation on Stevenson in the context of Mr. le Carré, and the very title of this novel should evoke classic schoolboy fiction as well as *The Honorary Consul* and Mr. Graham Greene. Mr. le Carré has not gone into detail about the matter, but he is known to have a very fine collection of schoolboy literature—Jerry Westerby's name is surely an appreciative salute to Percy Westerman, every single one of whose works Mr. le Carré appears to possess. (Did it start as 'Westerboy'?) *Treasure Island* is distinguished for the force and sharpness of its portraits of the successive pirates encountered by Jim Hawkins—Black Dog, Blind Pew, and Israel Hands as well as the grand ambiguities of Silver—and something of this seems to have gone into the making of the successive unpleasant acquaintances Jerry Westerby is forced to meet in his own pilgrimage before he reaches his private heart of darkness. Black Dog, Pew and Hands all mean destruction to Jim, and so, from time to time, will Silver, but for various reasons all are forced to withhold their murderous intent until it cannot be fulfilled; in the process of the needful delays they engage in conversation which gives more food for thought while it places more strain on nerves (since we know that the outcome may at any stage prove to be a direct attempt to kill Jim)—and these are the methods of Mr. le Carré in the Westerby Odyssey. But there is a supreme *volteface*. It is Drake Ko who has provided the equivalent of the Silver ambiguities as the complexities of his record assert themselves, just as it is Drake Ko with whom Jerry Westerby's meeting at the moment of truth must provide that heart of darkness. But anything like detailed exploration of one another's minds is made impossible here, and it is Jerry, not Ko, whose life is cut short before there is a construction of understanding beyond the briefest necessities. Mr. le Carré turns an agreeable trick on his reader by suddenly providing a climax of staccato one-liners from Jerry by which Ko is forced into acceptance of his alliance; and the obligation here is to Hemingway, much abused by Jerry's literary agent in the cameo early in the book to enable discussion of its place in the tradition of the eastern adventure novel. (This anxiety to claim that place seems to supply the only reason for the introduction of the literary agent—apart from the human desire to throw in a satirical portrait of a literary agent.)

The direct allusions to Conan Doyle's self-declared emulator John Buchan (see the remarks of the Literary Innkeeper in *The Thirty-Nine Steps*) are on the surface very clear. It would be interesting to know whether Mr. le Carré followed *Mr. Standfast* to its avowed parent lake, John Bunyan's *The Pilgrim's Progress*; it looks a little like it. Certainly if Smiley—justly—calls himself Mr. Standfast, Jerry Westerby points a terrible irony in 'passing over to the other side' (in all of its meanings) because he shows himself Mr. Valiant-for-Truth. Buchan certainly made that distinction, but missed its potential implications in promoting the dead Peter Pienaar from the first category to the second. Mr. le Carré may have seen clearer to Bunyan's intentions in making the distinction than did Buchan, and I think he needed a reading of Bunyan to do it. It is critical to Mr. le Carré's general theme of spy fiction that in the end his Mr. Valiant-for-Truth does find himself on the opposing side from Mr. Standfast. Leamas, Avery, Turner, Leo Harting, Prideaux and Jerry Westerby all finish at odds with the Smiley orthodoxy (although Smiley himself is not mentioned in Turner's quest for Harting, *A Small Town in Germany*); it is difficult not to admire, and even to be very fond of, Smiley, but Mr. Julian Symons is surely too crude in the revised edition of his *Bloody Murder* when he criticizes the Karla trilogy

> this was Smiley with a difference, no longer a faceless organization man but now almost unequivocally a hero. . . . The work of the Centre is now distinctly idealized, and although spying may still be a rather dirty business, the men of the Centre are now seen as modern patriots defending the bad against the worse. In early books the security services, both bureaucrats and men in the field, are shown as conscienceless people playing destructive games. The revelation of *Smiley's People* is that even the Russian spymaster Karla is human.

I am not clear whether Mr. Symons is objecting to this last discovery on literary or zoological grounds, but the case hardly stands up. Smiley was hardly 'faceless' in *Call for the Dead*, which Mr. Symons, having termed it 'unjustly neglected', here unjustly neglects. Leaving aside the treacherous Bill Haydon, the Circus leaders in *Tinker Tailor Soldier Spy*—Alleline, Bland, Esterhase—are a very peculiar selection to term 'patriots', however modern, and Lacon, their superior, is little better. The supervisory committee in *The Honourable Schoolboy* is a wickedly satirical set of wholly credible portraits, chiefly of absurd and morally empty people. There is a bleak, ruined dignity in Smiley's memory-bank, Connie, though it is hard to build it much beyond very appreciative caricature of the type that Charles Dickens and Edgar Wallace both did well. The ex-Jesuit Sinologist is as near to an attack of the Fu-Manchus as Mr. le Carré gets, and it is significant that it is with a government agent he gets it.

Smiley's hit-man Fawn ends up as a horrible psychopath, breaking the arms of a poor Chinese sneak-thief. The C.I.A. men and U.S. Narcotics officials are ruthlessly played for comedy in some of the funniest lines ever written by Mr. le Carré, but unlike most British treatment of Americans, whether friendly, openly hostile or (as is most frequent) covertly hostile, they are devastating in their fidelity. (Mr. le Carré is far above all great British traditions here, apart from those spies who came into the cold, Henry James and T. S. Eliot.) Wodehouse knew Americans and could present them with realism, but not until Mr. le Carré has the *American*-ness of bureaucracy been managed so well by an outsider, if only because Wodehouse when engaged on such an enterprise (as with 'America's Number One Plasterer' (process-server) in *Summer Moonshine*), is interested in light comedy, not the ultimately destructive comedy required for Mr. le Carré's work. (There is a pretty horrifying American lady in *Summer Moonshine*, but her evident professionalism in human destruction is presented in universal black-widow-spider terms, not specifically American.) As for Smiley himself, the whole point about the books is that Prideaux (a figure of archaic moral values) and Westerby (a figure of archaic cultural origin) end by thwarting that phase of Smiley's quest for Karla, and in their ethical decisions they are superior to Smiley, although one of them bows out after committing murder, the other after committing treason. *Smiley's People* itself concludes with Smiley victorious and by now scientifically convinced of his tranferrence of rôle with Karla, having at the end of the previous novel acknowledged that his own destruction is by means comparable to those employed by himself. Mr. Symons may think that Smiley is almost unequivocally a hero; Smiley does not. Certainly he is no more the hero than in *Call for the Dead*. Mr. Symons's range of reading has had to be large for his useful book. None of us is perfect. Even Rohmer sometimes nods.

The question of Mr. le Carré's use of Bunyan via Buchan brings us back to the more general question of epic forces lying at back of the tradition altogether. If Conan Doyle's parallel writing of chivalric and detective fiction gave them mutual strengthening (and *The White Company* was composed just after *The Sign of Four*, just before the first Sherlock Holmes short stories), what was the impact of chivalric literature in general? In some ways Holmes (especially the Holmes of 'The Final Problem') is more Arthurian than the cheerful realism of Sir Nigel's associates, however dignified in his protocol may be Sir Nigel himself. And this Arthurian dimension seems critical for Mr. le Carré, more especially in the Karla triology. Dr. David Monaghan observes in his *The Novels of John Le Carré* (1985):

> Le Carré is exploring the gap between the mythic vision of man's relationship to society and the more cynical analysis of the modern condition, associated with Conrad and Greene. His technique is, in essence, much the same as that employed by Joyce in *Ulysses* or Eliot in *The Waste Land* in that they, too, judge twentieth-century society by how far it falls short of a mythic ideal, supplied for them by the *Odyssey* and the grail legend respectively.

I grant the accuracy of much of this diagnosis; I am less persuaded by the mutual relations ascribed to its components. I would find Greene anything but cynical save in manner, or Joyce scarcely starry-eyed in classical idealism. But the various elements are undoubtedly present. Smiley is an Arthurian figure, conspicuously in relation to his Guinevere. He is also Joycean: he possesses something of the humanity, the decency, the absurdity and the cuckoldry of Bloom. Guillam is more definitely Telemachus than Stephen, but their association has a little of the limited accord of Bloom and Stephen, especially at the close of *Smiley's People*. The Arthurian antecedent, so frequently articulated in references to the Grail, is presented as no primeval beauty in itself, as the omnipresence of allusion to Guinevere's infidelity by means of Lady Ann Smiley bears witness. The salvation of Dieter by his raising himself from the bestial order to which he has fallen is answered in the melancholy cadence of the final meditation of *Smiley's People*:

> On Karla has descended the curse of Smiley's compassion; on Smiley the curse of Karla's fanaticism. I have destroyed him with the weapons I abhorred, and they are his. We have crossed each other's frontiers, we are the no-men of this no-man's-land.

'And all my realm goes back into the beast, and is no more', mourns Tennyson's Arthur. In one sense the entire Smiley corpus is a meditation on another of Arthur's thoughts: 'Authority forgets a dying king.' There remain also the symbols of Arthur's knights who from time to time find themselves in opposition to Arthur—Lancelot, Tristram, Gawain—and we find it again in the choices that ultimately divide Leamas, Prideaux and Westerby from Smiley. There are details such as the adversary (and *his* ambiguous wife) proving to be the truant knight's friend rather than enemy—the legend of Gawain and the Green Knight, as presented in Westerby's relationship with Drake Ko's mistress and subsequently with himself. There is the constant emphasis on the apparent universal destruction caused by one traitor: Modred, Haydon. There is the terrifying innocence of Galahad or Parsifal (Mr. le Carré is inclined to stress German rather than English influences, and his training in literature, diplomacy and investigation as regards Germany was extensive), particularly as revealed in Westerby; it is a suitable ironic comment on the sexual revolution of the contemporary world that Westerby is consciously presented as Galahad with appropriate purity of heart, despite a marital record of Hollywood proportions. And Prideaux is the knight–hermit, with the touching little portrait of Bill Roach as the squire only subconsciously aware of what calling he has assumed.

I have not pursued Wodehouse so far, because Mr. le Carré makes it clear that his closest obligations here, in 'rhythm and timing', would require very narrow analysis of specific passages.

Mr. le Carré's creative criticism enables him to see the values of Wodehouse's methods for his own operations, although his work seldom involves comedy. Wodehouse recognized common frontiers with the literature of detection and espionage; Jeeves and Wooster are the most successful descendants of Holmes and Watson (though Conan Doyle's wit, irony and comedy made this transition much less surprising than might at first sight appear). Wodehouse produced some light-hearted but nonetheless hard-hitting critiques of thriller conventions. Wodehouse directly inspired specific writers of detection, mystery and thriller fiction in his turn; Agatha Christie's thrillers *The Secret of Chimneys* and *The Seven Dials Mystery* at times involve almost explicit looting from the Wodehouse cast of characters, and Dorothy Sayers picked up several ideas from Wodehouse, *The Unpleasantness at the Bellona Club* possibly deriving from Bingo Little's *aperçu* in *The Inimitable Jeeves* when the Drones is temporarily rehoused in the Senior Liberal Club: 'I believe that old boy over by the window has been dead three days, but I don't like to mention it to anyone.' Mr. le Carré may in his turn have derived something from both of these writers. Jerry Westerby's adventures in Italy with the orphan, as somewhat over-facetiously presented through the eyes of the locals, recalls Sayers's 'The Incredible Elopement of Lord Peter Wimsey', also set in a Latin country, and the note of genial condescension to foreign inferiors, rare in Mr. le Carré, is strongly in keeping with the Sayers style. Wodehouse presenting his monocled fools in foreign parts not only suggests music-hall, but even foreign-language phrase-book foreigners—but this is a device to keep the perspective of his genial imbeciles before the reader. In *The Honourable Schoolboy* Mr. le Carré has the same intention: the chapter is his Westerby overture to a work which also has a Hong Kong overture and a Circus overture, the several 'Leonoras' to his *Fidelio*. Since Jerry Westerby must rise to something more than a Drones Club level of intelligence, innocent though he be, Lord Peter Wimsey, the intelligent woman's Bertie Wooster, may supply the appropriate vibrations. Christie memories are less certain: one man pursuing another begins *A Small Town in Germany* with the escape of the pursued forcing the novel's train of events by the course of action it throws on the pursuer, and this is also the means by which Christie began *The Mystery of the Blue Train*; both novels end with the destruction of the pursuer, who is by profession a trusted minor clerk or secretary, and who shows a remarkable degree of ingenuity in secret organization as well as considerable if unexpected amatory propensities. The idea in *The Little Drummer Girl* of having the plot of a cover given to an agent being itself written by a professional author was used by Christie in *Parker Pyne Investigates* (the writer in question being a self-caricature). Neither of these works are Christie favourites, but both were reprinted by Penguin to the tune of some 100,000 copies apiece in the 1950s when Mr. le Carré was presumably looking over the field before girding up his loins, and as *A Murder of Quality* reminds us, he himself was initially stretching between detective and thriller fiction.

To reduce a passage of Wodehouse to proportions necessary to demonstrate its specific use to Mr. le Carré is a little like tearing a minute fragment of a butterfly for microscopic examination, an odious and probably misleading action. One passage strikes me forcibly, perhaps because with its counterpart in Mr. le Carré's work, it ends a chapter. Bertie Wooster, having escaped from imprisonment in the millionaire J. Washburn Stoker's yacht in *Thank You, Jeeves* by means of boot-polished face, must for various reasons conceal himself not only from Stoker, but from the police, and from his friend, the owner of the house, Lord Chuffnell. He lacks food and liquids. Apart from Jeeves, the servants are a hostile quantity, one of them engaged to a policemen (who later will be holding him in custody):

> The door opened. A female voice spoke. No doubt that of the future Mrs. Constable Dobson.
> 'Mr. Stoker,' it announced.
> Large, flat feet clumped into the room.

*The Spy Who Came in from the Cold* shows Leamas in prison, with a similar if far more physically perilous omnipresence of surrounding enemies:

> He must have lain there hours before they came. It grew hot from the light, he was thirsty but he refused to call out. At last the door opened and Mundt stood there. He knew it was Mundt from the eyes. Smiley had told him about them.

I do not present what I find as a rhythmical similarity with confidence in its general acceptance, simply as the record of my instinct. But it does underline one point. Bertie's situation is hilarious, however infuriating for himself; Leamas's is horrible. Yet the writer in the process of creation is a cold-blooded scientist. Hence the epiphany of a new and terrible enemy by emphasis on a physical attribute can be moved from a source of hilarity to one of horror without any particular sense of incongruity. There is in any case quite a bit of the horrific about Stoker, were the context less funny:

> He eyed me musingly.
> 'There was a time, when I was younger, when I would have broken your neck,' he said.
> I didn't like the trend the conversation was taking. After all, a man is as young as he feels. . . .

> Mundt's appearance was fully consistent with his temperament. He looked an athlete. His fair hair was cut short. It lay mat and neat. His young face had a hard, clean line, and a frightening directness; it was barren of humour or fantasy. He looked young but not youthful; older men would take him seriously.

> 'She must have been with you a few moments before I arrived. Now, perhaps, Mr. Wooster, you can understand what I meant when I said that when I was a younger man, I would have broken your neck.'
> I hadn't anything much to say. One hasn't sometimes.

> 'I wanted to see Fiedler's report of his own interrogation of you, you see. I told him to send it to me. He procrastinated and I knew I was right. Then yesterday he circulated it among the Praesidium, and did not send me a copy. Someone in London has been very clever.'
> Leamas said nothing.

The trouble about a dual presentation of this kind, apart from the danger of Mr. le Carré's indignant rejoinder that J. Washburn Stoker had not the slightest influence on Hans-Dieter Mundt, is that the creative artist may take a richly comic source and transpose it into brutal tragedy, but the critic, endeavouring to follow his footsteps, feels about as elegant as a brontosaurus suffering from St. Vitus's Dance.

There is a dreadful similarity between the schemes of Wodehouse's Ukridge to make money and those of Rick Pym, or with his counterparts who fathered Jerry and Charlie. The children's situation invites some comparison with Eve Halliday in *Leave it to Psmith*:

> '. . . I expect he wasn't always up to time with fees, was he?'
>
> 'Well, my dear, of course I was only an assistant mistress at Wayland House and had nothing to do with the financial side, but I did hear sometimes . . .'
>
> 'Poor darling father! Do you know, one of my earliest recollections—I couldn't have been more than ten—is of a ring at the front-door bell and father diving like a seal under the sofa and poking his head out and imploring me in a hoarse voice to hold the fort. I went to the door and found an indignant man with a blue paper. I prattled so prettily and innocently that he not only went away quite contentedly but he actually patted me on the head and gave me a penny. And when the door had shut father crawled out from under the sofa and gave me twopence, making threepence in all—a good morning's work. I bought father a diamond ring with it at a shop down the street, I remember. At least I thought it was a diamond. They may have swindled me, for I was very young.'

Wodehouse's use of such material may have sharpened Mr. le Carré's reflections on the creative possibilities of his own background; and it is also possible that the easy self-mockery of Wodehouse (denied a university education when his father failed to live up to expectations), made it easier for Mr. le Carré to consider the objective comedy in experiences which must have been horrific for him at the time. The Mundts to whom his father abandoned him may not have been quite as awful as his fictional Mundt, but their menace must have been sickening enough.

Wodehouse gave him the best of all gifts if he offered him a tranquillity and laughter in which to reassess and redeploy his own past. And while it is agreed that Mr. le Carré is famed for his fascination with, and detestation of, elaborate contrivance with its ruthless sacrifice of the lives of others, his study of the schemes of Jeeves would give him greater objectivity as well as humour in its assessment which soliloquizing on his own boyhood traumas could never bring. He needed that crackle of anger which ennobles *The Spy Who Came in from the Cold*, and *The Looking-Glass War*; but if he was not to wither in his own blaze of indignation he had to celebrate the comedy as well as the tragedy. Your story gets further dimensions when you can see yourself as a Bertie Wooster sent out by Jeeves on an utterly useless night bicycle-ride with its intended failure as an indispensable part of its overall scheme. *Right Ho, Jeeves* would therefore join *Thank You, Jeeves* as potential progenitor. Its sequel *The Code of the Woosters* demands attention if only for Aunt Dahlia's cry, 'Good old blackmail!', although Mr. le Carré knows how to make that ugly enough in *The Honourable Schoolboy* and *Smiley's People*. One wonders if he was ever inspired to have a Circus employee blackmail a Russian operative for having secretly designed ladies' underclothing, à la Roderick Spode and Eulalie Soeurs. If so, his variants on it have been cautious. *Summer Lightning* may very well have supplied the idea of a tarnished Galahad proving himself worthy of his name: the Hon. Galahad Threepwood in his own innocence, charm and self-sacrifice might well be added to the Buchan, Sapper, Westerman, Greene and Conrad origins of the Hon. Gerald Westerby. Gally Threepwood also possessed a good deal of the schoolboy, and his absorption in the memories of a long-vanished era has its counterpart to Jerry Westerby's distinguished and obsolete style.

Wodehouse plays frequently with impersonation, and Galahad Threepwood's *protégé* Sue Brown in *Summer Lightning* offers a blend of courage and vulnerability which may have helped to bring to life Charlie, the Little Drummer Girl (her antecedents are a little mixed for Wodehouse, her father being Cotterleigh, her mother Henderson, her impersonation Schoonmaker, and Galahad's sister asks him in *Heavy Weather* if he is her father). A comparable heroine, Jill the reckless, shares theatre training with Sue and Charlie, and is called the Little Warrior (U.S. title of *Jill the Reckless*). Sue's impersonation itself is short-lived if closely analysed, and no bravura performance such as 'Uncle Fred Flits By' where Lord Ickenham impersonates the man who came to clip the parrot's claws, the owner of the house Mr. Roddis, and a Mr. J. G. Bulstrode from down the road, his greatest subsequent regret being that he did not also impersonate the parrot. That achievement seems more in the true Circus style, worthy of Smiley or of Toby Esterhase. The incessant catechism of Charlie by her Israeli secret-service trainers, to make her word-perfect in her identity before they send her loose, suggests another possible source from the popular literature of the early 1950s: Josephine Tey's *Brat Farrar*. Here, as with Charlie (and Sue), the author skilfully deploys maximum sympathy for the impersonator although— unlike Sue—the object of the impersonation, that of swindling out of his inheritance an heir who has done no harm to the impersonator, is in some ways even nastier than the betrayal of Khalil who is, after all, a very ugly civilian murderer. Josephine Tey had given much thought to the question of impersonation, having previously produced a fine study of an unsympathetic impersonator from the standpoint of her victims in *The Franchise Affair*. Another even more likely source for Charlie's training is Cecily's diary in Wilde's *The Importance of Being Earnest*, with its chronicle before the action of the play of a love-affair that had never happened between two people unknown to one another (and one of them, again unknown to the other, actually being non-existent).

So far I had, with some minor excursions, been ready to play the hand dealt by Mr. le Carré; arguably, I had played it badly, but I had played it. I began to feel some uneasiness, a little akin to Smiley's at his exchange of motives and weapons with Karla. Mr. le Carré has been conspicuous as a barbed critic of the Establishment, notably in his introduction to *Philby: The Spy Who Betrayed a Generation* by Bruce Page, David Leitch and Phillip Knightley in 1968, for which he was later made the recipient of an Establishment eelskin wielded by its most eminent hit-man of the day, Professor Hugh Trevor-Roper (later Lord Dacre). The attack was a silly one, reaching its apogee in the author's sudden citation of Kim Philby for a hostile critique of *The Spy Who Came in from the Cold* in the midst of a work, *The Philby Affair*, intended to express detestation of him and inspire others to the same. Why believe Philby's denial of *The Spy*'s likelihood? Beelzebub is hardly the appropriate authority for literary exorcism, even for a historian with such peculiar ideas about primary sources as Lord Dacre. But it underlined the condition of Mr. le Carré as intellectual alienated alike from the Philbys and Dacres of the Establishment. *The Spy Who Came in from the Cold*, and *A Small Town in Germany*, reflect Mr. le Carré's unease at the indifference of the British (and

American) Establishments to the phenomena of Nazi survival and revival; and quite apart from their additional message as to the moral flabbiness of the Establishment in its Machiavellianism, these were undesirable messages to see transmitted to a mass audience, especially by the formidable literary powers, cultural knowledge and diplomatic experience of Mr. le Carré. He could not be dismissed as a Jew (the Establishment in the 1960s was still quite good at dismissing people as Jews), although he clearly liked Jews—Jewishness is the first call of Dieter Frey and Fiedler on the reader's sympathies, and if *The Little Drummer Girl* is bitterly critical of Israeli policy towards the Palestinians, its anger is the anger of a friend, and an informed one. In fact, *The Little Drummer Girl* suggests a much deeper psychological involvement with Israel than Mr. le Carré tends to show with Britain. (It is not, I would think, that he is anti-English; he is sufficiently sure of his Englishness not to prate about it, as Fleming demanded of Bond.) I did not read *The Little Drummer Girl* until I had visited Israel and fallen in love with it; I had been told (in Britain) the book was the work of an enemy, but I thought it breathed a love of the country. It was also love, I felt, that was still deeply involved, not disillusion and rejection. I had known too many Americanophiles who bitterly denounced the U.S. Government's actions in Vietnam to mistake the work's emotions. Of course there would be pro-Israeli chauvinists, as there were endless pro-American chauvinists, to denounce any criticism; I preferred the honesty of the critical Americanophiles and I believe that many Israelis would prefer that kind of love for their country.

But where were Mr. le Carré's own antecedents of criticism of the English Establishment? The sources of alienation in spy fiction are numerous, but he hardly seemed to fit into any. Maugham's homosexuality, Buchan's Scottishness, Ambler's Popular Front liberalism, Greene's Catholicism, Erskine Childers's Irishness, Conrad's Polishness—these all offered vantage-points. They were only flickering vantage-points, certainly. Buchan might occasionally grind a tooth or two over the imbecility of conventional English attitudes (as does his South African hero Richard Hannay at the beginning of *The Thirty-Nine Steps*) or expertly convey how alone and even alien he could feel in London town (by making his hero a conspiracy-target in

63

*The Power-House*). These moods evaporated. Childers's *The Riddle of the Sands* is a masterly assault on the backwardness of English security, no doubt from the greater wisdom of the concerned periphery, but it would be many years before he became an Irish nationalist propagandist and still more before he faced an Irish nationalist firing-squad. Ambler played the artistic effects of shrewd reflections on arms manufacturers and their machinations, and showed more humanity in his lovable Russian-American Communist agent Zaleshoff that in his English adversary who has graduated from public school and the Black-and-Tans' Auxiliaries, a savage point of confrontation in *Background to Danger* (English title: *Uncommon Danger*); but when the time of the post-war Stalinist purges of the satellites began he wrote his dissent with far more integrity than most revisionists in the humane and perceptive *Judgment on Deltchev*. Maugham was much more the Establishment's critic of its lack of subtlety than anything else, writing as an Establishment person (after all, his brother became Lord Chancellor, hate one another as they might). Conrad, having mastered the language, reflected a conqueror's sense of possession. Greene's Catholicism was adopted, not inherited; it symbolized his alienation but not its cause, although it certainly strengthened it. With him the question of alienation's origin remains unanswered, as does that of Mr. le Carré. There does seem a sign of a desire to duel with God in occasional moments of Mr. le Carré, and it is not entirely a Greene thought in his shade. Of course Mr. le Carré grew up in a world which could no longer afford the illusions of Buchan, Childers, Ambler and Maugham. He is where he is because their Odysseys are no longer feasible.

Thus far had I reached when I got down to *The Naïve and Sentimental Lover*. And at this point I came to realize that it was not, after all, Mr. le Carré who had stacked my hand. Like so many others, I had swallowed all too readily the consensus that the book was wretched. I found it a distinguished work, and one which for me shared with François Mauriac the terrifying quality of entering into my own emotions to a depth unknown in most other writers. Although Professor Rutherford is not one of its admirers, his essay speaks of the general conflict between Dionysiac and Apollonian emotions; and this the book brings to magnificent fruition. It takes the attraction of Bohemia against bourgeois and conveys its self-fulfilling denunciation of the treachery of reason and order. It shows the magic of anarchy as the artistic conscience, and the inability of the half-conquered votary to answer its indictments. It comes to terms with beguilement at which writers as various as Shakespeare with Puck, and Barrie with Peter Pan, have only hinted. It exhibits a beauty, cruelty, nihilism and Nietzcheanism—and above all, terror—in love. It is exceedingly courageous, and I suspect extremely allusive. Thus the protagonist Aldo Cassidy is supposedly Mr. le Carré (but after all there is a good deal of Mr. le Carré in many of his own creations, as there is of all authors) but he is not a writer. He is a pram-manufacturer. A pram suggests Wilde, with Miss Prism—a lady of as fully geometrical a nomenclature as Mr. le Carré—having placed her novel in the perambulator and the baby in the handbag. We are therefore in Wilde's world of deception and mask, one where impulse is king and logic must first prove its insanity to prevail. The Establishment turned on it tooth and nail. It is a little hard to assign the reasons, but some may be suggested. The Establishment does not like it when the butcher's boy instead of his normal delivery arrives with a somewhat thorny rose-bush—it insists these must be spurious roses. Mr. le Carré, if he is to be tolerated, must be pigeon-holed. If he is only a writer of amusing thrillers, then their content, however disturbing for a time, will be subordinated to the thrills of the plot. Beyond this general bourgeois morality there was the disappointment that Mr. le Carré had not provided the usual corpse into whom the reader might, as Wodehouse would say, sink his teeth. Wanting another thriller, few people would accept substitutes. And the book may have seemed to many as an intrusion on their private beings; the heterosexual novel could be pigeon-holed in one direction, the homosexual novel in another, but the disturbing bisexual frontiers of this novel—where the bisexuality might not be sexual at all, but simply loving, as it said, which could be more alarming still—these things were definitely Not Wanted. Mr. le Carré may actually have portrayed some of this reaction later when in *The Little Drummer Girl* Charlie finds the Cecily-like diary the Israeli secret service have invented for her to have supposedly kept in the past: 'She felt dirty and invaded.'

There is irony in this, for Mr. le Carré does possess a

formidable Establishment quality himself. His anxiety to have his work judged by the highest standards makes him very quick to deny its origin in literature beyond the Critically Acceptable. E. Phillips Oppenheim is now no longer read and (like *The Naïve and Sentimental Lover*) is therefore a target of abuse by people who have not read him. And perhaps also by those who have. Mr. le Carré mocks the Establishment reading of Oppenheim in his youth. Yet *The Great Impersonation* turns on a man pretending to be himself who finally accomplishes his mission by proving it; it is in many ways crude and ill-thought, but is *The Spy Who Came in from the Cold* absolutely immune to its influence? And the last sight of Shamus in *The Naïve and Sentimental Lover* has a remarkable similarity to the final disappearance of the ambiguous eponymous protagonist of Oppenheim's *Michael's Evil Deeds*, a figure inviting repulsion and fascination, betrayer of one of his lovers to another, homicidal yet irresistible, ultimately saved by his most hated enemy. Mr. le Carré in *The Naïve and Sentimental Lover* on the one hand defied the Establishment by doing the unexpected, entering the forbidden territory and finally having as a thriller writer the impudence to try his hand at an un-classifiable novel. On the other hand, he virtually laid himself before it as a candidate for acceptance by coming forward for its examination in Serious Fiction. He was sharply reminded that Trespassers Will Be Persecuted. He had not, after all, taken the precaution of clothing himself in something like Catholicism which would immunize him by acknowledging he could never hope to be taken absolutely seriously.

*The Naïve and Sentimental Lover* carries with it one further problem. It is acknowledged that it has in part-origin aspects of the involvement of Mr. le Carré with the writer James Kennaway. But since Mr. le Carré is not, save in a purely Prismatic sense, a pram-manufacturer, the novel's plot does not indicate where Kennaway as writer influenced the younger and evidently impressionable Mr. le Carré (who, when the two men became close, had just rocketed to stardom without warning with *The Spy*). Kennaway was in one respect a very remarkable author: he was extraordinarily experimental. His various books show exceptionally drastic alterations of style and method. It is significant, I think, that Mr. le Carré in his turn became much more experimental after the careful and conventional structure of his first three novels: *The Looking-Glass War*, where we might expect Kennaway's influence to be strongest, shows great courage in its playing with anti-climax. Kennaway, the dedicatee, may also have inspired what I suspect is a clue in its title, largely ignored: that certain of the characters have origins in Lewis Carroll's *Through the Looking-Glass*—Taylor perhaps, as Lily, who never becomes a pawn, Avery as the White Queen, Leclerc as the White Knight, Leiser as Alice, Control as the Red King whose awakening must end the dream, Smiley as the Red Queen with her helpful if donnish instruction. This kind of masquerade would have a subtle allusiveness of a kind Kennaway seems to have enjoyed. Mr. le Carré had broken with Kennaway by the time of *A Small Town in Germany* but here again his impish former friend would have relished the idea of a work whose central character never appears save as a silhouette in the prologue and as a quickly murdered mute in the epilogue. *The Naïve and Sentimental Lover* is an experiment; it may be intended as a final repudiation of the now dead Kennaway, killed in a motorway accident, but I think it was intended to stand as a monument to their relationship. And to this reader, at least, it is a generous as well as a courageous one. Kennaway would surely also have been entertained at Mr. le Carré's return to his old orthodoxy; accepted as the penitent come back 'tail between his legs' (in the somewhat embarrassing phrase of Dr. Eric Homberger's admirable, if not always accurate, monograph), Mr. le Carré turned prodigal in his father's house and inflated the fatted calf to Brobdignagian proportions. *The Quest for Karla*, taken as a totality, effectively sank his critics in three instalments. As Miss Prism observes, never speak slightingly of the three-volumed novelists; the pram had come home. He then achieved a triumphant transposition of *dramatis personae* to Israel and the insurgent Palestinians, and for the first time looked at the world through female eyes. And he finally swept the board with a work of compassion and mockery, autobiography and fantasy, self-analysis and social anatomisation, which he magnificently refused to have entered for the notorious Booker Prize.

*The Naïve and Sentimental Lover* ends on the tender and terrible sentence: 'For in this world, whatever there was left of it to inhabit, Aldo Cassidy dared not remember love.' Mr. le Carré

67

dares. It was love—the love of Smiley and Dieter—which raised *Call for the Dead* to its greatest heights, and it was love that continued to distinguish his writing. Leamas dies for it, Avery cries for it, Turner in a strange sense professes it for a man he meets only after his death, Prideaux kills for it, Westerby is killed for it, Charlie is hurled out of her own identity by it. If spy fiction is belittled, love stories are the last word in the unacceptable to the Great Tradition. Yet in a wholly different sense from the pawing, predatory, pseudo-pornography which has so demeaned spy fiction, Mr. le Carré has been talking about love from the first, whether his readers and critics would recognize the fact or not. Above all, most of his novels are reflections of Wilde's 'each man kills the thing he loves.' Like the good and conscientious craftsman he is, he was simply exploring his most important theme when he sought to come to terms with it for its own sake in *The Naïve and Sentimental Lover.* And it is because he has given so much to it that he has earned his way to consideration in that great rank of writers who bring an entire civilization under their scrutiny, in politics, in society, in diplomacy, in culture, in the human trading in all of these things; those writers who recognize that however great the creator's canvas, and however momentous the issues which it depicts, its real achievement must lie in the revelation of truth and dignity in showing the highest relationship human beings can have with one another. 'Where Love Is, God Is', is a very small story; its author also wrote *War and Peace.* Neither in stature nor in belief is Mr. le Carré a Tolstoy; but for various reasons he is one of the very few English writers of our time who can look at Tolstoy without shame.

## NOTE

I would like to thank Alan Bold, Mark Kennedy, Elizabeth Balbirnie Lee, Patrick Cosgrave, Philip French, Ruth Dudley Edwards, Mhairi Mackenzie-Robinson, Trevor Royle, Peter and Liselotte Marshall, Alison Munro, Helena Jack, Alan Taylor of the Central Branch of the City of Edinburgh Public Libraries, the National Library of Scotland, Edinburgh University Library and above all the late Martin Goldman of the B.B.C. to whose dear memory this essay is dedicated.

# 3

# Women's Place in John le Carré's Man's World

by MARGARET MOAN ROWE

Let me begin with Margaret Atwood in 'Just Like a Woman':

> Men's novels are about how to get power. Killing and so on, or
> winning or so on. So are women's novels, though the method is
> different. In men's novels, getting the woman or women goes
> along with getting the power. It's a perk not a means. In
> women's novels you get the power by getting the man. The man
> is the power.[1]

Now let me turn to John le Carré. His espionage novels are
certainly about 'how to get power'—and in post-war Britain,
how at least to keep some of it. Whether or not women are
merely 'perks'—that is, relatively powerless characters in his
novels—is another story. It is a story that I propose to tell by
paying particular attention to female characters and their place
in the espionage fiction le Carré has written over the last three
decades.

## 1

In the five novels written in the '60s—*Call for the Dead* (1961),
*A Murder of Quality* (1962), *The Spy Who Came in from the Cold*
(1963), *The Looking-Glass War* (1965), and *A Small Town in
Germany* (1968)—women are less and less consequential
presences. And except for Liz Gold in *The Spy Who Came in from*

69

*the Cold*, that greater and lesser consequence is attached to their
rôles as wives in what David Monaghan describes as 'the
battleground of marriage'.[2] Le Carré presents a cavalcade of
wives as betrayers—sexual, social and/or political: Else Fennan
and Lady Ann Sercomb in *Call for the Dead*, Stella Rode who is
victim and victimizer in *A Murder of Quality*, and the absent
Mrs. Turner and the minimally present Hazel Bradfield in *A
Small Town in Germany*. Sarah Avery in *The Looking-Glass War*
escapes the weight of the betrayer: she is merely nagging and
unhappy. Except for Elsa Fennan, wives are pretty clearly
stereotyped as what Katherine Rogers would term 'troublesome
helpmates'[3] in le Carré's '60s fiction.

But twice I used the preposition 'except', so I feel compelled
to describe how the women in le Carré's first and third novels
escape the limitations of other women characters. Simply put,
Elsa Fennan and Liz Gold have significance apart from their
relationships with husband and lover in their respective
novels.

Fennan, in fact, is the traitor who uses her husband's work in
the Foreign Office as source for the material she passes to the
East Germans. As active participant in the events (suspicions of
her husband's disloyalty that seem to lead to his suicide) that
George Smiley comes to investigate, Fennan has power in the
narrative. Le Carré grants her complicated motives and shows
her impressive skills, skills that allow her a temporary out-
witting of the formidable Smiley:

> Smiley, looking at her, felt he had broken something he should
> never have touched because it was so fragile. He felt an obscene,
> coarse bully, his offerings of tea a futile recompense for his
> clumsiness.[4]

Fennan's past as a German Jew—'I'm the wandering Jewess,
. . . the no-man's land, the battlefield of your toy soldiers' (*Call*,
p. 147)—is presented in some detail in the novel, making her at
once sympathetic and forbidding for Smiley and reader. She has
a view of history that comes out of past oppression: 'Look at
me,' she said; 'What dream did they leave me? I dreamed of
long golden hair and they shaved my head, I dreamed of a
beautiful body and they broke it with hunger. I have seen what
human beings are, . . .' (*Call*, p. 95). She is also capable of

exploiting that past with both husband and Smiley to achieve her ends in the present. As Peter Lewis aptly notes:

> By the end of the book, when Smiley finally reveals that Elsa, not her husband, is the Communist spy, it is clear that she has been engaged in an extraordinarily complex piece of rôle-playing throughout this interview, in which the genuine and the hypocritical are blended. In order to protect herself from Smiley, she has to condemn her real self.[5]

Elsa Fennan certainly proves troublesome enough in *Call for the Dead*, but in granting her a more complex rôle than that of helpmate, le Carré makes her an exception among the wives in his '60s novels.

Liz Gold, a librarian, is not a wife but comes into the action of *The Spy Who Came in from the Cold* through her involvement with Alec Leamas. And like Leamas, she becomes a pawn between the espionage systems of Britain and East Germany; for both sides her significance comes through her attachment to Leamas, the spy. But within the narrative, she attains her own significance through her views of the world and of human relationships. Like Elsa Fennan, Liz is a Communist; she is not, however, a traitor. Indeed, le Carré delineates a process of recognition in the character of Liz Gold who moves from the abstract belief in 'History' she mentions to Leamas in her Bayswater flat through her distaste for the Party's 'secrecy, it seemed dishonest'[6] to an ugly encounter with the Party apparatus in East Germany in the person of the anti-Semitic prison warder who tells her: 'We cannot build communism without doing away with individualism. You cannot plan a great building if some swine builds his sty on your site' (*Cold*, p. 200).

Faced with the double-dealing of East and West, however, she finds herself in a moral no-woman's land as she waits for escape at the Berlin Wall. Ironically, Leamas uses the Party line to defend the intelligence operation:

> But don't complain about the terms, Liz; they're Party terms. A small price for a big return. One sacrificed for many. It's not pretty, I know, choosing who it'll be—turning the plan into people. (*Cold*, p. 210)

But Liz's commitment has always been to people over plans, a loyalty that le Carré captures earlier in internal views of Liz's response to party work in England. (Indeed in the minimalist characterization in *The Spy Who Came in from the Cold*, le Carré devotes a good deal of his narration to capturing the doubleness in Liz Gold who resents Party secrecy but lies about her sales of the *Daily Worker*.) Before her senseless death, she reaffirms her faith in people when she tells Leamas:

> You don't understand. You don't want to. You're trying to persuade yourself. It's far more terrible, what they are doing; to find the humanity in people, in me and whoever else they use, to turn it like a weapon in their hands, and use it to hurt and kill—. (*Cold*, p. 211)

So convincing is Liz's characterization in the novel and so sympathetic does the reader become to her that many readers— even careful critics—are tempted to read the novel's close as a validation of her view over any other. I quote Peter Lewis:

> At the end of *The Spy* le Carré upholds Liz's positive values while stressing their extreme vulnerability and helplessness in a world of power blocs, bureaucratic institutions, and political ideologies, whether Communist or democratic, poised on the brink of madness and universal destructions. She lives up to her surname in being a nugget of gold in a world of dross.[7]

I submit that Lewis, like many other readers, is overly responsive to Liz Gold and wants to make her the undisputed heroine of the novel.[8] But this is le Carré country, a terrain that thrives on ambiguity.

Liz's values are certainly presented for the reader's admiration, but Leamas's view of the necessity for 'bureaucratic institutions'—'We're a tiny price to pay . . .' (*Cold*, p. 212)—is not repudiated by the narrator. Lars Ole Sauerberg accurately describes the strange doubleness that exists in the novel when he notes:

> Despite its critical tone, the story is also a defense of values which makes the sacrifices of Leamas, Liz, and the sometimes quite sympathetic Fiedler necessary. The critical tone [in the novel] is directed against the way the plan is executed, not against the reasons for its execution. In SWCIFC le Carré pities the characters for their private fates, but this is something that takes place on the level of formula variation only. On the level of the formula there remains the ideological and political conflict

without which the genre could not exist. The story should not, I believe, be read as a complete denunciation of secret-agent activities, but rather as an experiment to transfer the perspective to the victim.[9]

Yet, so successful is le Carré in making Liz Gold a person as well as a victim in his narrative that readers are very much inclined to avoid the strange doubleness in *The Spy Who Came in from the Cold*.

No such compelling women characters issue from the two novels—*The Looking-Glass War* and *A Small Town in Germany*—that close le Carré's work in the '60s. In fact, the sexual relationships that prove to be most interesting are the male bondings between John Avery and Fred Leiser in the former and between Alan Turner and Leo Harting in the latter. David Monaghan captures the situation when he observes that 'Avery, in *The Looking-Glass War*, finds much more satisfaction in his relationship with the agent Leiser, than with his unhappy and complaining wife.'[10] Liz Gold's condemnation of systems that have 'contempt for love' (*Cold*, p. 211) resonates in *The Looking-Glass War* wherein John Avery, a young functionary in the 'Department', is ordered to seduce Leiser back into espionage for a run into East Germany. I use the verb 'seduce' because no other word so exactly captures Avery's work to win Leiser's loyalty and affection. Told that 'Leiser is not one of us. Never make that mistake',[11] Avery must still seduce Leiser into believing that they wear the same old-school-tie.

Male bonding also preoccupies le Carré in *A Small Town in Germany*. Leo Harting, like Leiser, believes that he is 'one of us' in the British system, and, like Leiser, he finds himself an object in the espionage game. But, unlike Leiser, Harting has some control over his destiny and exercises his freedom by temporarily upending British and German security systems. Sent to find a file Harting has stolen, Alan Turner, le Carré's most proletarian agent, uses his work as an escape from a broken marriage. In what seems like a reversal of the movement in *Heart of Darkness*, Turner moves from contempt for Harting—heretofore a small-time con man and operative in the British embassy—to recognizing 'a kind of integrity about him'.[12] Turner ultimately sees Harting as a double.

The women characters—Hazel Bradfield, Jenny Pargiter, *et al.*—who flit in and out of *A Small Town in Germany* have their significance as sexual objects with little or no attempt on le Carré's part to give them any complexity. But that must be seen as a realistic presentation, not necessarily an endorsement, of the way many women function in the world of espionage that le Carré seeks to portray. As David Monaghan observes: 'Le Carré's spies are misfits, men whose emotions have been stunted by lack of love in childhood or twisted by unsuccessful adult heterosexual relationships.'[13] In his '60s novels, le Carré's focus is very clearly on the male side of 'unsuccessful adult heterosexual relationships' so the psychological complexity that would enrich characterization is very much a male preserve.

## 2

In Muriel Spark's *The Abbess of Crewe*, Alexandra, the aristocratic abbess, pontificates: 'Here, in the Abbey of Crewe, we have discarded history. We have entered the sphere, dear Sisters, of mythology.'[14] Something of the urge to myth-making overtakes John le Carré, the realist, in his extremely long '70s novels: *Tinker Tailor Soldier Spy* (1974), *The Honourable Schoolboy* (1977), and *Smiley's People* (1979).[15]

In those three novels, the extraordinarily ordinary George Smiley, who first enters le Carré's fiction in *Call for the Dead*, achieves apotheosis as the epic hero of le Carré's male myth of the Circus. Smiley wins his heroic stature as he moves from cleansing the Circus of its internal weakness, notably Bill Haydon—the mole, in *Tinker Tailor Soldier Spy*, to bringing the Circus back into Western espionage through co-operation and contest with its American 'cousins' in *The Honourable Schoolboy*, until finally transcending the Circus and its vacillating values in *Smiley's People*, as he moves outside and structures his own army for final combat with Karla, his double and nemesis in Russian espionage. In the end, Smiley is like the ageing Beowulf fulfilling his own quest.

What of women characters in this epic world? Basically, they fall into three categories: women who help the hero, women who hinder the hero, and background figures—notably Peter Guillam's sexual targets. I wish to focus on the first two

categories, paying particular attention to Connie Sachs and
Lady Ann Sercomb; then I wish to turn to the characterization
of Elizabeth Worthington, the woman who begins to move
outside of le Carré's myth.

Connie Sachs is Smiley's Sybil. Through her remarkable
memory, she gives coherence to seemingly random events in the
present. She enters the epic in *Tinker Tailor Soldier Spy* when
Smiley, now a Circus outsider, goes to Oxford to visit his old
mate Connie, 'formerly queen of research',[16] and herself in exile
from the Circus. She had been removed for 'losing . . . [her]
sense of proportion' (*Tinker*, p. 99). But Connie is a genuine
grotesque who has neither talent nor use for proportion—'I *hate*
the real world, George' (*Tinker*, p. 99). Le Carré presents her
through long stretches of dialogue,[17] a technique that fits
Connie who is not 'a human wreck' as Lars Sauerberg maintains[18]; rather she is metonimized as a memory and comes to life
through her voice:

> She began her story like a fairy-tale: 'Once upon a time, there
> was a defector called Stanley, way back in 1963,' and she applied
> to it the same spurious logic—part inspiration, part intellectual
> opportunism—born of a wonderful mind that had never grown
> up. Her formless white face took on the grandmother's glow of
> enchanted reminiscence. Her memory was as compendious as
> her body and surely she loved it more, for she had put everything
> aside to listen to it: her drink, her cigarette, even for a while
> Smiley's passive hand. (*Tinker*, p. 100)

The essentially sexless Connie—'she had a low belly like an old
man's' (*Tinker*, p. 97)—presented as a memory with a voice
provides aid to but makes no demands of Smiley.

Indeed, so right an assistance does Connie offer in *Tinker
Tailor Soldier Spy* that le Carré expands her rôle as Smiley's
companion through the rest of his quest. Connie, alone, stays
with the silent Smiley as he broods in *The Honourable Schoolboy*,
and it is she who through her memory and voice puts him in
touch with the 'decent company' of the past:

> Smiley had closed his eyes and his brow was drawn into a rigid
> knot above the bridge of his nose. For a long while Connie said
> nothing at all. . . .
> 'Karla wouldn't give two pins, would he, dearie?' she mur-
> mured. 'Not for one dead Frost, nor for ten. That's the difference,

really. We can't write it much larger than that, can we, not these days? Who was it who used to say, 'We're fighting for the survival of Reasonable Man'? Steed-Asprey? Or was it Control? I loved that. It covered it all. Hitler. The new thing. That's who we are: reasonable.'[19]

She is the historian—handmaiden serving the hero.

Connie's rôle in *Tinker Tailor Soldier Spy* and in *The Honourable Schoolboy* makes her conversion to love in *Smiley's People* difficult to accept. Still serving Smiley as racial (in this case the Circus, a race apart) memory, Connie now spends her exile in a tortured (witchlike) country setting with Hilary and animals, and le Carré would have us believe that the dying Connie has found love. But the love interest—'Get yourself a bit of love and wait for Armageddon'[20]—is contrived. More believable is the Connie who begs Smiley to 'take me with you' (*People*, p. 211) in his quest for Karla. And Smiley does in the form of information about Karla's personal life; the physical Connie is dying but her precious memory ('Her memory was as compendious as her body and surely she loved it more') goes with Smiley.

Memory, too, plays an important part in le Carré's presentation of Lady Ann Sercomb, George Smiley's faithless wife. Connie Sachs brings memory to Smiley's aid; Smiley's memory essentially brings Ann into being for the reader. Time and again from *Call for the Dead* onwards Smiley invokes Ann's presence through his memories of past experiences with her, or her name is invoked by others to annoy or to comfort Smiley. Peter Lewis maintains that 'Smiley is haunted by memories of his former wife and their short married life together at the end of World War II before she deserted him, leaving him in possession of a broken world.'[21] That, I think, is also an accurate description of Ann's place in Smiley's epic—she can never be anything more than a haunting memory.

Lady Ann is essentially a type rather than a character in Smiley's journey towards heroic stature. She is Smiley's 'bitch goddess' (*People*, p. 292) as Saul Enderby notes and as such has both positive and negative effects on Smiley. He had married her 'in search of the kiss that would turn him into a Prince' (*Call*, p. 1), but le Carré's interest is in writing an espionage epic not a fairy-tale. The transformation of George does not then come through Ann's rather limited magic (she is a promiscuous aristocrat) but through his own internalization of his suffering over his broken marriage among other things. Ann has more meaning for Smiley as an absence than as a presence, and le Carré himself has called her 'that absent sexual force'.[22]

Yet despite his stated interest in sex as one of the greatest realities,[23] le Carré is content to typecast Ann Sercomb as a wilful and randy aristocrat. Incapable of controlling her own passions, she seems to have no hesitation in betraying Smiley with Bill Haydon and a legion of others. But even in writing the preceding sentence I find myself asking: how do you know this about a character who is never revealed as having any motives for her actions? Indeed she is so much a creature of Smiley's recollection that one becomes wary of the evidence against her.

But perhaps an 'absent sexual force' needs no motive; certainly Lady Ann Sercomb is never given any. She remains as remote and slightly baffling to the reader (even the few instances of Ann's cryptic dialogue further distances her) as she does to George Smiley. Connie Sachs is a more comprehensible type because of her contribution to the quest that links the three novels. Le Carré brings the reader close to Connie through dialogue; she literally speaks her way into an identity, an identity at Smiley's service. Connie is not simply a perk on the way to power but a remote means to that power: her memory is one of Smiley's weapons in the quest.

Elizabeth (Lizzie) Worthington in *The Honourable Schoolboy* is not so central to Smiley's quest, a fact that helps her elude the limitations imposed on the presentations of Connie Sachs and Lady Ann Sercomb. Part of her escape lies in the two levels of narrative in the novel[24]: Smiley's work in London tracing Karla's activities in Hong Kong and Jerry Westerby's work in the Far East as an agent for Smiley. The levels converge near the end of the novel but by then Lizzie has been established as a character apart from the mythic trappings of the quest.

But established how? Lizzie Worthington, wife and mother, leaves her family to seek her fortune in the Far East where she becomes embroiled in Smiley's attempt to refurbish British Intelligence in Hong Kong. Like Ann Sercomb, she betrays her marriage, but unlike Ann, Lizzie is given an involved background, a complex context that does much to explain her conduct. She is also directly involved in the action in Hong Kong where she becomes the idealized love of Jerry Westerby, the book's title character and forerunner of Magnus Pym in *A Perfect Spy*.

Let me first turn to Lizzie's background, cleverly mapped by le Carré in two interviews conducted by Smiley. First Smiley interviews the obtuse Peter Worthington, Lizzie's abandoned husband, and through a careful pacing of questions and silences breaks through the defences Worthington has set up to save face: 'You never knew your Elizabeth, Smiley thought, still staring at Peter Worthington; and I never knew my Ann' (*Schoolboy*, p. 219). The sympathy that Smiley maintains through that interview, however, gives way to shudders when Lizzie's parents, the Pellings, are interviewed. Retired to Arcady Mansion in north London, the Pellings—'She wore flat shoes and a mannish pullover with a belt that made her shoulders broad. . . . Mr. Pelling was the kind of small man who would only ever marry tall women' (*Schoolboy*, pp. 221–22)—are beasts. Each encouraged Lizzie to see herself as a potential celebrity. Mr. Pelling, whose relationship with Lizzie suggests incest, blithers on about her career, her '*commercial* experience' (*Schoolboy*, p. 228). Mrs. Pelling sings a hymn to her daughter's promiscuity: 'My little Lizzie went behind the hedge with half of Asia before she found her Drake. But she found him' (*Schoolboy*, p. 232).

Given such parentage, Lizzie's passion for fantasy has reasonable psychological explanation. I agree with David Monaghan who observes that

> Lizzie Worthington in *The Honourable Schoolboy* lives almost entirely in an invented version of reality that allows her far more spiritual and emotional scope than do her real social circumstances, as the daughter of a retired Post Office employee and the wife of an Islington schoolteacher.[25]

But Monaghan does not adequately capture the destructiveness of Pelling, a destructiveness that far exceeds 'social circumstance'. Pelling is the terrible father whom le Carré pursues with such vigour in *A Perfect Spy*.

In addition to a past, Lizzie has a present in the very complicated plotting of *The Honourable Schoolboy*, and in that present she has some complexity. Involved with men—Mellon, a British agent, and Riccardo, an American pilot, for example—who see her as little more than a perk in their power plays in Vietnam and Hong Kong, Lizzie still evolves a rudimentary code that makes her capable of loyalty. She shapes a deal to save Tiny Riccardo because 'He was one of us. . . . Although he was a sod' (*Schoolboy*, p. 495). And she wants Drake Ko told that 'I kept faith. . . . It's what he cares about most. I stuck to the deal' (*Schoolboy*, p. 515). In a world where so little faith is kept, Lizzie Worthington is at least the honourable whore.

### 3

When Jerry Westerby visits Tiny Riccardo's jungle hideout, he discovers how much Riccardo prides himself on his power over Lizzie Worthington: '*Pygmalion*—know that movie? well, I'm the professor, I tell her some things. . . .' (*Schoolboy*, p. 413). Infinitely more than the benighted and self-deluded Riccardo, Kurtz and Gadi Becker of Israeli Intelligence act as Pygmalion and Son in *The Little Drummer Girl* (1983). Their Eliza is Charlie, an English actress 'recruited' into their plot against Palestinian terrorists. But the preceding sentence suggests too much passivity on Charlie's part, a suggestion I want to qualify. First of all as title character (le Carré's first woman character to so function), Charlie has a primacy, a power in the narrative, and le Carré goes well beyond titling in empowering Charlie by making her consciousness the primary filter for much of the action.

Objectively, however, within that action Charlie is very much a 'perk' attached to men who have and want more power. On Charlie's first entrance, for example, the narrator notes 'a central meekness . . . somewhere that seemed to attract her fatally to bullies. . . .'[26] Meekness and poor taste in men are not her only qualities; she is also an actress of talent and a woman of chaotic passions and even more chaotic politics. In short, she is a perfect target for a psychological takeover—or as Kurtz puts it, 'An *acting* job' (*Girl*, p. 126).

That takeover occupies much of *The Little Drummer Girl*, so the reader's attention is riveted on Charlie and on the means that Kurtz and Becker use to transform her into the ultimate 'honey trap'. I say ultimate because Charlie has a more elaborate rôle to play than the girl picked to lure Salim, the brother of Charlie's target: 'In the end they came down in favour of the dark girl, on the grounds that she had the better backside and the saucier walk, and they posted her where the road works ended' (*Girl*, p. 52). Charlie, whose 'sexuality shone through' (*Girl*, p. 58), is certainly picked to supply the honey, but the nature of the way in which she is to act as trap is infinitely more complicated.

Even before being offered Kurtz's 'acting job', Charlie intuits just how different everything has become when she becomes discomposed by the presence of Gadi Becker (Joseph): 'He's come to collect my soul, she thought as she swung jauntily past him in order to demonstrate her immunity' (*Girl*, p. 62). She does not prove immune, and if not her soul, at least her personality is collected and altered by Pygmalion and Son. Simply put, if that can be done of so elaborate and brilliant a strategy, Kurtz takes over Charlie's fantasy life and has her fall in love with Gadi Becker who plays both Joseph the Israeli and Michel the Palestinian. No less than Control in *The Spy Who Came in from the Cold*, Kurtz demonstrates what Liz Gold termed a 'contempt for love'. To Kurtz, Charlie is an object to be used against the enemy; the situation with Gadi Becker is quite different.

Gadi Becker and Charlie become lovers, and for the first time in his espionage fiction, le Carré gives substance to present sexual energy, an energy suggested in the earlier involvements of Liz and Leamas, Ann and Smiley, Lizzie and Westerby, and Ostrakova and her husband and lover. At the beginning of 'Just Like a Woman', Margaret Atwood makes another distinction between novels by men and novels by women:

> Sometimes men put women in men's novels but leave out some of the parts: the heads, for instance, or the hands. Women's novels leave out parts of men as well. Sometimes it's the stretch between the belly button and the knees, sometimes it's the sense of humour.[27]

I do not think that the difference is really quite so clear-cut; perhaps Virginia Woolf was closer to the situation of both men and women novelists when she wrote of her problems of 'telling the truth about my own experiences as a body'.[28] At any rate, le Carré is freer in capturing the sexual energy between Charlie and Becker precisely because he does not leave out the woman's head in the exchange: the presentation of Charlie's sexual fantasies and yearnings accounts for much of the present sexual energy in the novel.

Essentially, then, in offering a subjective level on which Charlie's perspective is so important, le Carré counters the objective level on which she is seen by most of the participants in the action as a perk. In maintaining that view, however, I do not agree with David Monaghan's assertion that Charlie

> comes very close to completing her quest for self and emerges at the end of the novel as a richly mature human being capable of entering into and sustaining a satisfying love relationship.[29]

The quest in the novel is not Charlie's but Gadi Becker's, the disaffected Israeli hero/agent. The change that takes place in Charlie is also a good deal more ambiguous than Monaghan maintains. I quote the end of the novel:

> She was leaning on him and she would have fallen if he hadn't been holding her so firmly. Her tears were half blinding her, and she was hearing him from under water. I'm dead, she kept saying, I'm dead. I'm dead. But it seemed that he wanted her dead or alive. Locked together, they set off awkwardly along the pavement, though the town was strange to them. (*Girl*, p. 515)

Whatever the change in Charlie, it comes through Gadi Becker. The important point that le Carré is making is not about Charlie as questor but about Becker as moral agent. Becker comes to see Charlie as neither a means to power nor a perk that comes with power; rather, he views Charlie as a moral end in herself.

No such moral niceties seem to concern Magnus Pym in *A Perfect Spy* (1986). Pym, title character and one of the novel's narrators, leaves his post as a British agent/diplomat in Vienna and makes his way back to Devon where he spent much of his strange boyhood. (Strange, too, is the manhood he has spent as a double agent for Czech Intelligence.) Ostensibly, he drops out in an attempt to drop back into and to try to understand his past: 'To tell it straight, he rehearsed. Word for word the truth. No evasions, no fictions, no devices. Just my overpromised self set free.'[30] A big order for anyone, but a bigger order for Pym

81

whose whole life has been a series of lies and betrayals. A key word in the quotation above is 'rehearsed' because Magnus Pym is le Carré's consummate actor/agent described by his lover Kate as 'a shell . . . All you have to do is find the hermit crab that climbed into him' (*Spy*, p. 190) and by his Czech contact, Axel, as someone 'put together from bits of other people' (*Spy*, p. 392).

Ironically, Pym plans to free himself from fiction through fiction—writing his autobiography and an autobiographical novel. Those aims involve Pym in both first- and third-person narrative which along with sections of omniscient narration make up le Carré's most experimental novel to date. The narrative is a bit confusing at the beginning but essentially captures what le Carré is after: the portrait or pathology of a sociopath—the perfect spy. Pym is the perfect spy because he is the embodiment of lability, a quality that has fascinated le Carré from the beginning of his career when he had Smiley comment in *A Murder of Quality*: 'And there some of us—aren't there—who are nothing, who are so labile that we astound ourselves; we're the chameleons.'[31]

Adept at shifting 'personality and premises' (*Spy*, p. 19), Pym, nonetheless, settles down as 'Mr. Canterbury' in his final retreat in Devon and prepares to explain himself to others—principally male others. Spurred by his father's (Rick's) death, he begins his stories as a way of connecting to his son Tom and to Jack Brotherhood, his superior in the 'Firm'. Brotherhood is, in fact, a surrogate father for Pym whose own father, a full-blown monster, had robbed his son of childhood. Pym's great need to explain is directed towards men because the important people in his life are male; after his first heterosexual encounter, Pym thinks 'I'm whole and I've joined the men at last' (*Spy*, p. 350). His greatest love is the Czech Axel who actually seduces him through friendship into work as a double agent. Clearly, Pym has strong homoerotic tendencies which find their outlet in all the bonding offered by espionage. And since the book is centred on Pym, le Carré gives a great deal of attention to his relationships with men, what Frank Conroy terms 'personal loyalty among men'.[32]

Yet if Magnus Pym can be termed 'a perfect spy', Mary Pym, his second wife, can be termed 'a good spy'. Among the novel's multitude of mother figures (Pym is searching for a mother in his unresolved Oedipal conflict with his father) and lovers (Pym shares two with Jack Brotherhood), Mary Pym is the most fully developed woman character. Le Carré presents Mary as a strong woman (she comes from a family of soldiers) who must quickly come to terms with her husband's departure and his betrayal, personal and political. In many ways, she must face the immediate consequences of his actions; as 'Mr. Canterbury' sits in Devon working on his autobiography, Mary Pym must deal with the 'Firm' in the person of Jack Brotherhood, her lover before her marriage to Pym:

> Mary had prepared herself for everything except for this. Except for the pace and urgency of the intrusion and the number of the intruders. Except for the sheer scale and complexity of Jack Brotherhood's anger, and for his bewilderment, which seemed greater than her own, and for the awful comfort of his being there. (*Spy*, p. 43)

And the 'Firm' is not her only problem: Mary must play point woman with American Intelligence represented by the Pyms' 'friends', Grant and Bea Lederer. (*A Perfect Spy* offers le Carré's most involved and most virulent assault on the American 'cousins'.) The Americans had become concerned, and rightly, about Pym's loyalty, and the work of delaying full recognition falls to Jack Brotherhood and Mary Pym.

Earlier I noted the term 'rehearsed' as an important one in describing Pym's psychological make-up. Now 'work' seems to be the operative word in le Carré's characterization of Mary Pym. Betrayed by a husband with whom she thought she had made a good life—le Carré does much to create a 'present sexual energy' between the Pyms—Mary Pym must literally work to stay psychologically alive. Interestingly enough, she does this by taking what Connie Sachs called 'back-bearings' of her own and Magnus Pym's past. Mary must relearn ways of surviving as her domestic world is turned into a foreign terrain by her husband's treachery. Le Carré offers Mary as the amateur sleuth whose pursuit of Pym parallels the professional enterprise of Jack Brotherhood.

Early in his career, le Carré had Alex Leamas describe spies as 'a squalid procession of vain fools, traitors too, yes; pansies, sadists and drunkards, people who play cowboys and Indians to brighten their rotten lives' (*Cold*, pp. 210–11). By the writing of *A Perfect Spy*, le Carré is prepared to do more than just describe 'rotten lives'; he is able to dramatize what goes into the making of one such life. Le Carré's characterization of Mary Pym, whom he presents as a woman of 'wit' and 'cunning' (*Spy*, p. 394), is an important part of his indictment of Pym's 'perfection'.

Within Pym's first- and third-person narratives Mary is objectified as both perk and remote assistance to power. As he describes his life to his son, Pym notes:

> So Pym, with both his mentors pushing in the same direction, followed their advice and took Mary, your mother, to be his truly wedded partner at the High Table of the Anglo-American alliance. And really, after all that he had given away already, it seemed a very reasonable sacrifice. (*Spy*, p. 447)

Within the omniscient narration, however, Mary Pym has much greater primacy, indeed independence. Her consciousness is significant enough to be given subjectivity, and she is an important participant in the pursuit of Pym, the external action which parallels Pym's internal pursuit of his 'overpromised self'. The omniscient narration brings in some of the missing parts that Margaret Atwood mentions; in Mary Pym's case head and hands allow her to work effectively and to survive.

In the '80s, John le Carré's fiction is still centred on men, but women characters grow more complex. That complexity is related to an interesting doubleness in le Carré's presentation of women. On one level—certainly the view of most of the male characters in the novels—Charlie and Mary Pym are still perks on the road to power. On another level, however, a level made possible by his more sophisticated control of narration, le Carré privileges women's views. Such privileging gives women characters a status and independence which the world of espionage, a world of men and power, would deny them.

## NOTES

1. Margaret Atwood, 'Just Like a Woman', *Harper's*, 270 (June 1985), 27.
2. David Monaghan, *The Novels of John le Carré: The Art of Survival* (Oxford: Basil Blackwell, 1985), p. 31.
3. Katherine M. Rogers, *The Troublesome Helpmate: A History of Misogyny in Literature* (Seattle: University of Washington Press, 1966).
4. John le Carré, *Call for the Dead* (New York: Bantam, 1979; © 1961, Victor Gollancz), p. 98. Subsequent quotations will be identified in the text as *Call* with page number.
5. Peter Lewis, *John le Carré* (New York: Frederick Ungar, 1985), p. 33.
6. John le Carré, *The Spy Who Came in from the Cold* (New York: Bantam, 1975; © 1963, Victor Gollancz), p. 137. Subsequent quotations will be identified in the text as *Cold* with page number.
7. Lewis, p. 77.
8. Peter Lewis refers to 'Leamas and Liz's love, [as being] . . . like Romeo and Juliet's', p. 71. While in 'John le Carré: Murder and Loyalty', *New Republic* (31 July 1976), George Grella likens the lovers to Orpheus and Eurydice, 24.
9. Lars Ole Sauerberg, *Secret Agents in Fiction: Ian Fleming, John le Carré and Len Deighton* (New York: St. Martin's Press, 1984), pp. 54–5.
10. David Monaghan, 'John le Carré and England: A Spy's-Eye View', *Modern Fiction Studies*, 29 (Autumn 1983), 576–77.
11. John le Carré, *The Looking-Glass War* (New York: Bantam, 1975; © 1965, D. J. M. Cornwell), p. 137.
12. John le Carré, *A Small Town in Germany* (New York: Dell, 1983; © 1968, Le Carré Productions), p. 272.
13. Monaghan, *The Novels of John le Carré*, p. 30.
14. Muriel Spark, *The Abbess of Crewe* (Harmondsworth, Middlesex: Penguin Books, 1975), p. 16.
15. Lars Sauerberg comments on 'Le Carré's subtle support of patriotic attitudes in his trilogy . . .', p. 175.
16. John le Carré, *Tinker Tailor Soldier Spy* (New York: Bantam, 1975; © 1974, Le Carré Productions), p. 97. Subsequent quotations will be identified in the text as *Tinker* with page number.
17. Peter Lewis notes that 'In *Tinker Tailor Soldier Spy* le Carré gives more individuality to his many minor characters than in his early fiction by dwelling on them for longer and by equipping them with verbal mannerisms of their own', pp. 129–30. Such is certainly the case with Connie Sachs.
18. Sauerberg, p. 129.
19. John le Carré, *The Honourable Schoolboy* (New York: Bantam, 1978; © 1977, Authors Workshop), pp. 323–24. Subsequent quotations will be identified in the text as *Schoolboy* with page number.
20. John le Carré, *Smiley's People* (New York: Bantam, 1980; © 1979, Authors Workshop), p. 212. Subsequent quotations will be identified in the text as *People* with page number.

21. Lewis, p. 18.
22. Le Carré made the comment in an interview with Miriam Gross, 'The Secret World of John le Carré', *Observer Review* (3 February 1980), 35. Peter Lewis calls Ann 'an absentee from the Smiley novels since she usually features as part of George's consciousness rather than as a dramatically realized individual', p. 182.
23. Talking to Melvyn Bragg, le Carré made the following curious observation: 'One of the greatest realities is sex, but we almost never succeed in betraying our sexuality to one another fully.' Melvyn Bragg, 'The Things a Spy Can Do—John le Carré Talking', *Listener* (22 January 1976), 90.
24. A two-level narrative also works to make Maria Ostrakova a more fully realized character in *Smiley's People*.
25. Monaghan, *The Novels of John le Carré*, p. 27.
26. John le Carré, *The Little Drummer Girl* (New York: Bantam, 1983; © 1983, Authors Workshop), p. 59. Subsequent quotations will be identified in the text as *Girl* with page number.
27. Atwood, 27.
28. Virginia Woolf, 'Professions for Women' in *Virginia Woolf: Women and Writing*, ed. Michèle Barrett (New York: Harcourt Brace Jovanovich, 1979), p. 62.
29. Monaghan, *The Novels of John le Carré*, p. 195.
30. John le Carré, *A Perfect Spy* (New York: Alfred A. Knopf, 1986), p. 22. Subsequent quotations will be identified in the text as *Spy* with page number.
31. John le Carré, *A Murder of Quality* (New York: Bantam, 1980; © 1962, Victor Gollancz Ltd.), p. 148.
32. Frank Conroy, 'Sins of the Father', *New York Times Book Review* (13 April 1986), 24.

# 4

# Le Carré and the Idea of Espionage

by TREVOR ROYLE

Treachery, not deception, lies at the heart of John le Carré's view of the espionage game. Certainly, the players are deceivers all, and certainly, the rules are governed by deceit, but the hidden goal of all the actors is treason. What is there to say then about a man who acts the traitor, who betrays not only his country but also those who trust him? That is the central question which le Carré has been addressing ever since he published *The Spy Who Came in from the Cold* in 1963. In *A Perfect Spy* (1986) he goes some way to illuminating, if not the complete solution to the conundrum, then at least a glimmering of his own thinking on the matter.

On the surface, *A Perfect Spy* contains several features which le Carré has marked out as his own territory. The central character, Magnus Pym, an agent not quite burned out but badly singed by a lifetime's work in espionage, goes to ground taking with him a curious collection of biographies, unintelligible secrets and more than an ample supply of disgust and self-hatred. The pattern of insinuation, of making himself indispensable, of using others, emerges as le Carré builds up a comprehensive picture of Pym's lost life. We learn that he has been something of a star turn in the nation's intelligence service, a public schoolboy and an Oxford man, a linguist with an eccentric, though vaguely upper-class, English background; in other words, he possesses the virtues which our intelligence

87

services find intensely exciting in their recruits.

Le Carré, though, is too old a hand at the intelligence game to allow Pym to be quite so straightforward a creation. Having invited us to make generalizations about Pym and his background, he then frustrates them with a keen flash of insight. When Pym, at that time a National Service subaltern dabbling in Czech counter-espionage, performs his first act of treachery by photographing classified documents, he experiences a moment of glowing exultation.

> I am here to administer a caress. Folders, loose-leaf manuals. Signals instructions marked 'Top Secret, Guard' which Pym has never seen. I am here to borrow, not to steal. Opening his briefcase he extracts an army issue Agfa camera with a one-foot measuring chain fastened to the lens front. It is the same camera that he uses when Axel brings out raw material and Pym has to photograph it on the spot. He cocks it and sets it on the desk. This is what I was born for, he thinks, not for the first time. In the beginning was the spy.[1]

That moment of self-realization, sensed by Pym as he makes the betrayal which will set him up as a double agent, finds an echo in the creation of Jack Brotherhood, the man who runs him. It is Brotherhood who keeps alive the possibility that Pym has not defected, that his disappearance is simply an unfortunate aberration, and it is this morally upright man (as he sees himself) who refuses to believe that their work is anything less than honourable. Confronted by Lederer, an American agent, who sees through the 'great game', he has nothing to say in reply. 'Hell, Jack,' he is told after refusing the bait, 'we're licensed crooks, that's all I'm saying. What's our racket? Know what our racket is? It is to place our larcenous natures at the service of the state.'[2] Quite. Where then does patriotism end and criminality begin?

It is at this point that le Carré starts to consider the reasons why Pym has gone to ground, and his conclusions emerge against a dramatic background in which Pym's colleagues try to find him before he falls into the clutches of the Americans who distrust him and the whole British set-up, or the Czechs who have been running him as a double agent since his days as a National Serviceman.

In the foreground, meanwhile, the shadows begin to take on some substance. Through an autobiography he is writing for his son, we can piece together the hidden story of Pym's life: his eccentric con-man father, his fears and fantasies, his sexual hang-ups, his earnest craving to be honoured and respected, the fatal flaws which lead him—the casual player—into the game of spying. No other writer has drawn such a sympathetic, though unnerving, picture of intelligence work, or has felt so intensely the problems of idealism, innocence and practical politics which serve as the ground rules. The conclusion of this remarkable novel is all too dreary and predictable, but Pym's end matters not; the main concern is what has gone before, the feeble motives and faulty ideals, the wishful thinking and the absence of love.

*A Perfect Spy* is a well-nigh flawless novel about the seedy world of intelligence gathering and the corruption of human values that it encompasses. Whereas earlier novels like *The Spy Who Came in from the Cold* and *The Looking-Glass War* were more concerned with the minutiae of the world of espionage, the training of spies and the beastly undercurrent of fear that runs through their lives, *A Perfect Spy* addresses itself to the idea of espionage. In that sense it is more about the creation and the *raison d'être* of the spy than it is about the preparations which turn an ordinary man into a man capable of betraying those he loves and that which he holds most dear. It also highlights some of the interest that British novelists have taken in the nation's security services, a literary interest which came into being almost as quickly as military intelligence, as a regular institution, was born.

From the very outset of organized warfare, military intelligence has been central to the strategy of the commander in the field and the politician at home. In 1887 Britain recognized the importance of such work by creating the post of Director of Military Intelligence in charge of an intelligence branch at the War Office; he was responsible for co-ordinating the gathering of information about foreign armies and for overseeing home defence. Because Britain's international strategic policies rested on the pre-eminence of the Royal Navy, the Director of Naval Intelligence, founded at the same time as his army colleague, enjoyed not only seniority but also a better-funded department.

His specialization was anti-invasion planning and information-gathering along Britain's imperial sea-routes.

It was not until the creation of the Committee of Imperial Defence (C.I.D.) in 1903 that the Cabinet undertook to co-ordinate the activities of the various intelligence organizations, a move that removed them further from public or parliamentary accessibility. 'Locked away in the minutes of the C.I.D.,' says Nigel West, M15's historian, 'lie the origins of the British Imperial Intelligence Security Service which was later to become known as MO5 and then MI5.'³ As it became established, so too did the new organization seek ways to improve its standing, and in 1909 it assumed a shape which is still recognizable today. The Foreign Service of the Security Service Bureau, as it had become known, became the Secret Intelligence Service (later to be MI6), and the home section (later to be MI5) took over matters of home security.

Because the military intelligence department was concerned with anti-invasion counter-espionage it induced the earliest literary interest in its activities. (In 1904 the Director of Military Intelligence had been abolished and responsibility for military counter-espionage had been handed over to the Military Operations Directorate, hence the original MO5.)

Throughout the nineteenth century fears of the invasion of Britain by a hostile power—usually depicted as France or Germany—had been a subject for popular fiction. Sometimes these tales were written by a military writer to help expound in un-technical terms the army's point of view; others were unashamed vehicles for increasing a magazine's or newspaper's circulation figures. When Colonel George Chesney published his 'The Battle of Dorking' in the April 1871 issue of *Blackwood's Magazine* his idea had been to describe

> a successful invasion of England, and the collapse of our power and commerce in consequence. An ex-volunteer in the year 1900, for example, might be telling his children his experiences of 1872, the battle of Guildford, and occupation and humiliating terms of peace.⁴

John Blackwood jumped at the opportunity of publishing it, but behind that literary intention lay Chesney's professional belief that Britain was militarily unprepared. Since the larger part of the Regular Army was serving abroad, the country was prey to invasion by a foreign power, in this case, Prussia. In that respect, 'The Battle of Dorking' served Chesney's and the army's purpose by reopening the debate inside and outside Parliament about the necessity for strengthening home defence. So popular did Chesney's work become that Blackwood had to rush through a reprint of the April issue and its publication gave rise to a host of imitators with equally unlikely themes and titles, 'Our Hero by Sergeant Blower and Cheeks the Marine' and 'After the Battle of Dorking or What became of the Invaders!' being typical examples.[5]

More sensationally, the *Daily Mail* published another invasion story, 'The Siege of Portsmouth', which ran for three weeks from 17 June 1895. It increased the newspaper's circulation to such an extent that a similar story, 'The Invasion of 1910', written by Queen Alexandra's favourite novelist, William le Queux, appeared in the same newspaper in March 1906. To make a more telling impact the story was advertised by sandwich-board men wearing German army uniforms. By 1908 the invasion scare had reached new heights of popular concern with even papers like *The Times* publishing warnings that Britain was being infiltrated by a secret German army posing in the guise of bandsmen, waiters, jewellers and such like. So universal was this fear that when Guy du Maurier, a Major of the Royal Fusiliers, presented his 'invasion scare' play, *An Englishman's Home*, in London's West End, the War Office arranged for a recruiting booth to be placed in the foyer.

Other writers like Erskine Childers (*The Riddle of the Sands*) and E. Phillips Oppenheim were also attracted to the anti-invasion counter-espionage novel, and their work was deservedly popular in its day. Childers, in fact, served as a naval intelligence officer during the First World War. Partly, their public success can be seen as a reflection of the very real fear of invasion by a foreign power—in 1908 the C.I.D. debated the problem but concluded that 'a bolt from the blue' would be stymied both by Britain's naval superiority in the North Sea and by the creation of Haldane's Territorial Force which had been earmarked for home defence. Partly, too, enthusiasm for the 'invasion-scare' literature had been whipped up by a series of real-life incidents involving the infiltration of British naval dockyards by German agents in the years before 1914. In 1910 a German army officer was arrested while sketching defences at Portsmouth; two years later naval intelligence dealt with its first German defector, and in 1913 a German-born dentist was discovered trying to purchase naval secrets, arrested and jailed. All these activities were reported at the time and helped lay the foundation of British counter-intelligence work during the First World War.

During the war the nation's security services were expanded greatly. Military intelligence, reformed in 1916 as MI5, assumed complete independence and enjoyed direct access to the Prime Minister. It operated at a lower key than the S.I.S. and was generally considered to be less glamorous because it worked in less publicized areas of activity. One of its key members, though, was a man who was not averse to publicity and who had carefully employed it during his rise to prominence in the years before the war: John Buchan.

At the outbreak of war in August 1914 Buchan was working in London as a publisher for the Edinburgh-based firm of Thomas Nelson. Physically unfit for active military service, yet anxious to emulate those of his friends who had donned uniform, Buchan contributed to Britain's war effort by overseeing the production of *The Nelson History of the War*, which was published in serial form at fortnightly intervals. Written by Buchan himself, the publication created a great deal of interest in political and military circles because it was one of the few histories to show a keen grasp of strategy. A series of public lectures followed, which won the attention of Sir Edward Grey and A. J. Balfour, and in May 1915 Lord Northcliffe, the proprietor of *The Times*, invited Buchan to visit the Western Front as a special correspondent. There he won the ear of the British generals in the field—Haig, French, Allenby, Plumer—and from them he was able to discover the extent of the Shells Crisis which almost ended the career of the Secretary of State for War, Lord Kitchener.[6]

Gradually he was sucked deeper into the vortex of wartime military intelligence: in October 1915 he was back in Flanders as the official government reporter for the Battle of Loos, this time wearing the uniform of an officer of the Intelligence Corps. Despite gnawing ill-health, he kept up his intelligence work in

1916, writing a resumé of the Battle of the Somme for the new Commander-in-Chief, Sir Douglas Haig, and generally making himself useful with the men who mattered—throughout his life Buchan was able to promote an easy understanding between himself and the men who occupied positions of power and authority. His reward was an appointment as Director of the newly established Department of Information in February 1917, one of the first results of Lloyd George's premiership. (He had come to power as Prime Minister at the end of the preceding year.) The post made Buchan virtual head of Britain's propaganda effort and brought him into close contact with the nation's security services. In that capacity he formed a close working relationship with Sir Reginald Hall, the head of naval intelligence, and Buchan's letters to his mother at that period reveal the extent of his work, part propaganda, part politics and part espionage.[7]

Internal squabbles between the ministers of Lloyd George's Cabinet meant that the Department of Information was always going to be a political hot potato, and Buchan soon found that his loyalties were stretched to the limit. Because his department was only semi-official, Buchan could not answer directly criticisms of its work but had to rely instead on the uncertain protection of his political boss, Sir Edward Carson. A solution was found in January 1918 when Buchan's responsibilities were taken over by Lord Beaverbrook in a new Ministry of Information. At the same time John Buchan was appointed Director of Intelligence, a post he was later to describe as being something of a conundrum: 'I have some queer macabre recollections of those years—of meeting with odd people in odd places, of fantastic duties which a romancer would have rejected as beyond probability.'[8]

Buchan may well have rejected many of the episodes he encountered during that last year of the war but the experience did fire his literary imagination. During the war he wrote and published *The Power-House* and *Greenmantle* and gathered in the material for *Mr. Standfast* (1919) which is based directly on many of his experiences as an MI5 officer. Central to these espionage thrillers—'shockers' Buchan called them—is a belief that civilization is a thin veneer, a narrow dividing line between the forces of good and evil. He had first expressed the notion in

*The Watcher by the Threshold* in 1902, but it finds its real expression in his short story 'Fountainblue', which had appeared a year earlier in the August issue of *Blackwood's Magazine*. The speaker is Maitland, a man torn between the two worlds: 'There is a very narrow line between the warm room and the savage out-of-doors . . . you call it miles of rampart; I call the division a line, a thread, a sheet of glass.'

The war had served to increase Buchan's certainty that the forces of evil were only kept at bay by the combination of good men, and that below surface appearances of normality there lurked a dark and dangerous world. In *The Power-House*—a thriller originally conceived in imitation of Phillips Oppenheim— Lumley makes this belief clear from the very outset.

> You think that a wall as solid as the earth separates civilisation from barbarism. I tell you the division is a thread, a sheet of glass. A touch here, a push there, and you bring back the reign of Saturn.[9]

Other motifs crowded in to establish the formula which Buchan was to employ so well in his spy fiction—the intelligent and respectable citizen who finds himself beyond the law's protection, the apparent honesty and distinction of the spy, the chase through a familiar landscape which assumes satanic proportions, the experience of pain and the practice of courage.

When he came to write *Mr. Standfast* Buchan drew heavily not only on his experiences as Director of Intelligence, but he also welded his knowledge onto a structure created by those early shockers. The background to the novel is authentic enough and well delineated by Buchan who knew it well— Clydeside, Skye, London during an air raid, the Western Front—but it is the author's mastery of suspense that marks *Mr. Standfast* as being one of the prime early examples of British spy fiction. Moreover, Buchan demonstrated a fine appreciation of the tactics used by the German spy ring and the ways in which they were able to cross frontiers at will:

> In a back street of a little town I would exchange passwords with a nameless figure and be given instructions. At a wayside inn at an appointed hour a voice speaking a thick German would advise that this bridge or that railway crossing had been cleared. At a hamlet among pine woods an unknown man would clamber up beside me and take me past a sentry-post.[10]

As the Director, first of Information, and then of Intelligence, Buchan was also in a good position to gauge the state of morale within wartime Britain. Early in 1918, for example, he had been able to reassure Gilbert Murray that he could see no reason to ban a performance of *The Trojan Women*, telling his friend that 'the audience who will attend the Repertory Theatre is not likely to be driven into a pacifist frenzy by Euripedes.'[11] A similar concern drives Hannay, the engineer turned spy-catcher, who goes to Glasgow in the aftermath of the 'Red Clyde' strikes of 1915. There, he finds that all is well, that although the strikers might hate the profiteers, they hate the Germans first and foremost. Le Carré, too, was to use this device in the character of Bill Haydon who yields to the temptation of Moscow because he has come to believe that the pillars of his life have been knocked from beneath him, that Britain has surrendered her position as a world power, thus leaving the thinking man with a direct choice between the U.S.A. and the U.S.S.R. In his case it is the malaise he encounters in British society that helps to tip the balance.

Buchan was not the only literary man to be recruited into the fledgling MI5; John Dickson Carr, the American-born thriller writer who specialized in 'sealed room' mysteries was another. Other authors who gravitated towards the world of espionage at that time included Compton Mackenzie and Somerset Maugham, but they chose the more glamorous S.I.S. largely because it offered the chance of foreign service. Both were destined to write about their experiences, Mackenzie in *The South Wind of Love* and Maugham in his *Ashenden* stories.

After an unsuccessful attempt to get a commission in the Seaforth Highlanders Mackenzie served in Gallipoli in 1915 before being recruited into the S.I.S. as the head of its Aegean station, an experience he described in *Extremes Meet*. It also gave him the background for the second volume of his *Four Winds of Love* quartet in which his hero John Ogilvy becomes a secret agent in the Aegean area and throws himself into the unseen world of British espionage, thereby escaping from the narrow confines of his past privileged life. Mackenzie was always careful to emphasize that *The South Wind of Love* was not 'veiled auto-biography', explaining to his friend Newman Flower in a letter of 2 July 1937 that the novel was more or less pure invention.

That I have drawn upon my own experience for certain historical incidents is obvious, but it will be a waste of time for people to try to identify characters or search for facts in what is a work of fiction. One or two of the subsidiary characters have been drawn from life, but the originals of such are no longer alive. The principal characters are pure creations of my fancy and are not even founded upon models. The two islands of Lipsia and Icaros are adumbrations of real islands, but all their inhabitants are fictitious and also much of their topography. Mileto is a cloud-cuckoo place of my own. So is Citrano. These remarks on places apply to ships, and even when I have occasionally used actual incidents the people who played their parts in such incidents have not appeared. I was never in Salonica, and that portion of the tale which concerns Salonica might have been placed equally well at any Base. Salonica happened to be the Base geographically necessary.[12]

Mackenzie's protestations have the ring of truth but it is difficult to believe that he had been entirely untouched by his work for the secret services. He possessed a natural love of the exotic and was drawn to the bizarre or the dramatic gesture—hence, one suspects, his involvement in intelligence work during the First World War. Maugham, too, offered similar excuses in the preface to his *Ashenden* collection of stories, but he went a step further by pointing to the necessary transmogrification of experience by which a literary work is born.

The work of an agent in the Intelligence Department is on the whole extremely monotonous. A lot of it is uncommonly useless. The material it offers for stories is scrappy and pointless; the author has himself to make it coherent, dramatic and probable.[13]

Maugham had enjoyed a brief flirtation with the secret services in 1917 when he was sent to Russia in an unsuccessful attempt to halt the Red revolution. Out of that disillusion came the *Ashenden* stories which give a realistic—though, it has to be admitted, romantic—picture of the 'Intelligence Department' during the First World War. (Buchan's portrayal of Hannay's activities in *Mr. Standfast* is equally flamboyant and inventive.) Moreover, it gives a clue to the growing interest which British writers were taking in the espionage novel. If we are to believe the memoirs of senior spymasters, such as Sir Percy Sillitoe's *Cloak without Dagger* (1955), then much espionage work is 'extremely monotonous'; but the point is that the writer is able to use that material to good effect as the base matter for true fiction.

What then is the attraction of espionage to the writer? In the first place, there seems to be a natural relationship between the world of the intelligence agent and the world of the novelist. Both are caught between the reality of day-to-day life and the day-dreaming make-believe which they themselves create. For example, a novelist will draw upon the experiences of his own life for much of his fictional output, just as the agent's metier is intelligence-gathering of everything around him. This is not to say that the novelist carefully hoards every detail of the daily round and then reproduces it, undigested, as a work of fiction or that every fictional work is related to direct experience. Rather, the novelist observes, notes, collects and then transposes the evidence when he comes to write fiction. In the same way, the agent gathers in the information and from the detritus emerges a plausible story which reaches a logical conclusion through cause and effect.

A corollary of this symbiotic relationship is that the novelist, like the agent, betrays real life—his family, friends, those he meets in the casual daily round—in much the same way that a spy betrays his country. These are often his links between fiction and reality.

> It's quite certain to me now that an Author is not a character worth talking about, worth analysing because the contradiction is one too many: he is the actor to end all actors because he is driven by the people within, that vast family of cousins. . . . He's a kind of rickety candelabra in which all the lights don't work all the time. They come off and go on again due to outside circumstances. The man in the street, the girl in the bed, whatever sets a light. She or he resembles closely enough the character already hidden in the head for there to be illumination bright enough to demand attention: to be written about or *acted out* sometimes, so close do fiction and fact become.[14]

Le Carré's friend James Kennaway expressed that point of view in a notebook which he kept in 1965 during a period of mental anguish brought on by the breakdown of his marriage. (His wife Susan had had a brief affair with le Carré.) What he appears to be saying is that the novelist collects people, uses them and then, in a sense, betrays them. Le Carré, too, is aware of this conundrum. 'Love is whatever you can still betray', thinks Pym in *A Perfect Spy*. 'Betrayal can only happen if you love.' Is that an echo perhaps of the indifference with which the senior professionals abandon their scheme—and their agent—in *The Looking-Glass War*? Kennaway worked with le Carré on a planned film version of that novel, and at the end of the working notes appear the words, written in le Carré's hands: 'Jim. You have done more for me in a week than I have done for anyone else in a lifetime.'[15] That same year, he had fallen in love with Kennaway's wife.

In the second place, writers have a well-developed fantasy life and sometimes show a tendency to identify with their heroes. When the hero is a spy, this entails a respect, even an admiration, for his activities. Mackenzie certainly thought very highly of John Ogilvy and he is a mouthpiece for many of the opinions held by his creator. In much the same way Ian Fleming admired James Bond and went to great lengths to place his hero in the real world. His novels employ brand names, they are set in fully realized geographical locations and they brim over with snippets of information drawn from Fleming's work in naval intelligence. Le Carré does this, too, but unlike le Carré's characters, Bond is pure fantasy, a superman who has been 'packaged' instead of merely being created by the imagination. He is a marvellous sportsman, understands all the complexities of the international jet-set, dresses beautifully, is irresistible to women and always triumphs over evil. In other words, he is the perfect cypher for the fantastic world inhabited by the secret agent. Once he had placed Bond in it, Fleming's imagination could take over completely and allow him to confront any number of impossible, or downright unbelievable, missions. Curiously, Fleming's own career in naval intelligence seems to have been blessed by a similar brand of make-believe: one of the dafter notions on which he worked was the possibility of freezing clouds to construct mid-air gun platforms.

In the third place, writers are not usually men of action but prefer, instead, to write about it. Yet in times of national crisis of war the very nature of their craft means that they tend to gravitate towards activities which can make use of their talents.

Daniel Defoe, for example, worked as a government spy in Scotland in the period of unrest prior to the passing of the Act of Union in 1707. His task was to test the political climate for his political boss Robert Harley and he brought to his work a good deal of gusto, as well he might have done, it being part of his own political rehabilitation.

When the Second World War broke out in September 1939, Evelyn Waugh tried unsuccessfully to gain a position in naval or military intelligence, feeling that his abilities as a writer could be best used in the field of intelligence or counter-intelligence. At the Admiralty he was interviewed by Ian Fleming and at the War Office by General John Hay Beith, the novelist who wrote under the pseudonym of 'Ian Hay'. To Waugh's dismay, neither man was able to offer him employment and after a period of mixed fortune he ended up in the somewhat unlikely company of the Royal Marines. From the tone of his diary, written at that time, the rejection was a sorry cross for Waugh to bear, especially as most of his friends and acquaintances were 'in uniform'. Another writer who applied unsuccessfully for British intelligence was Claud Cockburn, but his rejection was due to the fact that he was a member of the Communist Party of Great Britain and had been involved actively on the Republican side during the Spanish Civil War. (For the Comintern in 1938 he had invented a non-existent battle in Morocco in an attempt to persuade the French Prime Minister to allow the passage of Russian field guns over the border into Spain.) It is intriguing to imagine what they would have made of such ruses as 'The Man Who Never Was' or 'Monty's Double' which were worked out by MI5 to sow doubt and confusion in the enemy's mind.

Other writers drawn into security work during the Second World War included Dennis Wheatley, Tom Driberg and John Bingham; they gravitated towards the activities of 'B' Division which dealt mainly with counter-espionage activities in the United Kingdom. There they worked in counter-subversion for the colourful Max Knight and generally considered themselves to be an élite group, part intellectual, part amateur in outlook but never less than professional.

They were generally youthful, attractive and rich. Knight himself had married twice, his first wife having committed suicide after an occult experience with Aleister Crowley. His second wife, Lois, spent most of the war working at the headquarters of the Oxford-shire Constabulary. Perhaps his greatest talent, in spite of his eccentricities (which stretched to training cuckoos and sharing his flat with a bush-baby), was his ability to select and recruit very reliable women agents who became devoted to him, a remarkable feat because he was always essentially homosexual.[16]

One of Knight's tasks was to infiltrate his group into organizations sympathetic to the German cause and their most celebrated coup—widely reported at the time because it was such a success—was the breaking of the Right Club, a small but influential collection of British fascists.

During the Second World War the anti-fascist tenor of the times meant that it became easier for Communists to infiltrate MI5. Unknown to the authorities, underground party members and N.K.V.D. recruits found their way into Britain's security forces, the most notorious of these being Anthony Blunt and Guy Burgess. Their task was made easier by the sea-change that had taken place within the organization itself, for by 1945 MI5 was a complex business involving different divisions with different responsibilities which were often out of kilter with each other. It was a far cry from the investigative responsibility it had assumed when it was founded; the manpower and the range of its work had also increased. The world of international espionage had changed, too, until its motives had almost become unrecognizable. Blunt's treachery might have been little different from that practised by Wilhelm Klauer, the dentist who had tried to purchase secrets in 1913, but its ramifications were much greater and in the long term much more damaging to his country.

The much-publicized activities of betrayal perpetrated by men like Philby, Burgess, Maclean and Blunt naturally gave a field day to outside observers who suddenly found that fiction was being surpassed by reality. They also helped to bring into sharper focus such matters as loyalty and duty, and to question deeply held beliefs like honour and patriotism. Once it had been recognized that espionage was not the glamorous occupation it had been portrayed by the first generation of thriller writers, the business of spying became altogether more human and vulnerable. At the same time it became less easy to comprehend, frontiers became blurred in Europe's Cold War landscapes and the vocabulary of the writers became punctuated by concepts such as deceit, betrayal, doubt. These are the words employed by le Carré in his delineation of that world and each novel has redefined and illuminated the process for his main protagonists. When George Smiley confronts his opposite number, Karla, in *Smiley's People*, his reaction is very different from the bluff enthusiasm displayed by Richard Hannay in *Mr. Standfast*.

> He looked across the river into the darkness again, and an unholy vertigo seized him as the very evil he had fought against seemed to reach out and possess him and claim him despite his striving, calling him a traitor also; mocking him, yet at the same time applauding his betrayal. On Karla has descended the curse of Smiley's compassion; on Smiley the curse of Karla's fanaticism. I have destroyed him with the weapons I abhorred, and they are his. We have crossed each other's frontiers, we are the no-men of this no-man's land.[17]

By his admission John le Carré has had links with the nation's security forces; by his own admission, too, he has said that the autobiographical approach to his work should be resisted. Like his literary predecessors, Maugham, Mackenzie and Buchan he has been drawn to the idea of espionage and in so doing has helped his readership to a better understanding of its many complexities. He may have played at being a spy through his fiction, but like all the best writers that fascination has only fuelled his literary output. In other words, he has remained, first and foremost, a writer and has transformed the reality of the world of espionage into a fictional world inhabited by his own men of action.

## NOTES

1. John le Carré, *A Perfect Spy* (London: Hodder & Stoughton, 1986), p. 363.
2. Ibid., p. 246.
3. Nigel West, *MI5: British Security Service Operations, 1909–1945* (London: Bodley Head, 1981), p. 33.
4. F. D. Tredrey, *The House of Blackwood, 1804–1954* (Edinburgh and London: William Blackwood, 1954), p. 139.
5. See I. F. Clarke, *Voices Prophesying War* (London: O.U.P., 1966).

6. See Trevor Royle, *The Kitchener Enigma* (London: Michael Joseph, 1985), Chapter 11.
7. Janet Adam Smith, *John Buchan: A Biography* (London: Rupert Hart-Davies, 1965), pp. 204–5.
8. John Buchan, *Memory Hold-the-Door* (London: Hodder & Stoughton, 1940), p. 179.
9. John Buchan, *The Power-House* (Edinburgh and London: William Blackwood, 1916), pp. 64–5.
10. John Buchan, *Mr. Standfast* (London: Hodder & Stoughton, 1919), p. 353.
11. Smith, p. 212.
12. Compton Mackenzie, preface to *The South Wind of Love* (London: Chatto & Windus, 1937).
13. Somerset Maugham, preface to *Ashenden* (London: Heinemann, 1928).
14. Susan Kennaway, *The Kennaway Papers* (London: Jonathan Cape, 1981), p. 97.
15. Ibid., p. 18.
16. West, pp. 123–24.
17. John le Carré, *Smiley's People* (London: Hodder & Stoughton, 1980), p. 324.

# 5

# Information, Power and the Reader: Textual Strategies in le Carré

## by STEWART CREHAN

The liberal humanism articulated in le Carré's spy fiction has convinced at least one critic that he is 'a writer with ambivalent politics . . . reluctant to take sides'.[1] Set, however, against a more democratic perspective, this self-questioning, liberal stance amounts, in effect, to little more than giving Western imperialism a human face. The Soviet critic V. Voinov[2] was correct when he spotted in le Carré's

> ordinary 'Little man' . . . with his doubts, weaknesses [and] vulnerability, a less 'frontal' and therefore more acceptable defender of the modern capitalist state than the phallocentric killer-heroes of Micky Spillane, Nick Carter and Ian Fleming.

In 1980, le Carré said: 'I do believe, reluctantly, that we must combat Communism.'[3] As an adverb of manner, the scrupulous conscience of the English liberal helps to vindicate hardened loyalties, sustained despite the author's well-known contempt for the British establishment. In the novels themselves, bureaucratic collectivism and 'absolutism' (whether of the East or the West) are seen to corrode moral honesty, genuine feeling and authentic individuality. According to some, this takes le Carré's work outside the Western spy genre, whose 'ideological assumptions' are consequently 'subverted'.[4] At the end of the narrative process, 'enemy' figures such as Dieter Frey, Jens Fiedler,[5] Leo Harting, Drake and Nelson Ko, and Karla, are made to appear vulnerably and emotionally human. Initially viewed as 'other', the enemy becomes incorporated into a liberal-humanist discourse, part of a broader strategy of assimilation which, as I hope to show, operates with varying degrees of success throughout le Carré's fiction.

From a combative standpoint, assimilating the enemy might seem a contradictory and dangerous project, one that makes too many concessions. If the enemy and ourselves are basically the same, employing the same methods, if the opposition reflects the uneasy marriage within our own camp of absolutism and relativism, of cold bureaucratic dogma and flesh-and-blood human-ness, why, one may ask, the need for 'combat' at all? In fact, the enemy, *qua* enemy, is always other *until* he is assimilated. What, through various textual strategies, le Carré's spy novels try to enact, is a many-sided process in which the other is absorbed into the circle of the known and the familiar. If le Carré's novels function as props of Western 'culture' and 'civilisation', they do so not merely through their thematic content, but through their textuality. Against Tony Barley's claim that the 'open-ended method' in le Carré 'allows positions to be examined angle by angle in a constantly unsettling process',[6] I would argue that le Carré's ultimate aim is not to unsettle but to reassure, and that the 'interaction of perspectives', to use Iser's term,[7] is not open-ended and dialogic (at least not in the sense in which Bakhtin employs that concept), but moves towards a resolution; and that these perspectives are textualized with a view towards their ideological assimilation, liberal dilemmas and internal debates notwithstanding. Thus profound historical, social and ideological contradictions are, by the very nature of the genre, simplified from the outset into individual manhunts and conspiracies. Le Carré has admitted that 'the conspiracy alone is some kind of solace to the reader or to the audience: people want to interpret their lives in terms of conspiracy.'[8] One way of reassuring the reader is to demonstrate that the enemy is personally identifiable—more, that he is a human being just like ourselves. (This implies, theoretically, that he can be won over, although it also carries the danger—seen in Smiley's almost pathological obsession with Karla—of the hunter being 'taken over' by the hunted.)

The strategy of assimilation in le Carré's spy fiction works on various levels. At the level of plot, divergent strands are woven into a logical system which, in accordance with the reader's horizon of expectations, is made accessible—after some effort— to rational explanation. From a situation where mystery and the enigmatic predominate, a coherent pattern of human events and motives is gradually built up. Since this pattern must also be deduced by the agent, whose reasoning we must follow, the reader is reconciled to a logically ordered and knowable universe. This world may, of course, be *unjust*, as the political universe of *The Spy Who Came in from the Cold* is unjust; what matters from the reader's standpoint is that a complex puzzle is solved: 'And suddenly, with the terrible clarity of a man too long deceived, Leamas understood the whole ghastly trick.'[9] The sudden *frisson* of pleasure we experience when this 'trick' is revealed is directly proportional to the ingenuity of the trick itself, regardless of our affective response (such as moral outrage). This is guaranteed by the genre.

At the level of fictional illusion, the 'top secret' world of intelligence is brought as close as possible to that of the reader. It is rendered credible, plausible, at times even humdrum, though never unabsorbing. Verisimilitude, narrative voice, focalization and the cultural-referential code combine in positioning the reader *within* the intelligence world, ideologically as well as imaginatively. (This, incidentally, is not true of Conrad's two 'spy novels'.) Le Carré's fiction provides the reader with no alternative position from which to judge the spy world, apart from the liberal-humanitarian attitude referred to which, inevitably, proves to be no alternative at all, either for the likes of Leamas and Westerby (who fall in love and die), or for the reader. Le Carré's 'endogenous' realism—based, we know, on the author's professional experience—is achieved at the cost of some loud political silences. The continued existence of MI6 and the C.I.A., and the continued need to 'combat Communism', are neither rigorously justified nor radically questioned, despite the occasional 'philosophical' debate. Indeed, the whole business of espionage and counter-espionage, of agents and moles, cut-outs and case officers, coat trailers and honey-traps, acquires the character of an autonomous activity; the political, economic and military issues at stake tend to become peripheral to a game that is played for its own sake. The need for spies is understood; it is a 'fact of life'. Endogenous realism and the limitations of the genre thus co-opt the reader into a fictional world that is, in the strictest sense, constituted by ideological closure. Any options for change made available to the reader are, at best, reformist. In *A Small Town in Germany*, for example, the routinized institution headed by Bradfield and de Lisle has lost all sense of purpose apart from self-survival and obediently pursuing the policies of Her Majesty's Government. Some revitalizing is therefore necessary. The trappings of bureaucracy are made familiar to us, then magically brought to life; the routinized is de-familiarized, not only by the situation that sets the plot in motion, but by the manner in which the narrative is focalized, both through the questing Alan Turner and through the absent, formerly questing Leo Harting. The novel succeeds in 'keeping the humdrum alive'[10] by injecting into the quotidian world of officialdom a new meaning and purpose, recharging tired batteries in those jaded readers whose lives are governed by the same bureaucratic reality which the novel criticizes and, implicitly, upholds. (The idea of tracking down a Nazi war criminal, used in thrillers such as Forsyth's *The Odessa File*, is suitably embellished with the wider theme of history repeating itself, but this is not allowed to detract from the central notion of an individual's compulsive quest conducted within a bureaucratic context.)

At the level of genre, a strategy of assimilation still operates, though not always successfully. Defining the spy genre will not concern us here, apart from pointing out that, in reacting against the action-packed, high-tech spy thriller—which Bruce Merry calls 'a form of readable evasion'[11] and which really belongs to an adventure genre—le Carré returns to a more hermeneutic genre: the detective mystery, from which much spy fiction is in any case derived. Summarizing the detective mystery, Todorov says:

> The investigation consists in returning to the same events over and over, checking and correcting the slightest details, until at the end the truth breaks out with regard to this same initial history.[12]

Alan Turner's investigations in *A Small Town,* and Smiley's in *Tinker Tailor Soldier Spy* and *Smiley's People,* also involve a painstaking digging-over of past events; the principal difference, however, is that whereas in a detective mystery a crime— usually a single event—has to be solved, in the le Carréan spy novel a multiple train of facts and appearances, actions and circumstances, including criminal acts such as murder, have to be unravelled as part of a mission: a manhunt, identification of an enemy agent, exposure of a 'mole', or, in *The Spy,* protection of a double agent misconstrued by the deceived agent as the enemy. Instead of breaking the genre, le Carré renews it, bending and parodying[13] the conventions of the spy thriller while foregrounding certain 'novelistic' elements, notably, a highly crafted 'literary' style.

Renewal, as Bakhtin has said, is the essence of genre:

> A genre is always the same and yet not the same, always old and new simultaneously. Genre is reborn and renewed at every stage in the development of literature and in every individual work of a given genre. This constitutes the life of the genre.[14]

Discussing Conrad's *The Secret Agent* and *Under Western Eyes,* Bruce Merry concludes:

> As great psychological studies with a relaxed development and a full cast of equally drawn characters, these novels enact the conventions of future espionage writing at the same time as they break them. And this, surely, is the way in which a popular genre can find its way to 'literariness': to understand the conventions but to surpass them in style and structure and manner. . . . 'Literariness' is a capacity to extract the maximum from a popular genre and still write about a man who is *also* a spy rather than about men who are defined by spying.[15]

The last two sentences apply more to le Carré than to Conrad, whose two novels in no sense 'enact the conventions of future espionage writing'. Each popular modern genre and sub-genre of the novel is a branch or twig of what was once a tree. Adorning one of these branches with 'literariness' does not make it into a tree, although I would agree with Andrew Osmond that le Carré at his best is 'much better' than most current British ' "literary" novelists'.[16] The question is whether a demarcation exists between 'spy fiction' and 'fiction that happens to be about spies', and whether le Carré's work, through its 'novelistic' qualities, surpasses the conventions of the former and crosses into the latter.

In his characterization of Smiley, le Carré certainly *attempts* to write about a man 'who is *also* a spy' rather than a man who is 'defined by spying'. But the grafting strategy fails with embarrassing results when, as in *Smiley's People*, the ageing Lady Ann telephones her 60- or 70-year-old husband, and we read: 'He rang off. He imagined her crying.'[17] Even more incongruous is Smiley's reflection a paragraph later: 'in his limited experience of women, earrings were what they took off first. Ann had only to go out of the house without wearing them for his heart to sink.'[18] The emotional side of Smiley's relationship with Ann is not merely tiresome; it exposes the limitations of writing within a spy genre. Like Sherlock Holmes, George Smiley is first of all a proper name, upon which is predicated a set of memorable traits, attributes and mannerisms (plump with short legs; 9 Bywater Street; German literature; wiping his glasses on the thick end of his tie). Most importantly, he is the model of a certain kind of reasoning intellect, whose function in a text such as *Smiley's People* is to drive the narrative forward. As a serial figure, Smiley does not develop. He is eternally middle-aged, and once the 'Ann problem' finds its groove it stays there for thirty years. The 'Ann problem' becomes another of Smiley's attributes, an original bound motif which, as long as it remains a bound motif and nothing more, helps to renew the genre. (If Smiley had had a loyal wife and children he might have been too 'social', or his need for dissimulation might have alienated our sympathy; on the other hand an eccentric English bachelor would have been too commonplace. Le Carré presumably wanted a lonely married bachelor who gains our sympathy. The answer was a childless cuckold.) The bound motif becomes embarrassing, then, precisely at the point where it pretends to explore the feelings of 'a man who is *also* a spy' rather than a man who is 'defined by spying'. The psychology of Smiley's involvement with Karla (the feminine name hints at a repressed sexuality) is quite a different matter, for this bears directly on Smiley's rôle as an intelligence agent.

Other motifs that become uncomfortably extraneous when they try to act as seams for the 'human condition', irrespective of their function in the plot, are Guillam's fraught relationship with his flute-playing girlfriend in *Tinker Tailor*, and passages such as the paragraph in the same novel beginning: 'Middle children weep longer than their brothers and sisters.'[19] Assimilating these personal and familial concerns into the narrative fails because they are 'unsettlingly tangential'[20] to the plot. With *A Perfect Spy*, on the other hand, le Carré solves the problem of writing a spy novel about a man 'who is *also* a spy' by having the spy retreat, after his father's death, to write what Lederer guesses to be 'twelve volumes of Pym's answer to Proust'.[21] Family matters—fathers and sons, husbands and wives—become legitimately central. When Brotherhood, hunting for the missing Pym, gives the railway clerk—an Indian who speaks in highly dignified sentences—a wedding photograph of Pym and his bride that shows Brotherhood ('Uncle Jack' to Pym's son Tom) in the background, the clerk asks: ' "Are you sure you are engaged in an official enquiry? This is a most irregular photograph." '[22] This time, however, the reader sees nothing incongruous. In *The Spy*, the coming together of Leamas and Liz turns out to be one of the components in 'a filthy, lousy operation'.[23] Their love affair is thus both intrinsic to the plot and thematically productive. The relationship between Jim Prideaux and the schoolboy Bill Roach in *Tinker Tailor* is similarly well woven in. Although it is not part of the main plot, its assimilation into the narrative succeeds because it revolves around 'watching', secrecy, and the gathering of information—and *information*, as I shall argue, is the key to le Carré's spy fiction. In its various manifestations it becomes the guiding narrative principle, determining the actantial rôle of each character in the story and providing the most crucial structuring link between text and reader.

The politics of information are familiar to all of us. Monopoly and state control of the media, disinformation campaigns, censorship, data banks, official secrets and intelligence operations are part of the ideological environment in which we live. Information in capitalist societies has also become fetishized. The owner of 'hot' information has wealth and power in his hands. The popularity of the spy thriller may, in fact, have as much to do with the so-called 'Information Society' as it has with espionage. Fiction often *refracts* rather than reflects reality.

Although le Carré's spy fiction is characterized by its 'endogenous realism', what engages the reader may be something other than the 'authentic', extratextual reality (though sticklers for the authentic detail are also catered for[24]). As Iser puts it:

> [No] literary text relates to contingent reality as such, but to models or concepts of reality, in which contingencies and complexities are reduced to a meaningful structure. We call these structures world-pictures or systems.[25]

This is echoed by le Carré when he says: 'Authenticity is frightfully boring but credibility is what novel writing is about, and plausibility.'[26] Elsewhere he says:

> [People] know that they live in an increasingly secretive society in many ways where they're cut off from the decisions of power—so that a story like *Tinker Tailor*, or for that matter, *Smiley's People* does lay out a massive conspiracy for them and lead them to some kind of conclusion, and they have that sense of resolution: 'Yes, that is how the world is, that is how my firm is. . . .'[27]

This is extremely illuminating, but I want to argue for a slightly different model of reality governing the narrative strategies in le Carré's spy novels, a model that is enacted in the interplay between text and reader, in the 'interaction of perspectives' and in the focalization.

Underpinning most of le Carré's fiction, especially the 'hermeneutic' novels (the 'proairetic'[28] elements in *The Honourable Schoolboy* and *The Little Drummer Girl* veer more towards an adventure genre), is a model of reality that relates to a political economy of information based on the principle of *scarcity* and *ownership*. The model can be summarized as follows. Information of the right kind has great value, and is scarce. Certain people compete for its ownership, and those who possess it are, with a few significant exceptions, either niggardly in parting with it, or have an anal-retentive habit of not parting with all of it. When all the information of the right kind has been put together it forms a complete picture. The reader believes that a complete picture exists; that the agent, on behalf of the reader, will eventually come to own all the pieces, and that when this happens, the narrative will end and the reader will enjoy a feeling of quasi-omniscience. On the way, pieces will be introduced which, we discover, do not belong; we may be aware that particular pieces are missing, but there will be times when we do not know that there *is* a piece missing, so that our vision of the completed picture is modified at every stage in the narrative.

Using this information model, we can begin first by sketching out some of the primary actantial rôles in le Carré's fiction. An *actant* has an unambiguous function within the story. A *psychological personality*, on the other hand, invites a broader assessment of 'character' in which a variety of conflicting rôles may be involved, and where the summary of events may give us only partial clues as to the character or personality in question. (Thus Magnus Pym in *A Perfect Spy* is more of a personality than an actant.) In his study of spy thrillers, Bruce Merry accepts the conventional terms of 'The spymaster, the Control figure, the agent, double agent, mole, sleeper, cut-out, informant'.[29] Our information model, however, requires us to find terms that describe more accurately the *actantial rôle* of each character. ('Control' is a misleading term if Control does not control events, though he undoubtedly does so in *The Spy*.) Our first rôle is that of the Seeker, who seeks out information, and who slips readily into the rôle of interrogator. Alan Turner, Smiley in *Call for the Dead, Tinker Tailor* and *Smiley's People,* Jerry Westerby and di Salis in *The Honourable Schoolboy*, and Brotherhood in *A Perfect Spy*, are examples. The Seeker need not be the hero: in *The Spy*, for example, Peters and Fiedler, not Leamas, are the Seekers and interrogators. Next there is the Holder, or keeper of information. A Holder is either an unwilling or reluctant informant, or one who holds something back. Leamas, Bradfield in *A Small Town*, Sam Collins in *The Honourable Schoolboy*, and on occasions Smiley himself, are examples of Holders. In *Smiley's People* Smiley remembers that Toby Esterhase 'had never once volunteered the truth, that information was money to him; even when he counted it valueless, he never threw it away'.[30] Ricki Tarr in *Tinker Tailor* provides invaluable information about the Circus mole through the would-be defector Irina, but fails to tell Guillam and Smiley that his daughter and her Eurasian mother are travelling to London on fake British passports, information that Guillam learns from Alleline ('It may sound to you like ordinary flight information but it isn't that at all. It's ultra, *ultra* sensitive.'[31]). Guillam also learns from Alleline that Tarr has instructed his daughter and her mother to go to Guillam should Tarr fail to make contact with them. Guillam's reaction is violent: 'he would have been tempted to beat the daylight out of Tarr and if necessary he would have brought Fawn in to lend a hand.'[32] The second interview with Tarr, concerning the Poole passports, is much more hostile. Holding onto information is a pervasive theme; it is even encapsulated in a brief exchange between Leamas and Fawley.

> 'Do you know?'
> 'Of course.'
> 'Then why the hell don't you tell me?'[33]

Other actantial rôles in le Carré include the Requester, who delegates or commissions others to seek out information (Smiley in *The Honourable Schoolboy*, and in *Tinker Tailor* when he delegates Guillam to steal files), and the Carrier, who acts as a vehicle of information (Villem in *Smiley's People*). Much more important, however, is the Provider, or liberal dispenser of information. Unlike the Holder, the Provider is a generous giver, and it is a curious fact that le Carré's Providers tend to be naïve, trusting and childlike, with an other-worldly innocence. Examples are Mr. Hibbert in *The Honourable Schoolboy*, Irina, Grigoriev (*Smiley's People*), and Connie Sachs. (Liz, the child-woman heroine in *The Spy*, is a browbeaten witness, a would-be Holder who innocently reveals all.) Mr. Hibbert, the ex-missionary, is full of warm, woolly, Christian sentiment, unlike his bitter and unforgiving daughter. His generous outpourings about the brothers Ko betray a forgiving, almost ludicrously indulgent paternalism: 'Oh, the slogans they dream up!'[34] he says, talking of the Communist riots that led to the destruction of his church in Shanghai. Irina in *Tinker Tailor* pours out her testimony in 'fast urgent writing with no erasures'[35] in her secret diary, and is naïve enough to believe that Ricki Tarr loves her, while Grigoriev, weak and ridiculous in his entrapment, seems to forget that he is being held by British agents who are black-mailing him, and launches into a full-scale 'confession', 'liberally volunteering information'[36] that is apparently elicited by Smiley's rôle-playing as the 'bureaucratic messenger of the inevitable',[37] but which surely has its cause in the Russian soul: 'In the catharsis of confession, Grigoriev once more forgot his own peril.'[38] (In fact, it is not really a 'confession' at all, certainly not in the Dostoevskian sense; the hapless Grigoriev is simply spilling the beans. Although this may be an anti-climax for the reader, we are clearly intended to admire the brilliance of Smiley's psychological technique.)

The most famous of le Carré's Providers is Connie Sachs. In *Tinker Tailor* and *Smiley's People* she is an eccentric old dear, girlish and emotional, liable to burst into tears at the drop of a hat. 'I *hate* the real world, George. I like the Circus and all my lovely boys.'[39] George, knight errant (in *Smiley's People* she gazes at him 'as if he were an erring son she loved'[40]), relies on vital information from Connie concerning Polyakov, then Karla's daughter, in his two quests; structurally, therefore, she plays the rôle of helper who provides the key—an actant found in countless legends and folktales. The reader intuits this sub-consciously, and it reveals another of le Carré's narrative strategies: his 'mythmaking', with its patriotic, at times Arthurian overtones. Yet behind Connie's 'fairy-tale' narration, 'her grandmother's glow of enchanted reminiscence',[41] her playful use of gushing terms of endearment, her mimicry, and her frustrated sexuality (in *Smiley's People* there are strong hints of lesbianism)—behind all this, there is something quite sinister and deadly: a killer's instinct, honed into a precision instrument by the Circus environment. (Her memory is as sharp as a razor.) There is, one feels, something rather repulsive and nasty in this gushing, mocking-bird grandmother. Yet whatever it is, Connie's actantial rôle prevents the narrator from emphasizing or exploring it. The narrator simply treats her as a 'wonderful mind which had never grown up',[42] and the chance of creating a complex personality (rather than an assemblage of traits, attributes and mannerisms) is lost.

Like Hibbert, Irina and Grigoriev, Connie is carried away by her flights of narration. Lacking the built-in dynamism and tension of an interrogation, an outpouring of information holds the reader's interest more if there is something frantic and urgent about it. In *Smiley's People*, Connie's sudden 'Spot of *timor mortis*',[43] and her occasional meanderings and lapses at critical points in her narrative, are a le Carréan device for creating suspense. Elsewhere, le Carré's narrative skills are demon-strated by the way in which signifiers operating at the meta-story level are inserted at strategic points, triggering off appropriate responses in the reader:

> '. . . Plus the Green and that's Formal and Informal
> Conversations—'
>> 'Bradfield told me.'
>> 'They're like pieces, believe me, pieces in a puzzle . . .
>> that's what I thought at first . . . I've moved them round in
>> my mind. Hour after hour. I haven't slept.'[44]

If Meadowes moves these pieces of bureaucratic information round in his mind, so do we; and if Meadowes cannot sleep, neither can the reader. And when Turner says to himself, 'You will not go to bed until you are at least aware of the trail you must follow',[45] the reader, who is inside Turner's mind, takes this as an order.

So far we have used the term 'information' to mean a set of data forming the basis of the plot, data which the reader, together with the hero or Seeker, must retrieve by following interrogations with Holders, the intradiegetic narratives of Providers, and the retrospective thoughts of the hero or Seeker himself, such as those of Smiley in *Tinker Tailor*. But 'information' in this context also means *narrative* information. Narrative perspective, to quote Genette, is a 'mode of regulating information, arising from the choice (or not) of a restrictive "point of view"'.[46] In Todorov's three-term typology, the narrator either knows (and therefore says) more than the character knows, says only what a given character knows, or says less than the character knows. This is schematized as follows:

$$\text{Narrator} > \text{Character}$$
$$\text{Narrator} = \text{Character}$$
$$\text{Narrator} < \text{Character}$$

Avoiding 'the too specifically visual connotations of the terms *vision, field,* and *point of view*',[47] Genette employs the term 'focalization' to mean any restriction of field and hence of narrative information, either internal (where the narrative is focalized through the eyes and mind of a particular, usually major character), or external (where the character is viewed from the outside). 'Variable focalization' is where the focalization shifts from one character to another.

Applying these concepts to le Carré's spy fiction yields some interesting results. *The Spy Who Came in from the Cold*, a novel of classical concentration and richness, is based on a double deception, both of the characters and of the reader. The reader is kept in the dark or deceived through restrictions of field, delayed exposition, tactical reticence, and *paralipsis*, where the narrative does not merely skip over a moment of time, as in ellipsis, but '*sidesteps* a given element',[48] or omits information that should be given according to the focalization—a device at its most 'blatant', says Barthes,[49] in Agatha Christie's *The Murder of Roger Ackroyd*, where the narrative is focalized 'through the murderer while omitting from his "thoughts" simply the memory of the murder'.[50] The double deception in the story of *The Spy* consists in the hero, Leamas, pretending to act as a defector in a 'put-up job'[51] that deceives Peters and Fiedler, when Leamas in turn is being deceived by his masters; the deception of the reader consists in the narrator making 'the great lie'[52] that Leamas lives seem (at times) genuine, and in focalizing the narrative through a hero whose plausible, yet wrong, deductions about his mission (e.g. that Fiedler is the 'special interest' Control is fighting to preserve) become our own until Leamas and we discover the truth.

The first chapter, focalized through Leamas, is a scene of terse dialogue and economical description, ending in a piece of tense, dramatic action. Coming before this climax is a passage of retrospective reflection ('That damned woman, thought Leamas'[53]) that slides into a flashback complete with dialogue. This passage hardly clarifies what is going on, however, for we are too much inside Leamas's mind (an example of what Genette calls 'excessive focalization'). Direct exposition follows in Chapter II, with some external views of Leamas—one from the air hostess—and then the dialogue with Control. Between Chapter II and III there is an important paralipsis. The briefing that Leamas has with Control and Guillam, in which Leamas's pretended defection and the spurring of Fiedler are worked out, is omitted from the narrative, and it is not until Chapter XII that this omission is supplied in a brief flashback. Had the information been provided in its proper place, much of the novel's atmosphere of tension and uncertainty would have been lost. Mystery surrounds Leamas in Chapters III, IV and

115

V with the switch to external focalization, testing our previous certainty that Leamas is on a mission. Leamas's 'decline' is viewed by 'uninformed' observers and commentators: Elsie in Accounts (whose gossip also turns out to be a put-up job), Circus colleagues and secretaries, then the representatives of a local London community, playing the same actantial rôle as the Tuscan community in *The Honourable Schoolboy*, for whom Jerry Westerby becomes a comparable object of gossip and speculation. Here, the narrator says *less* than the protagonist knows. We revert to some internal focalization when Leamas works in the library, but then we switch to Liz, through whose unsuspecting, innocent consciousness we follow Leamas's sickness, recovery, and farewell.

Thereafter Leamas is the focalizer, and his pretended rôle is understood, but the paralipsis is upheld: though we have almost unbroken access to his thoughts, all memory of his briefing is omitted. At one point in Chapter VIII we view Leamas through Peters: 'What was Leamas worth? What would break him, what attract or frighten him? What did he hate, above all, what did he know?'[54] Since we are as much in the dark as Peters about Leamas's information value, as well as unsure of Leamas's ability to sustain his rôle, and still uninformed of the details of his plan, suspense is maintained. The narrator again plays on the reader's uncertainty at the end of this chapter by implying that Leamas has, in fact, defected: 'when at last Leamas stumbled into bed the following night he knew he had betrayed all that he knew of Allied Intelligence in Berlin.'[55] Delayed exposition of Leamas's Berlin experience and the 'Rolling Stone' affair, milked out of him by his interrogators, does not relax the tensions, for the reader, knowing the dangerous game Leamas is playing, also hears about these things for the first time, unaware of how thoroughly the plan has been laid. The relationship between narrator and reader thus parallels that of Holder and Seeker, with the narrator holding back and the reader interrogating, kept on tenterhooks by Leamas's performance. Deception of the reader, as I have indicated, works on two levels. The first, analogous to Leamas's deception of Peters and Fiedler, creates uncertainty around Leamas; the second, analogous to Control's deception of Leamas, locks us inside the deceived focalizer.

There are two occasions—Smiley's visit to Liz and Liz's invitation to the G.D.R.—when we learn from the narrator more than Leamas knows; most of the time we know less. With Liz we know rather more, initially, but when she is invited to the G.D.R. we are on approximately equal terms, though we interpret the invitation less naïvely. It is during the cross-examination by Karden that Liz's blindness, relative to the reader's knowledge, becomes acute: 'like a blind child among the seeing she was cut off from all those around her.'[56] The reader's aching feeling of superiority as one of the 'seeing' is abruptly ended, however, when Leamas thinks: 'London must have gone raving mad . . . It was insane, fantastic.'[57] When Leamas, then Liz, are fully apprised of the 'foul, foul operation', the circuit of knowledge broken by Control's deception is restored, while the circuit of knowledge linking the reader and the narrator is also complete. Just as Control has no more tricks left, so the narrator can no longer deceive and tantalize the reader. At the end of the reader's interrogation of the narrative the truth is finally yielded up, and the reader—if he or she is a skilled interrogator—emerges as the victor.

In *A Small Town in Germany*, single internal focalization becomes 'double' as Alan Turner repeats the weekday routine and enters the mind of the absent Leo Harting, reading his handwriting and his books, sitting in his chair, and touching what he touched (cigars, keys, envelopes, buttons). Although the text largely consists of Turner's interviews with Leo's associates, the theme of an existential quest is conveyed phenomenologically, through objects, books and documents whose tangible presence mocks the searcher with an elusive, absent meaning, made present only when Turner 'becomes' Leo after discovering the missing files hidden in the Glory Hole.

The reader's assimilation into Turner's thought-processes is facilitated by Turner's *tabula rasa* mind. Focalizer and reader begin as equals, working on information that is presented for the most part in chronological sequence. Turner's long-term memory plays no part in solving the enigma; this frees the narrative from any need for the kind of interiorized reminiscence and historical interpretation that burdens the narrative of *Tinker Tailor*, where Smiley's solitary recollections play a key rôle in the resolution. In *A Small Town* all the relevant background history is presented in the direct and reported speech of Turner's interlocutors. Only at one crucial point in the narrative does Turner jump ahead of the reader: in Chapter XV, after telling Gaunt to leave him alone with the missing files. The reader also leaves him, and a paralipsis occurs. In Chapter XVI Turner gives Bradfield the evidence against Karfeld, collected during Turner's all-night reading session—to which the reader has not been privy.

Turner's eyes, we are told, 'were a swimmer's eyes, very pale, washed colourless by the sea'[58]; when he searches Harting's house a phantom observer notes how 'He remained motionless, head to one side, his colourless eyes vainly searching the gloom.'[59] Files, paper, envelopes and handwriting all have colours in this novel, but the eyes of its main focalizer are strangely 'colourless'. Colour is what Turner's eyes *see*; his eyes are what the reader *sees through*. This must be why they are colourless, for if we were told that they were, for example, brown (le Carré's favourite colour for eyes, it seems) we would be looking *at* and not through them.

In *A Small Town* reader and focalizer are more or less on equal terms; but when Smiley starts on the files given to him by Lacon in *Tinker Tailor* he retraces 'path after path into his own past'.[60] Unlike Turner's quest, Smiley's reading stirs memories the reader does not have, necessitating phrases such as 'Smiley reflected', 'Smiley now relived', 'Smiley recalled', and 'Smiley remembered'.[61] Action in the present becomes recollection, which in turn modulates, somewhat awkwardly, into flashback; devices such as 'With mounting interest Smiley continued his journey through Lacon's meagre records'[62] fail to trigger the responses elicited during Turner's quest. Smiley's mind may have been 'open as he read to every inference, every oblique connection',[63] but we have to take this on trust as second-hand testimony; we are *told* rather than *shown*. The presentation of the evidence itself gives no quarter to the inattentive. However, one wonders how many readers are able to see that Alleline's potted biography at the beginning of Chapter 16 is a vital piece of evidence. For an important paralipsis in the narrative is that Smiley has already discounted Alleline as a suspect because of the latter's lack of experience in Soviet and East European affairs. We are told at the end of Chapter 36 that Smiley 'had always known it was Bill'.[64] The political point—that cliques breed cover-ups—is clear. Still, one cannot help feeling more than a little cheated by the news.

The power relationship symbolically enacted between text and reader in these two novels might be described thus: in *A Small Town*, where focalizer and reader work together, it is egalitarian; in *Tinker Tailor*, where the reader is led to admire the superior, often inward workings of a sometimes intuitive intellect, it is élitist. For most of *Smiley's People* the relationship is more than equal: not until Chapter 9, for example, does Smiley learn what we have already seen in Chapter 2, when Villem carries the yellow envelope in a basket of oranges and the contact leaves a yellow chalk mark on the seat; and few readers can fail to keep up with and even surpass Smiley's methodical reasoning as he deduces, then searches for, then finds Vladimir's missing packet of Gauloises. Chapters 12 to 17 are focalized entirely through Smiley; Chapters 18 and 19, however, do a characteristic 'duck-dive'. First, the narrative is focalized through Ostrakova. Then external focalization, using characters such as Guillam and Enderby, draws a veil over thoughts we have had continuous access to for six chapters. The intention is not simply coy, as if Smiley's mind had suddenly acquired forbidden charms, but part of a narrative strategy. (Towards the end of the novel, sentences such as 'And Smiley, sitting so quiet, so immobile, as the party broke up around him, what did he feel?'[65] are typically myth-making, creating an aura of admiration around the hero.)

Enderby asks Smiley who Karla's 'dark lady' is:

> Again there is mystery about Smiley's decision not to reply to this question. Perhaps only his wilful inaccessibility can explain it; or perhaps we are staring at the stubborn refusal of the born caseman to reveal anything to his controller that is not essential to their collaboration.[66]

The 'mystery' exists only for Control and others not in the know. Recalling what Connie told Smiley about Tatiana in Chapter 15, the reader now enjoys privileged access to information not even Control possesses. Indeed, the reader can even feel superior to the narrator, who identifies with the uninformed 'we'. The narrator in this case seems to be some kind of objective

sycophant compiling a detailed Circus history for limited circulation, a public voice locked inside a private clique: 'the fact
is that Smiley kept his counsel.'[67] This historicizing and rather
pompous voice, addressing members of a group in which certain
events well known within the group have been frequently discussed, is also heard in *The Honourable Schoolboy*: 'The fact
remains that Saigon was the worst place on earth for Jerry to be
kicking his heels.'[68]

The function of this voice is first of all deictic, placing the
reader either close to an inner circle or somewhere on its fringes.
The reader enjoys the illusion of being a member of a special
club, of having access to its secret documents, files, conversations
and correspondence. Secondly, the narrator in *Smiley's People*
records for posterity events which, it is agreed, are already
legendary. The historian pretends to factual accuracy when
actually he is mythologizing: 'There is even a scale model of the
scene at Sarratt, and occasionally the directing staff will dig it
out and tell the tale.'[69] The narrative technique here is all the
more remarkable for its proleptic self-confidence ('For years
afterwards, and probably for all his life, Peter Guillam would
relate, with varying degrees of frankness, the story of his home-
coming that same evening'[70]), shifting the time of narrating to a
period long after the events in the story are supposed to have
occurred. The events of *Smiley's People* take place in 1978, and
the novel was published in 1980. The time of narrating therefore postdates the novel's publication by an indefinite number
of years. This creates a sense of permanence. It says that things
will remain basically the same, and that the Circus itself will
continue into the indefinite future. In a word, that the system is
indestructible.

Against this interpretation, there is Steven M. Neuse's con-
tention that le Carré registers a sense of 'despair over the
stultifying effect that bureaucratic organizations have on human
freedom, creativity and moral sensitivity'.[71] In terms of *narrative
discourse*, however (rather than 'theme' or so-called 'message'),
le Carré's fiction re-invests the bureaucratic with meaning,
working it into something *new*. Take the following:

> 'You are an operator, Leamas,' Fiedler observed with a laugh,
> 'not an evaluator. That is clear. Let me ask you some elementary
> questions.'

Leamas said nothing.

'The file—the actual file on operation Rolling Stone. What colour was it?'

'Grey with a red cross on it—that means limited subscription.'

'Was anything attached to the outside?'

'Yes, the Caveat. That's the subscription label. . . .'[72]

Files are not 'stultifying': they are objects whose detailed appearance is loaded with dramatic significance. In *A Small Town* Meadowes says of the 'Destruction' programme: 'That's the fascination of files; there's nowhere to stop.'[73] A sentence such as 'There was a sudden smell of hot wax from next door, and the muffled thud of a large seal being pressed on to a packet'[74] brings the office world vividly to life.

This relates to one of the central themes of *A Small Town*. In a context where millions of human lives are buried in files, and where book-burning echoes the Nazi past, affirming the 'life' in books, documents and files is a moral obligation. When Turner forces open Leo's bookcase, 'the brass came through suddenly like a bone through flesh'.[75] Examining the volumes, 'he grasped hold of the covers and with a savage twist wrenched them from the binding as if he were breaking the wings of a bird'.[76] (Earlier on we are told of Turner's notebook: 'It crackled sharply as he opened it.'[77]) But down in the Glory Hole, greeting the missing files 'as we greet old friends', Turner sees 'some grey with bloom, some wrinkled and bent with damp, column after column in their black uniforms, veterans trained and waiting to be called.'[78] It is a moving, powerful vision. Later, a boy in the Karfeld crowd breaks a book and throws it on the flames; the book 'burned badly, choking before it died. I shouldn't have done that to the books, Turner thought; I'll be doing it to people next.'[79] Meadowes's comment, that 'Destruction's a weird game',[80] takes on other, darker meanings. The theme is hardly original, but it is handled imaginatively, with artistry and skill, and it gives *A Small Town* a resonance few spy novels, or novels about the bureaucratic world, ever attain.

Elsewhere one notes a 'zoom lens' effect, with sudden, vivid close-ups, especially of bureaucratic objects, handwriting, letters and stationery; a grey file 'with a red cross on it'; hand-drawn words 'a good two inches high, ruled at the edges and cross-hatched in red and green crayon'.[81] 'Bringing to life' at times

121

seems to mean 'seeing close up', and it produces some strange effects in terms of focalization. In *The Honourable Schoolboy*, Jerry 'had seen Mama Stefano from a long way off. He had that instinct, there was a part of him that never ceased to watch.' In the next sentence we are told: 'He had seen very early the blue envelope she was waving. . . .'[82] These powers of vision are also possessed by Smiley. The original typescript (much altered) of a passage in Chapter 17 of *Smiley's People* reads:

> 'Isadora,' he said, and pointed at a jetty further down the shore.
> The planks of the jetty yielded alarmingly to Smiley's tread. The Isadora was a forty-foot motor-launch down on her luck, a Grand Hotel awaiting demolition. The port-holes were curtained, one of them was smashed, another was repaired with Scotch tape.[83]

The final version reads:

> '*Isadora*,' he said.
> He pointed at a rickety jetty farther down the shore. The *Isadora* lay at the end of it, a forty-foot motor launch down on her luck, a Grand Hotel awaiting demolition. The portholes were curtained, one of them was smashed, another was repaired with Scotch tape. The planks of the jetty yielded alarmingly to Smiley's tread.[84]

When Smiley reaches the end of the jetty he realizes that the *Isadora* is twelve feet out to sea. In the draft version, Smiley sees more detail as he walks down the jetty; in the final version, he can see that one porthole is 'repaired with Scotch tape' *before* he steps onto the jetty, and before he notices that the *Isadora* is twelve feet out to sea. The 'zoom lens' effect, though it breaks the rules of focalization, would seem to be deliberate. Bringing close up is cognate with 'bringing to life'.

Bringing to life and *coming back to life* are also kindred notions. The bureaucratically dead must become humanly alive. In this way the system will prove indestructible. Supplementing the textual strategies we have examined are certain recurrent motifs such as regeneration, resurrection and indestructibility, by which is meant, ultimately, the indestructible nature of the Eurocentric, bourgeois world into which le Carré's fiction seeks to assimilate its readers. Smiley's retirements and resignations, his apparently moribund physical condition, and his Buddha-like withdrawal into states of suspended animation, are like the Circus's 'duck-dive' in *The Honourable Schoolboy*. The empire only *seems* dead. In fact, like Smiley, it is indestructible. In Craw's analysis:

> The thinner her trade routes, the more elaborate her clandestine efforts to protect them. The more feeble her colonial grip, the more desperate her subversion of those who sought to loosen it.[85]

Connie Sachs is another whose nearness to death belies a tenacious grip: 'It seemed impossible that her racked and drink-sodden body could have once more summoned so much strength.'[86] Here, the 'apparently dead' come back to life. What is 'too dead', however, needs to be revivified, like Bonn, 'a dark house where someone had died, a house draped in Catholic black and guarded by policemen'.[87] (The false regenerator is Karfeld; but the main narrative focus is on Leo, and to some extent Turner, as representatives of a force needed to bring back to life a world gone morally dead.) Those who cynically accept their moral death or who merely express their own putrefaction, such as Fielding in *A Murder of Quality*, perhaps deserve to die: 'In me the process is complete. You see before you a dead soul, and Carne is the body I live in.'[88] Bradfield's defence of hypocrisy at the end of *A Small Town* is just as cynical in its way; however, it is certainly not an acceptance of decline and death, but a determination to hang on in the old way, and 'go down fighting', rather than turn virtuous and neutral:

> We are a corrupt nation, and we need all the help we can get. That is lamentable and, I confess, occasionally humiliating. However, I would rather fail as a power than survive by impotence. I would rather be vanquished than neutral. I would rather be English than Swiss.[89]

Finally, in *The Honourable Schoolboy* there is a character who is not only apparently dead—and who therefore comes back to life—but is *too alive*: Ricardo, the Mexican opium runner. In one of the best scenes in the novel, we meet Ricardo holed up in the jungle of North East Thailand, a bare-chested, hairy, oily Latino whose macho sexuality is simply *too alive*. The pattern holds: Ricardo is associated with *too much death*, with guns, violence, murder, and the attempted murder of Jerry.

In *The Honourable Schoolboy* le Carré's—or rather the narrative's—strategy of assimilation is at its most 'political' when the 'we-are-all-the-same' theme is cheapened by attributing to the Communists tactics that were in fact adopted by the C.I.A.; China Airsea is a Moscow Centre proprietary company in the novel, but in Indonesia in the 1950s Civil Air Transport and Southern Air Transport were C.I.A.-owned companies. On a more ideological level, the text of *The Honourable Schoolboy* displays to its readers a dazzling array of semes and signifiers whose goal is to expand our horizons while still keeping us within a Eurocentric consciousness. The East is a stage (Cambodia is a 'sideshow') and we are the audience, following a rapid succession of vivid, newsreel-style images relayed to us by one of our foreign correspondents. The people of the East—Thais, Laotians, Cambodians, Vietnamese and Chinese—have no eyes and no voice (a situation that le Carré tried to amend by giving the Palestinians a point of view in *The Little Drummer Girl*). The anglicized, mission-taught Drake Ko and his stereotyped bodyguard hardly count as spokesmen.

The paradoxical law of any assimilation strategy is that the more one tries to absorb, the less one assimilates. No narrating voice or focalizer in *The Honourable Schoolboy* really has a grasp of what is going on, other than a general notion that Communism is taking over. In a desire to embrace the globe, the novel's cultural-referential code runs amok, juxtaposing (to take a random example) broken cup handles and bar extensions in Tashkent, in what becomes a riot of artistically unassimilated information. The reader's powers of absorption break under the strain. In 'classical' le Carré, the textual organization of precise reference makes for the maximum of assimilation; in 'overblown' le Carré, superabundance of reference produces entropy. Yet even in the most indigestible passages an ideological intention is present. The clotted style bespeaks a consciousness for whom no part of the earth and no portion of humanity, in no matter what combination, are surprising or unfamiliar:

> Tarr's father was an Australian solicitor living in Penang, it seemed. The mother was a small-time actress from Bradford who came East with a British drama group before the war. The father, Smiley recalled, had an evangelical streak and preached in local gospel halls. The mother had a small criminal record in England but Tarr's father either didn't know or didn't care. When the war

came the couple evacuated to Singapore for the sake of their young son. . . .[90]

This could just as well have read: 'Tarr's father was a Canadian architect living in Bangkok, it seemed. The mother was a part-time ballet dancer from Falkirk who came East with a British dance troupe before the war. . . .' The congested prose is not difficult to parody because it implies that by putting a disparate collection of facts together—and the more ingenious the better—one has thereby created something meaningful.

When the world, or Communism, becomes too big to handle (Coca-Cola culture and imperialist 'global village' concepts aside), the honest thing to do is to look otherness in the face and accept it, before anxiously attempting to assimilate it into a Western, liberal-humanist discourse. Perhaps it is for this reason that Karla's adamantine silence in Smiley's account of their meeting in *Tinker Tailor* is so devastating. It is the nearest le Carré's text gets to admitting that the other side is morally stronger, that its ideological otherness is absolute and impenetrable. The reader takes small comfort in the consoling thought of Smiley, who is at this point the 'very archetype of a flabby Western liberal', that 'I would rather be my kind of fool than his for all that.'[91] Whatever Karla represents, it is unassimilable. The episode is a *locus classicus* of Western liberalism's failure to give a voice to the other. Yet the other cannot be spoken unless it speaks itself, and to allow that in a spy novel would be courting ideological and literary suicide. For behind the fictional silence of Karla lie other, even louder silences. Liberal-humanist, imperialist fiction cannot, of course, be expected to commit suicide. Perhaps, therefore, the most one can expect of it is that it acknowledges, honestly, its silencing of the other.

## NOTES

1. Tony Barley, *Taking Sides: The Fiction of John le Carré* (Milton Keynes: Open University Press, 1986), p. 23.
2. V. Voinov, 'John le Carré: Spy Tamer', *Literaturnaya Gazeta*, 16 October 1965.
3. Miriam Gross, 'The Secret World of John le Carré, *Observer*, 3 February 1980.

4. Barley, p. 9.
5. It may be objected that Mundt is the real enemy, but of course he is not; his cold-blooded ruthlessness, anti-semitism and diabolical cunning clearly mark him out as one of ours. The 'ideological assumptions' of the popular spy thriller are indeed subverted here, but a subtler strategy is at work: Fiedler, who is 'ideologically sound' according to Leamas, is 'not ours' (1964, pp. 215–16), but the point is surely that he *is* ours. He is basically decent, honest and human, and says things like: 'All our work—yours and mine—is rooted in the theory that the whole is more important than the individual' (p. 124) and: 'I myself would have put a bomb in a restaurant if it brought us further along the road. Afterwards I would draw the balance— so many women, so many children; and so far along the road. But Christians—and yours is a Christian society—Christians may not draw the balance' (p. 135) and: 'I like the English' (p. 135).
6. Barley, p. 22.
7. Wolfgang Iser, *The Act of Reading: A Theory of Aesthetic Response* (London: Routledge & Kegan Paul, 1978), p. 96.
8. Melvyn Bragg, interview with le Carré on *The South Bank Show*, London Weekend Television, 27 March 1983.
9. *The Spy Who Came in from the Cold* (London: Pan Books, 1964), p. 217.
10. 'Le Carré's Circus: Lamplighters, Moles and Others of That Ilk', *Listener*, 13 September 1979, p. 340.
11. Bruce Merry, *Anatomy of the Spy Thriller* (Dublin: Gill & Macmillan, 1977), p. 5.
12. Tzvetan Todorov, *The Poetics of Prose* (Oxford: Basil Blackwell, 1977), p. 135.
13. An expert knowledge of guns, according to Bruce Merry, is an indispensable attribute of the agent in the popular spy thriller. In *The Spy*, this knowledge is amusingly useless: 'As he fell, drifting warmly into unconsciousness, he wondered whether he had been hit with a revolver, the old kind with a swivel on the butt where you fastened the lanyard' (p. 162).
14. Mikhail Bakhtin, *Problems of Dostoevsky's Poetics* (Manchester: Manchester University Press, 1984), p. 106.
15. Merry, pp. 196–97.
16. Andrew Osmond, 'The Silent, Unlit Country', *Literary Review*, March 1986, p. 47.
17. *Smiley's People* (London: Hodder & Stoughton, 1980), p. 129.
18. Ibid.
19. *Tinker Tailor Soldier Spy* (London: Hodder & Stoughton, 1974), p. 79.
20. Barley, p. 102.
21. *A Perfect Spy* (London: Hodder & Stoughton, 1986), p. 246.
22. Ibid., p. 252.
23. *The Spy* . . ., p. 226.
24. When such sticklers are not properly catered for, they become indignant, like Craig S. Karpel, 'Time to bring Smiley back from the cold', *Listener*, 29 September 1983, reviewing *The Little Drummer Girl*.
25. Iser, op. cit., p. 70.
26. 'Le Carré's Circus . . .', op. cit., p. 340.

27. Bragg interview.
28. Defining the proairetic code as the sequence of actions, Barthes says that 'its basis is more empirical than rational': *S/Z* (New York: Hill & Wang, 1974), p. 19.
29. Merry, p. 1.
30. *Smiley's People*, p. 155.
31. *Tinker Tailor . . .*, p. 179.
32. Ibid., p. 183.
33. *The Spy . . .*, p. 17.
34. *The Honourable Schoolboy* (London: Hodder & Stoughton, 1977), p. 253.
35. *Tinker Tailor . . .*, p. 60.
36. *Smiley's People*, p. 291.
37. Ibid., p. 287.
38. Ibid., p. 303.
39. *Tinker Tailor . . .*, p. 100.
40. *Smiley's People*, p. 162.
41. *Tinker Tailor . . .*, p. 101.
42. Ibid.
43. *Smiley's People*, p. 172.
44. *A Small Town in Germany* (London: Heinemann, 1968), p. 104.
45. Ibid., p. 145.
46. Gerard Genette, *Narrative Discourse* (Oxford: Basil Blackwell, 1980), pp. 185–86.
47. Genette, p. 189.
48. Ibid., p. 52.
49. Roland Barthes, 'Introduction to the Structural Analysis of Narratives', in *Image–Music–Text* (New York: Hill & Wang, 1977), p. 113.
50. Genette, p. 196.
51. *The Spy . . .*, p. 214.
52. Ibid., p. 140.
53. Ibid., p. 10.
54. Ibid., p. 80.
55. Ibid., p. 90.
56. Ibid., p. 205.
57. Ibid., p. 210.
58. *A Small Town . . .*, p. 35.
59. Ibid., p. 185.
60. *Tinker Tailor . . .*, p. 125.
61. Ibid., pp. 128–32.
62. Ibid., p. 141.
63. Ibid., p. 143.
64. Ibid., p. 327.
65. *Smiley's People*, p. 307.
66. Ibid., p. 239.
67. Ibid.
68. *The Honourable Schoolboy*, p. 409.
69. *Smiley's People*, p. 279.
70. Ibid., p. 222.

71. Steven M. Neuse, 'Bureaucratic Malaise in the Modern Spy Novel: Deighton, Greene, and le Carré, *Public Administration* 60 (Autumn 1982), 295.
72. *The Spy* . . ., pp. 128–29.
73. *A Small Town* . . ., p. 96.
74. Ibid., p. 99.
75. Ibid., p. 183.
76. Ibid., p. 185.
77. Ibid., p. 46.
78. Ibid., p. 244.
79. Ibid., p. 293.
80. Ibid., p. 91.
81. Ibid., p. 69.
82. *The Honourable Schoolboy*, p. 44.
83. Reproduced in 'The Times Profile', *The Times*, Monday, 6 September, 1982.
84. *Smiley's People*, p. 203.
85. *The Honourable Schoolboy*, p. 33.
86. *Smiley's People*, p. 181.
87. *A Small Town* . . ., p. v.
88. *A Murder of Quality* (Harmondsworth: Penguin), p. 51.
89. *A Small Town* . . ., pp. 286–87.
90. *Tinker Tailor* . . ., p. 39.
91. Ibid., p. 205.

# 6

# *The Little Drummer Girl:*
# An Interview with
# John le Carré

## by MELVYN BRAGG

*Before discussing* The Little Drummer Girl *in detail with the author, Melvyn Bragg raised an issue that has fascinated readers of le Carré. Bragg observed that various commentators assumed that, while working for the Foreign Office, le Carré 'acted as a spy', in which capacity he encountered situations subsequently used in his novels. Le Carré's answer is the closest he has come to settling the issue:*

> Well, to an extent, it's true. I wasn't Mata Hari, and I wasn't Himmler's Aunt, but it would be stupid of me to pretend that I was not—like Somerset Maugham, Graham Greene and lots of other writers—for a time engaged in that work. And it was a natural continuum, really, of the life I had led . . . I've always tried to deny it, and keep away from the subject, and I intend to go on doing so. Firstly, because I simply don't want to commit a breach of confidence; and secondly, because it seems to me really to belong—it's so long ago—to an extension of my childhood, rather than adulthood. I loathe the notion that I'm some kind of literary defector from the secret world. That's really all I want to say about it.

*Bragg*: *The Little Drummer Girl* is set all over Europe but centred very heavily in the Middle East. And it's a non-Smiley book. Can you say why you wanted the Middle East as a subject first of all?

*Le Carré*: Well, my interest in the Middle East began after I'd written *The Honourable Schoolboy*, when I still had it in mind to take Smiley around the world and have him fighting it out with Karla, his Russian opposite number, in different theatres. So in 1978 I went to the Lebanon and to Israel and I tried to familiarize myself with the area and its problems. I simply could not find a plot which was not too Gothic, too manipulative—too silly really—to accommodate that conflict. The Soviet presence in the Middle East, at that time, was very slight indeed, I mean the Russians have goofed in the Middle East anyway and they were effectively thrown out of Egypt. I just couldn't find a point at which to come in with the story so I put it aside and wrote *Smiley's People* instead and then, when Smiley was tucked away, I thought I would go back without all that luggage of the Circus and some great British conspiracy, Russian conspiracy; all of that was swept aside and I just went and goofed around again. I went to Israel and then back to the Lebanon and stayed in Beirut and I went down to the Palestinian camps at Rashovdiyeh and Nabatiyeh, the camp in Sidon itself, explored the camps in Beirut, and out of that began to make quite a different story which drew upon totally different elements. I wanted also to write about much younger people than were given to me by the Smiley world, I also wanted to write more about women. So I took as my central character—through whom we perceived the Middle East and the Middle Eastern problem—an English girl, an actress. Actors and actresses were very much in mind too because of mucking around with actors and actresses over the two B.B.C. dramatizations, *Tinker Tailor* and *Smiley's People* and I have also a very beautiful sister, Charlotte, who is an actress and whose life was, in crude terms, the raw material that got me off the ground. Those were the things that came together.

*Bragg*: As you say, *The Little Drummer Girl* is about an English actress who is used by Israeli intelligence to penetrate Palestinian intelligence.

*Le Carré*: Not Palestinian intelligence, but a breakaway Palestinian group that is conducting anti-Jewish operations around Europe.

*Bragg*: An English actress is used by Israeli intelligence to get to an extremely successful Palestinian guerilla group.

*Le Carré*: Yes, that's right.

*Bragg*: Like a lot of your novels it has an enormous number of layers in it. It reads as if you've done an immense amount of ground research in the Middle East. Can you give us some idea of the sort of research you did?

*Le Carré*: I began with Israel because Israel is much more accessible. The Israelis help. They invited me, allowed me to see anybody I wanted to see. In many ways it's an extraordinarily open society. If you want to see General so-and-so, somebody calls him up, you get an introduction to go along, he gives you time. I wanted to meet chaps from the Israeli and Special Forces. People who'd been in secret outfits. The Israelis enabled me to go and talk to their Palestinian prisoners, they even allowed me to talk to a German girl they were holding in prison, who had been allegedly involved in a Palestinian terror operation in Kenya. Otherwise in Israel: moving, talking, thinking, spending time with people, just going where the wind blew. The Palestinians were a much more difficult nut to crack, in a way, because they have no Public Relations worth talking of—they speak very poorly for themselves, in my opinion, and you go so far and then somehow you get no further. But I did eventually manage to find the right connections and, through them, I was received by Yassir Arafat [Chairman of the Palestine Liberation Organization, leader of Al Fatah] in Beirut and had one of those celebrated nocturnal conversations with him. He said 'Please, why have you come to me, what do you want?' And I said, 'Well, Mr. Chairman, I'm trying to put my hand on the Palestinian heart.' And he grasped my hand and held it to his own breast and said, 'Sir, it is here, it is here.' I found him very interesting, very touching, very genuine and I don't think I'm as starry-eyed as I might appear. I did think he was a much maligned man by comparison with most of the people in his outfit. He's extremely moderate and, indeed, if we are to see his downfall—which is quite possible—it will be because of his moderation. He said 'What are you going to do tomorrow night?', which was New Year's Eve, and I said I had no plans and he said, 'Well, come up to the school for the martyrs', and so again I hung around in my hotel. Eventually cars came and we were whisked from one side of Beirut to the other, changed cars—it was all very exciting—and we got into a convoy and roared up the hill outside Beirut, up this snake hill in pouring rain behind a red Landrover. We shot through Syrian checkpoints, everybody's checkpoints, and finished at the school and we all leaped out of the car and went to greet the occupant of the red Landrover. The doors opened and out got a couple of boys I didn't recognize. Arafat was already at the school, he takes care of his personal security very well. So we sat in the audience at this packed school of orphans, children of people who have died fighting for Palestine. And the kids, on the stage, staged a Palestinian dance, and they were tossing wooden rifles back and forth. The dance has a very emphatic rhythm and the audience began doing this. . . . Suddenly Arafat, just down the row from me, put out his arms like this and two of his fighting men seized him and tossed him up onto the stage. He took the back of this *kaffiyeh* and began, to this hypnotic rhythm, leading this kind of weird congo round the stage. When it was over, and everybody by then was clapping and urging him on, he came to the edge of the stage and again spread out his arms and leapt straight into the air, straight off the edge of the podium and his boys caught him and put him back in his seat. He's a very infectious man; tremendously spontaneous and very witty and it's said Beirut is still full of stories about him, one of them being that when they came to him and said 'look, the seige is over, the deal is done and the Lebanese want to come and say goodbye', Arafat said 'Why, where are they going.' That was Arafat. I saw him a couple of times more, it was really only from a distance and through him and through his staff I was able to go down to the camps.

*Bragg*: The contact with Arafat gave you introductions to other areas.

*Le Carré*: Yes. Then I went South and things were extremely tense because by then everybody knew that it was only a matter of time before the Israelis would come, and it was just spoken of as an inevitable fact that the big invasion would come. As the Palestinians put it, they were going to try and wipe us out, it was no secret anywhere. I stayed again, not through Arafat but through other connections, in a house in Sidon which belonged to a Palestinian commander of troops. He had a lot of fighting kids around the house and some not-fighting kids, just students and people. I talked a lot to them and there was one who carried no gun and was a very studious-looking chap and hardly ever spoke, and I thought he must be the spook and made every kind of attempt to get alongside him. I asked him questions and always received very bland replies, and then we all went down to Sidon to watch the procession to celebrate the Palestinian revolution. Most of the kids who were looking after me or looking after the house were in the procession, but this boy was not, so I said to him 'Why were you not in the procession?' and he said, 'Please, I have night work.' I said 'What is your night work?' He said 'Special work.' I said 'What do you do at night?' He said, 'You notice the boy scouts, the little boys in the procession, they wear on their breast a photograph of our Chairman Arafat.' I said yes, I had noticed. He said 'I personally, all through the night, work with a hot iron on the photographs.' So I realized that perhaps he wasn't a spy. And I talked to people in the camps and got the feel of it, and became astonished really with one very simple perception that seems to me to have made no headway in the West at all: that one can, indeed as I am, be greatly in favour of the state of Israel and wish for its survival but that in the making of Israel a great crime was committed, not numerically commensurate with the crime that was committed against the Jews, but appalling all the same. Millions of people displaced, others subjugated with total alien types of rules, turned into second-class citizens. The image of the Palestinians, largely invented, as crazies carrying guns and so on, was so far removed from the reality of the majority of the Palestinian people that it needed saying, it needed demonstrating—and not by some maverick Trotskyist, or something, but by somebody like myself who has written extensively, with great passion I like to think, about Jews in the past but found in this situation an injustice which needs reporting.

*Bragg*: So that was one of the spurs of the book.

*Le Carré*: Yes. Like my character Charlie, I had a love affair with the Palestinians, exactly as in the past I've had a love affair with the Jews. It is my job to radicalize, my job to feel that way.

*Bragg*: So you have the ground out there, the revelation is the Palestinian problem, because the Israeli problem we know a lot about, it's well reported. The Palestinian situation is new territory, both in fact and in the perception it gives you of the fact.

*Le Carré*: And in popular fiction. I mean we've all had *Exodus* [the novel by Leon Uris, filmed by Otto Preminger in 1960] until it comes out of our ears. We all have that image of Israel in different forms but, as it happens, I don't think anybody's written with anything like compassion about the Palestinians.

*Bragg*: So you go there, you want to radicalize and report. Now the other big element coming in is an English actress who is somehow going to come together with this material. Can you give us some fix on why it was an English actress, where she came from and how you wanted to weld her to this material?

*Le Carré*: It didn't have to be an English actress, it had to be a Western one. Charlie is, in my book, about 28. She's a person of extremely strong conscience, she wishes for a moral anchor, she wishes for a discipline, if you will. But although she's rejecting, she really wants to join—a feeling that I know about—and what the Israelis offer her is all the things which I believe actresses, or for that matter women of that age, would fall for: a direction, a purpose, a mission, the family attachment; the mind control, if you like, which tells her what to think and who to be. She has loyalty in her pocket like loose change and they show her how to spend it, how to invest it, who to be. Now I'm not suggesting that every woman can be manipulated in such a way but there are people who have a surge towards an absolute, in the same way that, for instance, Patti Hearst was turned from (one assumes) a spoilt little millionairess into a radical fighter. It seems impossible, it's terribly hard to write, but we accept it in real life. Charlie, when she's first picked up by the Israelis, is loosely radical, pro-Palestinian. They don't discount that in the least; they like that part of her but they take hold of her and they control her and they recruit her and they turn her into a double agent. In that sense it's an exploration of the double agent which I began in *Tinker Tailor*.

*Bragg*: And it's also an exploration or a continuation of the idea of fiction working itself out in real life which is one of the things your books are about. Which is to say, that Charlie's also given a rôle.

*Le Carré*: Yes, that's right, a job, for an actress above all; a part, as they put it to her, in the theatre of the real, that as an actress you must always have had that appetite to experience real life; to play a part in real life, you must have felt the confinement of theatre: now join us and you can continue to act but it's the theatre of the real and you'll be doing good and we love you, all of us we love you.

*Bragg*: You have the circumstances that you found in the Middle East and you want to declare or bear witness to these. You have the actress and you've mentioned your sister Charlotte and being involved with actors and actresses in the productions of *Tinker Tailor* and *Smiley's People*. But with a book, a lot of its power has got to come from authenticity. Did you go back and check that it was at all plausible for an English Shakespearean actress to be recruited by Israeli intelligence for such an important job?

*Le Carré*: Well, I put it to the lads in Israel and they were enchanted with the idea and said: yes if it would work, yes they would do it. You see Israel, from an intelligence point of view, is the sandbox—you can do anything as long as it works. They see themselves as totally surrounded by hostile forces. Security is survival. If they lose a battle, they've already lost the war. If they lose the war, they've lost Israel. That's how they feel, and so the intelligence arm is an absolutely crucial one and the intelligence world in Israel is to be found everywhere. Dons get into it and come out of it the moment a war starts or a crisis appears; people put down their academic books and flood to secret offices around the place. They have a highly developed intelligence service and above all a highly motivated one and, of course, because it's a well-kept secret, I don't know how the devolution of power works. I don't know what freedoms the Mossad has or the Israeli security service has, but I suspect, however much they would deny it, that they're far greater than are available to the C.I.A. or to our own.

*Bragg*: *The Little Drummer Girl* is about a great number of things, but the main line of the story is that an English actress is picked up by Israeli intelligence, turned into a double agent and sent on a mission to destroy a particularly effective group of Palestinian guerillas. Now the fact that your sister, Charlotte, is an English actress and a redhead and that she was acting in the West Country, where we meet the Charlie in the book, is obviously relevant.

*Le Carré*: Yes. There is a scene in the book which is set in the West Country, where Charlie is on tour with an unnamed travelling company, and in fact my sister was travelling with the Royal Shakespeare Company and performing at Camborne [in Cornwall] at the Sports Centre there. I was here alone and I went up to see her and it was pouring with rain, the most unbelievable noise on the roof, and Charlotte was really having to belt it out. I thought she was very good but she was over the top. I mean she was booming in order to defeat the rain and it was actually the moment, I think, where I thought: yes, I'll use that. I'll have Charlotte for my character, at least this, and I kept the episode. It's absurd to say that it is my sister, but for most characters there is a point of departure and that was hers. It was that night really, that I brought her back here with a couple of kids from the touring company and we spent a pleasantly drunken night here, that the plot began to shape up.

*Bragg*: As you'd researched the Middle East, did you research the actress background? Let's leave your sister Charlotte to one side, but Charlie, in the book, is an actress figure who has been to a 'radicalizing' school in England and been taught about revolution and is a left-wing type of actress—of whom there are several in this country—who believes very passionately in extreme measures. Did that need finding out about?

*Le Carré*: I sort of knew about it really. Not to bring Charlotte up again, but it was, in fact, her experience also. She did go to one of those places. She went through a dotty time politically and emerged from it very fast, and she talked to me a bit about it. And I went up to Islington and mucked around various funny bookshops there that feed the extreme left, and the radical causes, and talked to one or two people in that world.

*Bragg*: Where did you decide that the book's perception should lie? You had two lots of material—the Middle East aspect and the actress side—and a desire to witness and depict a radical idea. Having got the mechanism of the intelligence service, you then have the point of view. Now what point of view did you decide on, and why?

*Le Carré*: I settled for the irreconcilability of the problem. I mined, first, my own feelings about it which are, very simply, that there is a terrible historical irony in the fact that because— very properly and far too late—the Jews engaged our Western conscience, we gave them a country which was not ours to give. And we in fact obliged the Palestinians to pay the price for the

Western conscience. It was not the Palestinians who persecuted the Jews, it was us. Us westerners. It was us Brits for not letting them in, it was the Americans for not letting them in, it was a whole mucky western conspiracy of which the Germans were the spearhead, but we are not without blame in the matter. That, on the one hand; then, on the other, the lamentable fact that in the protection of Israeli security Israel, in my opinion, has gone overboard, particularly under this government [in 1983]. I don't think it is allowable simply because the Jews have been persecuted that Mr. Begin can draw his own borders and turf out more people or subjugate them. That seems to me to be a modern monstrosity. So, one's conscience was doubly engaged. Beyond that I was determined to balance the story as perfectly as I knew how and so the point of view became Charlie's, it became the ambivalent perception. The capacity to fall in love, the twice-promised girl, and I don't think that there are any opinions expressed which do not actually proceed from characters because I knew this was going to be an egg-walk. As the Germans say, I would be dancing on eggshells and a lot of people would be very cross. The great heresy is not that I have said anything unpleasant about the Israelis, but that I have actually raised the Palestinians to the point where their claim is made clear. I think that that—particularly in the United States—is liable to upset a great number of people and I don't think it's been done before.

*Bragg*: Going through another layer, *The Little Drummer Girl* links up with *The Naïve and Sentimental Lover* in that the fulcrum of the whole thing is an idea of a commitment to a particular personal love affair. From my reading of the book, when Charlie, recruited by Israeli intelligence, falls in love with this man, Joseph, and goes to do her job behind Palestinian lines, she has, naturally, perceptions about Palestine which you've been describing yourself and is then totally torn and her loyalties given in the end to this particular man, Joseph.

*Le Carré*: Whose loyalties, of course, are ambiguous. As a fighting Israeli who has given the whole of his youth to the various wars, he feels now that the things he fought for are not there.

*Bragg*: Did you find that hard to write, in the sense that all writing is to do with committing yourself first? That this would be, that her commmitment to him could be so strong, that it could survive her education and radicalization and realizations in Palestine, in the Palestinian area?

*Le Carré*: I found it difficult to write. I found Joseph altogether—the character of her Israeli agent runner—the most difficult to deal with. For technical reasons, because we had to experience him in the first instance through her, I could not cut away into Joseph's own mind because to do so would destroy the mystery of who he was, which was kindled in Charlie.

*Bragg*: In the end you have got to believe as a writer, and we believe as readers, that for love of this man, Joseph, Charlie will in a sense deny the amazing and shocking experience of what she discovers behind the Palestinian lines. You're actually testing the strength of your own story. It's a mixture of loyalty, responsibility and credibility that you're looking for in Charlie, as a reader and as a writer.

*Le Carré*: That's right. The linch-pin is her relationship with her agent runner, her controller. I think there is, there must be, something quite extraordinary in the relationship between male agent runner and female agent: a kind of Pygmalion relationship. He's the link man, he speaks for the organization for her, he gives her a personal gloss, to her brief, he debriefs her, he must man-manage her emotions. He is the manipulator, he is the giver of love and the receiver of love. If that relationship doesn't work, no other relationship works. Therefore for Charlie, to be in love with him is almost a masochistic necessity of the operation for her, and the moment when she ceases to love him, she's done something perfectly dreadful. She's committed a betrayal on an unforgettable scale. Indeed, by the end of the story, she knows she's done that anyway, but Joseph holds her to the line until then, which is his job.

*Bragg*: But it's really two sorts of betrayal facing each other, because by betraying the Palestinians she gets a lot of people—who we come to like very much—killed. She holds to that but destroys that. There is a good deal of bleakness, unlike the Smiley novels where there's always Smiley, a good man. I mean, it's very bleak.

*Le Carré*: There is no consolation, Smiley isn't there to cheer us up and explain things and say we'll carry on another time.

When the curtain comes down, as Charlie is warned in the theatre of the real, nobody gets up and goes home. The bodies stay where they are. She learns that, so the end, I imagine, is bleak and ambiguous. But the feel of love betrayed has really gone on, I think, in most of the books all the way through. In *Tinker Tailor* love is abused, misused: the baddie had slept with Smiley's wife in order to put Smiley off the scent. People manipulate one another in so many of the books, by means of love, that I don't think it is out of line in that respect.

*Bragg*: No. There has always been the contrast between private and public morality. Is the reason you acclaim private morality because at least you might know the consequences of it?

*Le Carré*: At least you know what your feelings are. When you accept a larger institutional argument, of the sort Charlie accepted, there are complications: when they are recruiting her she asks who do we kill and the reply is—only somebody who has entirely broken the human bond. Who has lost our claim to compassion, him we must kill, say the Israelis. And she says, who are you to say that has happened? And their answer is glossed over. What was the first bond that was broken, who cast the first stone? God alone knows. So the institutional conflict cannot be resolved in the story and personal love suffers, is adjusted accordingly.

*Bragg*: We've been talking about some of the themes and the areas of material you've drawn on in this novel. Driving it through is a very tightly planned plot which is unravelled, checked back on: go in this direction, go in that direction, so it fools you. It's plotted in enormous detail, and at some length. What do you think the value of that is, to take it in so much detail, to plot it so ingeniously? What value do you give to that, as a writer?

*Le Carré*: It gives a monstrous logic to the manipulation of Charlie, I think. With a story of this kind the whole premise is that they take a girl like that and manipulate her life from beginning to end, so that we are constantly dealing with the taming of Charlie, the breaking in of Charlie, the winning of Charlie. To spread around her all the evidence of meticulous planning is actually to remind the reader all the time that they are doing that to Charlie as well, that there is no part of her life, no corner of her character that they have not taken into account, not examined, not studied, put into the scales before they recruited her, and while they are running her.

*Bragg*: That's one sort of value I can see you get from this sort of plotting. What value does it give your characters? Do you feel it gives them more room to breathe, gives them things to work against?

*Le Carré*: Well, Charlie's pulling all the time at the bridle. So I think that it gives a dramatic tension. It also, in pompous terms, gives them a relationship. The destiny that is being woven around Charlie is one which, in a sense, she wished upon herself. She is a girl whose bluff was called. But all the posturing and attitudes and all the lies she's told, all the little cheating that she's got up to, all of these things are now put into effect. Very well, if you are that kind of person, be it, but more so; be it in extension and put all your sins and all your virtues to our service. It's a very beguiling guide, it's a crusade, a mission, which takes up all the slack in this wayward, rather gooky, character.

*Bragg*: Would you say *The Little Drummer Girl* was, in any structural way, a departure from your earlier novels?

*Le Carré*: I think it's a far more passionate book, probably the most passionate. It's the maddest. I think that within Charlie, within that controlled schizophrenia, there are scenes which, when you start taking tham apart, are at the very edge of sanity. I found that very hard to write, and it's a very hard book for me to get out of mentally. Beyond that I think I would have to leave the answer to the critics. I don't know. I think it's the same as the other books, but more so, and of course the sexuality is much greater. It takes on things that I couldn't take on in the earlier books because of the characters I used, and perhaps, in some ways, because of my own nature. It's just the way I've changed.

*Bragg*: To come back to one of the starting points of the book, when you went to the Middle East you discovered the Palestinian cause which radicalized your thinking. Do you think your book represents and bears witness to the strength of feeling you had then, and do you think the work of fiction can do anything about it?

*Le Carré*: I am necessarily limited by a considerable concern for Israel also. It's enough, I think, to do what I've done. I think that, with any luck, I would have opened people's minds much more to the reality of the Palestinian tragedy without going overboard and, if I've done that, nobody but the most bigoted Israeli or Jew would attack me for it. I'm not afraid of that attack, but I'm very afraid of the book being characterized as anti-Israeli which is really, coming out of modern Israel, almost a cheap jibe. It drives me absolutely mad. A great number of books, some of them pulp, have almost blindly extolled the making of Israel and neglected entirely the Palestinian matter. Golda Meir, as you probably know, said the Palestinians did not exist; there was a slogan, a land without people for a people without land. Now these things were not fair and not just. I think that in terms of popular fiction, simply by putting a human face upon the Palestinians by revealing the human tragedy, it's enough. It's enough thus far. I haven't gone nearly as far in the book, for instance, as the Israeli left would go within Israel, but then I'm a gentile. There are other things I regret very much, which I can't control. One of them is the premise in the book that Beirut, around the time when the story occurred, was still the capital of terrorism which could be taken as a justification for the Israeli invasion [of the Lebanon in 1982]. It is a fact, of which I only recently became aware, that the Palestinians moved all their operational centres away from Beirut at the beginning of the cease-fire, so I would have written that differently too. But, by and large, the book does a job. I have reacted much more vehemently in the press at the time of the Israeli invasion. I did write a piece ['Memories of a Vanished Land'] in the *Observer* [of 13 June 1982] which attracted a great deal of flack, and so on, but when it comes to actually drawing the balance, it's almost enough to have corrected the cliché which required everybody to say piously 'I believe in the survival of Israel.' They forgot that they also believed, if they were even aware of it, in the survival of the Palestinians. So it's enough.

*Bragg*: There are those who would say that Arafat has committed acts of terrorism and so have the Palestinians and that, in a sense, by meeting him and—to a certain extent—taking his side, you are committing yourself to that aspect of life as well. What would you say to that?

*Le Carré*: I would say that it was nonsense. To talk to him, to try and understand him, is already the right thing to do whatever he's done, but I can't think, offhand, of many heads of States, or heads of organizations in that part of the world, with whom one could sit down with a clear conscience. I wouldn't really want to sit with Kissinger after the bombing of Cambodia. I don't think I would have been allowed to have sat with Jomo Kenyata, after his association with the Mau Mau. I would certainly feel a bit queezy about sitting next to Begin after the invasion of the Lebanon. The fact of the matter is, by exploring the roots of Palestinian anger one gets closer to understanding the acts of violence. Also, I do not know what terror is. I mean, is it an act of terror to send Israeli aeroplanes over a camp, to drop a cluster bomb, kill two or three hundred people, or is terror already legitimized by the fact that you have an air force?

If you are a displaced people, and you've got to make the world listen, that is the Palestinian argument. If you've been driven from camp to camp, if you've had the living daylight persecuted out of you by your own people—by the Israeli's but above all by your brother Arabs—I can understand that you would turn to violence. And very many people who have this cliché vision of the Palestinians would themselves, if they had been subjected to the same harrassment and persecution and humiliation, if they had no passport, no friends, no permanent home, if they'd been bombed out of one place after another all through their lives, from the age of practically nothing—many of those people would have taken the violent path. I think the amazing thing is, how little has actually happened on the Palestinian side. I think it's outrageous that the Israelis simply refer to the Palestinians now as terrorists. That really is a piece of propaganda overkill which I think will bounce back in time. In the second month of the Israeli invasion of the Lebanon, the Israelis killed more children than have died in all the Palestinian operations against Israel. So I don't know what terrorism means in this category. I certainly loathe, as we all do, these wanton acts against civilian people. They are appalling and unthinkable, and that is part of the awfulness of my story. But I really would not think of Arafat as having exceptionally bloody hands.

*Bragg*: In the fiction, in *The Little Drummer Girl*, what are you saying about Charlie's relationship with terrorism? What, in your opinion, justifies her in it?

*Le Carré*: They tell her specifically that she will save innocent life and, indeed, it is true, it's absolutely true, she prevents a maverick Palestinian bomber from bombing any more; in that sense she does right. But in the course of doing right she understands the roots of his anger, and she understands how he turned the corner and took the violent path. But there's absolutely no sense, anywhere in the book, of anybody condoning it, let alone myself doing that.

*Bragg*: Finally, then, could I come back to the idea of fictions? The book has references to the theatre of the real and the idea of people perceiving things in terms of inventions, that being the way they tackle things that are mysterious to them, that are unpalatable to them. That is also what you have done about this situation in the Middle East. What do you think are the consolations and benefits that come from that?

*Le Carré*: To whom? To me?

*Bragg*: Yes. As a writer of this particular novel.

*Le Carré*: I think I have externalized things in my own past about which I was intensely uncomfortable: forms of artificial behaviour if you like, a sense of dislocation between personal behaviour and internal reality. I think that by making the story function in so many different theatrical stages of the same stage I've maybe, in some quite therapeutic way, cut through personal deceptions to some sort of centre. I think that that is nothing new for any writer. Most of us are fairly weak creatures in one way or another; it's absurd to appoint us as great gurus but, after all, our job is to combine perception with internal fantasy and to spin out of it something which produces a new reality for other people and gives a narrative.

*Bragg*: And it's the story, finally, that carries the message of your idea of realities? By discovering the story the whole business makes sense for you and therefore, you hope, for someone else?

*Le Carré*: Yes. And to entertain, to stimulate, to cause to ponder, to excite, to stretch and to have that sense of company that people feel with you, any entertainer. As a comedian tries to fight off ridicule, so perhaps a thriller writer tries to cauterize tension or reconcile components within himself by setting them out in different characters. In the end it should be a story.

# 7

# The Hippocratic Smile: Le Carré and Detection

by GLENN W. MOST

Under her left breast and tight against the flame-colored shirt lay the silver handle of a knife I had seen before. The handle was in the shape of a naked woman. The eyes of Miss Dolores Gonzales were half-open and on her lips there was the dim ghost of a provocative smile.

'The Hippocrates smile,' the ambulance intern said, and sighed. 'On her it looks good.'

—Raymond Chandler, *The Little Sister*[1]

*1*

The true mystery in a mystery novel is not that of the crime committed near its beginning and solved near its end but instead that posed by the nature of the detective who solves it. To be sure, the crime is always puzzling, either because it is so bizarre or because it seems so simple, and the plot of the novel always moves from the absence of an answer for this puzzle, through a series of false answers, to a final and therefore presumably true one. But at the end, there always is that final answer, that solution which accounts both for the initial crime and for the various inadequate hypotheses to which it gave rise; and, at the end, the reader wonders why he had not seen the answer sooner. For the mystery of the crime is, in essence, simply a riddle, a question that seems obscure before it is

144

answered but oddly simple afterwards, a puzzle for which there is always allegedly one and only one solution. Its difficulty derives from the fact that a truth has been *concealed*, its ease from the fact that a *truth* has been concealed. For no concealment can be flawless (the fruitlessness of the genre's eternal search for the perfect crime is enough to show this), and the very measures that are taken to disguise the crime are the ones that in the end will point unmistakably toward its perpetrator. If one reason for the mystery novel's conventional preference for the crime of murder is that murder is perhaps the only human action in which there are usually only two participants, one absolutely incapable of narrating it later and the other disinclined to do so, then we may be tempted to explain this as part of an effort to make the puzzle as hard to solve as possible; yet the victim's unwilling silence is always more than compensated for by the murderer's onerous knowledge. The certainty of the latter's correct awareness of what really happened is the fixed point around which the novel moves and to which it can and therefore must inevitably return. The victim may have been duped by the murderer; but in the end, it is always the murderer who is the greater dupe: for he had imagined that merely concealing an answer would suffice to make it irretrievable, and had not realized that any process of concealment can be reversed and become, step by step, a process of discovery. The victim, whose corpse abashed survivors surround, may seem lonely in his death—but the criminal, to whom finally all point their fingers and proclaim, 'Thou art the man', is, in fact, in his utter nakedness, far more terrifyingly so.

But if the crime is, in essence, merely a puzzle, the detective who solves it is himself a figure of far deeper and more authentic mystery. All the other characters may be stereotypes and may turn out to have acted from the most banal of motives; but the detective fits into none of the categories with which the actions of all the others can be exhaustively explained, and his own motives are cloaked in an obscurity that is never finally lifted. He is fundamentally at odds with the society of which all the other characters are part; he is the bearer of true rationality, opposed to both the murderer (who degrades reason to the cleverness with which an irrational crime can never be adequately concealed) and the police (who represent a reason that is institutionalized, technocratic, and therefore quite futile); he is the figure of decency surrounded by selfishness and immorality, the sole searcher for truth in a world given over to delusion and duplicity. He is in every regard a marginal figure: his profession is not to have a profession but to investigate all those who do; he derives his income not from a steady and productive job but, case by case, from those who have such jobs but require his services; he alone can move, competently but never at home, through every stratum of society, from the mansions from which the poor are excluded to the slums that the wealthy abhor; he is almost always single or divorced (it is marriage that provides the most fertile soil for this genre's crimes); his parents are almost never mentioned, and he is invariably childless. It is his freedom from all such categories that permits him so clearly to see through their workings in all the other characters; but at the same time this dispensation from the rules that bind all others makes him an enigma without an answer, a mystery which is never solved. What does the detective do between cases?[2]

Poe, with his usual prescience, endowed the literary detective with this aura of mystery at his birth. The first sentence of the first mystery story, 'The Murders in the Rue Morgue', points the paradox nicely: 'The mental features discoursed of as the analytical, are, in themselves, but little susceptible of analysis.'[3] What is this analytical power to whose description Poe devotes the first pages of the story? His analysis of it juggles paradoxes of appearance and reality, means and ends, method and intuition, without even pretending seriously to provide a satisfactory answer. We are told that the man who possesses this power 'is fond of enigmas, of conundrums, hieroglyphics' (p. 141); but the power itself (which suffices to solve such trivial problems, though they may confound us) cannot be approached directly, but only through the detour of such examples as checkers and whist provide. Even Poe's final correlation of ingenuity with fancy and the analytical ability with imagination serves only to translate the dilemma into the terms of English romantic literary theory, not to resolve it. From the beginning, that is, Poe is at pains to show us that the mysteries that can be solved are not as mysterious as those posed by the power that solves them; and his method is to use answerable puzzles as a means of demonstrating the unanswerableness of the deeper puzzle of the power that can answer them. The celebrated anecdotes that follow this opening—Dupin guesses the narrator's thoughts and solves the double murder in the Rue Morgue—are introduced simply as being 'somewhat in the light of a commentary upon the propositions just advanced' (p. 143), and even they do not answer the questions that opening raises. They provide further, more extended, examples; they pretend to demonstrate by narrative rather than by analogy; but they multiply the enigma rather than resolve it. Hence, not the least of the red herrings in Poe's story is its very form: by its structure it seems to begin with a mystery (what is the analytical power?) and then to provide its solution (by the narrative of Dupin's exploits). But those exploits—by their bizarre mixture of reckless leaps to conclusions with scrupulously logical method, by their combination of erratic erudition and cheap theatricality, and above all by their wildly improbable success—serve only to deepen the mystery rather than to dispel it. We ought to have been warned by the very name Dupin (which does not quite conceal the French verb meaning 'to dupe')—or by the epigraph from Sir Thomas Browne that Poe brazenly affixes to his story and that propounds the solubility of questions to which no answer could possibly be found: 'What song the Syrens sang, or what name Achilles assumed when he hid himself among women, although puzzling questions, are not beyond *all* conjecture' (p. 141).

Hence, the mystery of who killed Madame l'Espanaye and her daughter is definitively, if oddly, resolved; but the mystery of Dupin never is. The details of his past are entirely obscure; of his income we learn only that it suffices to free him of any occupation other than reading, writing, and talking all night long; we do not even know what he looks like. Dupin is, of course, an extreme example; but in the way in which he penetrates all others' secrets while remaining opaque to us he provides the model for all his followers:

> He boasted to me, with a low chuckling laugh, that most men, in respect to himself, wore windows in their bosoms, and was wont to follow up such assertions by direct and very startling proofs of his intimate knowledge of my own. His manner at these moments was frigid and abstract; his eyes were vacant in expression; while

his voice, usually a rich tenor, rose into a treble which would
have sounded petulant but for the deliberateness and entire
distinctness of the enunciation. (p. 144)

The vacancy of his eyes seals him against our inspection; as the
oracle, filled with divine inspiration, of which this latter sentence
is designed to remind us, he offers us troubling insights into the
truths we conceal within us, but himself escapes our detection.

Such coyness is, of course, profoundly seductive; and, from
Poe onwards, the mystery genre has fascinated its readers at
least as much through the person of its detective as through the
ingenuity of its puzzles or the exoticism of its crimes. Future
historians of the genre could do worse than to point to the
striking proximity, in place and time, of the rise of the detective
story and of that of the modern biography, for detective stories
are, for many readers, instalments in the fragmentary biographies
of their heroes, each displaying his familiar virtues under a new
and surprising light. Every new case presents a challenge to the
detective's skills; we know he will meet it, and are pleased to
discover we had not foreseen how. The natural result is the cult
of the literary detective, so familiar in our time, whether that
cult is centred upon holy sites (like number 221B Baker Street)
or upon the gifted actor who has succeeded in incarnating the
detective on film (like Bogart's Sam Spade or Philip Marlowe).

But if the detective's essential enigmatic quality has persisted
now for almost a century and a half, the specific form it has
assumed has undergone radical transformation during that
time. For the sake of simplicity (and at the cost of a certain
schematism), we may distinguish between two basic and largely
successive traditions: one that may be called English (though it
begins with Poe) because it is brought to its classic form by
Arthur Conan Doyle and continued by other British authors
like Agatha Christie; and another, primarily American tradition,
founded by Dashiell Hammett, perfected by Raymond Chandler,
and prolonged by Ross Macdonald.

In the English tradition, every effort is made to keep the
detective free of any other participation in the case he is
investigating than that necessarily involved in his solution of its
perplexities. This is, indeed, one of the hallmarks of the early
modern detective story that separates it decisively from such

forerunners as *Oedipus the King* or *Hamlet*, in which the investigator is intimately bound up, by links at least familial and dynastic, with the case in question. The invention of the professional detective, who investigates not because anything is at stake for him (other than the discovery of the truth) but simply because that is his job, serves the purpose of keeping him free of any taint of complicity in the case.[4] In this way, investigation and event, thought and object, are kept entirely distinct from one another. The separation between these two realms engenders a narrative that can begin with the widest possible distance between them and moves, more or less haltingly, toward their identification. The standard plot within this tradition begins with the discovery of the crime in its apparently absolute inexplicability. The detective is brought into the case either by the accidental circumstance of his proximity or by a client who has been unjustly accused and whose innocence he is required to establish. The detective then begins to investigate, by means of perception (the discovery of clues), discourse (the interviewing of various parties), and the logically self-consistent interpretation of the material he thereby acquires. His activity proceeds until the mental construct of the original crime he has been gradually refining finally coincides with that crime; at this point there is at last an exact correspondence between his thought and the real event that had occurred before his entrance onto the scene, the discrepancies that had provided the impetus to his revision of earlier hypotheses have been resolved, and the truth can be announced. The criminal confesses and the innocent suspect is redeemed; the police enter and the detective exits; justice is done. In such plots, two particularly noteworthy kinds of exclusions tend to operate. On the level of the individual characters, relations of sex or violence between the detective and the other figures tend to be prohibited; the detective neither experiences nor exerts sexual attraction, and he neither inflicts nor is seriously endangered by physical violence. On the level of society, the characters tend to be isolated during the investigation from forces that would otherwise interfere with it; the result is a certain unity of place, which, at the limit, secludes all the possible suspects in a train, a hotel, or an island.

In all these regards, the contrast posed by the American

tradition could hardly be more striking. Consider the plot structure most frequently found among these latter authors. The novel begins, not with a murder, but with the client's hiring the detective in some far more minor matter: a painting has been stolen, a blackmailer must be foiled, a runaway teenager must be found. The detective begins to investigate, and only then do the murders begin. The detective relentlessly pursues his course on a path increasingly strewn with corpses until a truth is uncovered for which the original assignment represented at best a misunderstanding, at worst a ploy. It generally turns out at the end either that the client was himself the criminal and had attempted to lure the detective into becoming the unwitting accomplice of his designs or that the minor incident that had brought the detective onto the scene was merely a distant epiphenomenon of a deeply hidden, far more heinous crime, which cannot remain unsolved if that minor incident is to be adequately explained. Here the detective is not only the solution, he is also part of the problem, the catalyst who by his very introduction both provokes murders and solves them. In the figure of this investigator, the investigation and its object become inextricably intertwined. Correspondingly, the two exclusions we noted in the English tradition tend to be annulled. On the one hand, the detective's relations with other characters are free from neither sex nor violence; he feels acutely a disturbing erotic interest in the women of the case, which they are all too ready to exploit; and conversely, he can become the victim of considerable violence and be seriously threatened with death, just as he can employ methods of interrogation and coercion that the English novelists might dismiss as ungentlemanly. These features are not just sensationalistic but are designed to further implicate the detective in the case and to jeopardize his autonomy; a sexual involvement would abolish his status as outsider, whereas the scenes of violence turn him into a version of the victim or of the murderer. And on the other hand, the ever-widening circle of his investigation constantly draws in new characters and forces that might seem to hinder his initial task but, in fact, fulfil it by placing it in its full context; it is only by indirections that he finds directions out, and his travels through the extreme reaches of different social classes and different parts of the city, always in pursuit of a unified truth, link what might have seemed disparate and unconnected fragments into a complex and deeply corrupt social network.

It is tempting to accuse the English tradition of naïveté and its products of being sterile intellectual puzzles or to praise the American tradition for its sophistication and social realism. But this is short-sighted. Not only can the English authors produce plots of a deeply satisfying complexity and psychological richness; not only can the American novelists fall into the trap of identifying the bizarre or the sordid with the realistic and fail to recognize how stereotyped their own plots are. More importantly, both traditions provide valid, if competing, versions of the fundamental mystery of the detective without which the genre can scarcely be conceived. In both, the detective is, in fact, the figure for the reader within the text, the one character whose activities most closely parallel the reader's own, in object (both reader and detective seek to unravel the mystery of the crime), in duration (both are engaged in the story from the beginning, and when the detective reveals his solution the reader can no longer evade it himself and the novel can end), and in method (a tissue of guesswork and memory, of suspicion and logic). That is why the literary detective (as distinguished, one supposes, from the real-life one) tends so strongly to marginality, for he is quite literally the only character who resides at and thereby defines the margin between text and reader, facing inward to the other characters in the story and facing outward to the reader with whom only he is in contact; so, too, that is why he is so isolated, insulated from family, economy and his own past, for all such factors as these tend to be suppressed as distractions by readers during the activity of reading any literary text. To be sure, in cases where the story is told not by the detective himself or by an omniscient narrator but instead by the detective's confidante, the reader's identification may be split between the Holmes figure and the Watson one; but here the Watson character provides one pole of convenient stupidity that the reader is proud to avoid (though he must exert himself to do so), whereas the Holmes one represents the ideal pole of perfect knowledge, of an entirely correct reading, toward which the reader aims and which he ought never quite to be able to attain. In other regards as well (the suspense of the delay that intervenes between desire and fulfilment or between question and answer and without which the temporality of any plot is impossible), the detective story takes certain features inherent in any narrative and concentrates its textual operations upon their deployment; here, too, it exaggerates the reader's natural wish to identify with the characters in a story and offers him one character in particular who fulfils the criteria of an ideal reader, but tends to deny him all others. The reader of the detective novel, entranced by the impenetrable enigma of the figure of the detective, thereby forgets that he himself is a Narcissus, staring in wonder at the beauty of a disturbingly familiar face.

From this perspective, the difference between the English and the American traditions resides only in the way in which they conceptualize the activity of reading, for if the detective is a figure for the reader, different modes of detection can be construed as different implicit theories of reading. The English insulation of the detective from his case is designed to create one privileged discourse within the text that is capable of determining the value of all its other parts but that is not itself dependent upon them; the locus of truth is incarnated within the text in such a way that it can legislate to the other parts, so that it is in the text but not of it. Hence the tendency to unworldliness in the English detective, which contributes to his mystery and sometimes makes it difficult to imagine his existing in the same society as the other characters. His wisdom is essentially timeless, and his final correct understanding of the case takes the form of a momentary vision in which all its parts cohere; the time of the narrative of his investigation may mimic the temporality of reading but has none of the genuinely dialectic quality of the latter, none of its belatedness, duplicity, self-delusion, and hope. Unlike the American tradition, the English one can include the very short story, for the temporal deferral that separates crime from solution contributes in itself nothing to the latter and can be expanded, rearranged, or elided at will. It is this temporality of reading to which the American tradition accords so much importance; here the sequence of events may seem arbitrary but is, in fact, unalterable. Human time, in its despotic irreversibility, rules the American novels; the minor incident for which the detective is summoned must precede and cannot follow the murders that his entrance provokes, and his final account of the case takes the form of a narrative, of a chain of causes and effects in which the criminal became fettered more ineluctably the more desperately he sought to free himself. Here the detective is not the bearer of a higher wisdom but himself, at least in part, an imperfect agent. The threat of sex, like the actuality of violence, binds him to crimes for which he himself is in some sense responsible, for they would not have occurred (at least not in this way) if he had not entered the scene. His identification of the criminal is intended also to exculpate himself, but he can never be entirely freed of the burden of responsibility for having catalysed the criminal's actions; at the end of each of these novels, Spade, Marlowe, or Archer is terribly alone, for these detectives embody that aspect of reading in which it is a guilty and solitary pleasure. Part of their mystery is that they continue in their professions at all, despite the bitterness of their knowledge of their world and of themselves.

Hence, the American tradition focuses upon the pain of the process of interpretation and the English upon the joy of its result. The English novelists presuppose the certainty of a correct reading and project back from that end to an initial stage of ignorance from which the path to that goal of knowledge is in principle never in doubt. The Americans, on the other hand, are caught up in the uncertainties of the activity of interpretation itself, for which a final and valid result may be imagined but can never be confidently predicted. From the point of view of the activity, the result is a utopia we may never attain; from the point of view of the result, the activity was meaningful only insofar as it led step by step to that end. The miracle of reading, and the dilemma of the mystery story, is that both are right.

### 2

In his book on the tragic drama of the German Baroque (a period that will be of importance for George Smiley), Walter Benjamin describes the difference between symbol and allegory in a way that casts light upon this contrast between the English and American traditions:

> Within the decisive category of time . . . the relation of symbol and allegory can be defined with an incisive formula. Whereas in

the symbol destruction is idealized and the transfigured countenance of nature fleetingly reveals itself in the light of redemption, in allegory the observer is confronted with the *facies
hippocratica* of history as a petrified, primordial landscape.
History, in every regard in which, from the very beginning, it has
been untimely, sorrowful, unsuccessful, expresses itself in a
countenance—or rather in a death's head. . . . This is the heart
of the allegorical way of seeing, of the baroque, secular explanation of history as the Passion of the world; it attains significance only in the stations of its decline.[5]

Much of the conceptual framework Benjamin employs in this
section of his book has striking affinities with the differences
between the traditions of the detective novel outlined earlier; a
literary theoretical distinction could easily be elaborated between
the English authors' symbolic approach, with its non-historical
and redemptively synthetic view, and the secular temporality of
the Americans' allegory. Instead, I should like to call attention
here to a new element this passage introduces, to the *facies
hippocratica* Benjamin uses as a symbol for allegory. We may take
Benjamin's hint and ask what kind of countenance the literary
detective wears: more specifically, how he smiles.

The answer is only at first surprising. Within the English
tradition, perhaps only Poe's Dupin almost never smiles; despite
his chuckle in the passage quoted earlier, he is usually too much
the romantic *poète maudit* to engage in levity, and the only people
who laugh aloud in Poe's stories are fools who thereby betray
their incomprehension.[6] Elsewhere in this tradition, from Holmes
through Poirot and Nero Wolfe, the detective smiles frequently:

> 'It may seem very foolish in your eyes,' I added, 'but really I
> don't know how you deduced it.'
> Holmes chuckled to himself.
> 'I have the advantage of knowing your habits, my dear Watson,'
> said he.

> 'What is this, Holmes?' I cried. 'This is beyond anything which
> I could have imagined.'
> He laughed heartily at my perplexity.

> 'Well, well, MacKinnon is a good fellow,' said Holmes with a
> tolerant smile. 'You can file it in our archives, Watson. Some day
> the true story may be told.'

Our visitor sprang from the chair. 'What!' he cried, 'you know my name?'

'If you wish to preserve your incognito,' said Holmes, smiling, 'I would suggest that you cease to write your name upon the lining of your hat, or else that you turn the crown towards the person whom you are addressing.'[7]

This is the smile of wisdom, complacent in the superiority of its own power and tolerant of the weakness of mere humanity; the detective adopts it in the moment when he has understood something that no one else has, yet it signifies not only the incomparability of his skill but also the benevolence with which he will use it. Ultimately, this is the smile of the Greek gods in their epiphanies to mortals: the smile of Aphrodite asking Sappho what is bothering her now or the so-called 'archaic smile' on countless early Greek statues. In terms of our earlier discussion, it is also the smile of the reader who can close the book with the mixture of delight and satisfaction that a full understanding of it brings.

This smile is never found on the faces of the detectives of Hammett, Chandler, or Macdonald: they lack the requisite benevolence no less than the necessary superiority. To be sure, they do smile upon occasion, but only in two ways. Rarely, they smile to deceive, to pretend to a man they do not trust that they trust him so that they can lure him into their clutches. But more commonly, their smile is wry, bitter, helpless in the face of the corruption of the world and of their own complicity in it; it is the sardonic smile of the reader who knows that his own life is no less ambiguous and stalemated than the novel he is now reading. In Raymond Chandler, the Hippocratic smile is a recurrent symbol: the rictus of death, it suggests a fullness of wisdom that only the dead can have and that therefore comes too late to be of any use to the living. Hippocrates should be able to heal; but the man who wears the Hippocratic smile is past healing. One time it is Marlowe himself who wears it. This happens at a crucial moment in *The Big Sleep*. Marlowe has just witnessed, helplessly from the next room, a gangster's callous murder of a fellow detective, Harry Jones. Marlowe is partly responsible for Jones's death: it was he, after all, who had told the gangster's boss that Jones was following him; and though Marlowe had certainly not intended this result, he will feel it

155

necessary to expunge and compound his guilt for it, when the time comes, by gunning down the gangster without mercy in his turn. At the very end, in the eulogy to Rusty Regan, the only thoroughly decent man in the novel, whose corpse had already been decaying in a sump before the story had even begun, Marlowe will give voice to a deep envy for the dead, who have attained to a peace that the living seem foolish for so desperately deferring. But now the plot must go on, and it requires Marlowe to take over briefly the rôle of Jones, whose death was unnecessary and who in a sense died for him. Chandler writes:

> It was raining hard again. I walked into it with the heavy drops slapping my face. When one of them touched my tongue I knew that my mouth was open and the ache at the side of my jaws told me it was open wide and strained back, mimicking the rictus of death carved upon the face of Harry Jones.[8]

## 3

Despite his name, George Smiley is not given much to smiling. Even at the moment of his greatest triumph, the forced defection of Karla at the end of *Smiley's People*, he does not share in the jubilation of his colleagues. Most often he seems worried, tentative; he blushes often; people think him confused and shy. These appearances both are and are not deceptive. For his name is no less carefully chosen than are those of Dupin, Sam Spade (direct and disillusioned, with the gravediggers' humor), Philip Marlowe (literate and endangered), and Lew Archer (a straight shooter and good guesser, a modern Apollo), and of most other literary detectives. As George, le Carré's hero is the slayer of the dragon, like his pseudonymous creator a defender of the faith, the guardian of traditional values. No wonder he is worried, for in a fallen world these can only be preserved by recourse to methods those same values must condemn. But as Smiley, he is not only put into contrast with such competing models of the secret agent as James Bond (can one imagine Ian Fleming's hero with Smiley's name?), but also placed firmly in the tradition of the literary detective, who, as we have learned to expect, ought by profession to smile. Why doesn't Smiley?

It may at first seem odd to consider Smiley a detective; after all, le Carré has attained celebrity as a writer of novels of espionage, and Smiley has entered the annals of world literature as a master spy. In fact, stories about spies and about detectives have much in common. As the two major subgenres of the thriller, they share many features: the interpretation of clues and the construction, revision, and eventual confirmation of hypotheses; an atmosphere of deceit, where treachery is the rule and trust a sometimes fatal mistake; a curious fascination with the many varieties of violent death. And historically there have been many crossovers between the two modes: already Dupin's services were enlisted in affairs of state in 'The Purloined Letter,' as were Holmes's in 'The Naval Treaty' and 'His Last Bow'; and Nazi agents turn up in Chandler's *Lady in the Lake* and many other detective novels of the 1940s.

Yet considerable differences separate the modes of espionage and of mystery, and clarifying these will suggest the degree to which many of le Carré's novels, though full of spies, no less clearly belong to the tradition of detective fiction. These differences are not only thematic, in the sense in which we can say, for example, that mystery novels tend to centre upon the destinies of individuals, whereas in spy novels the interests of nations are at stake.[9] They are also, and even more clearly, formal. The plot of a mystery is retrospective: it looks backward to an event that happened before, at or shortly after its beginning and, knowing that it has already occurred, asks how it happened. The plots of spy stories, on the other hand, tend to be prospective: they are directed toward an event that has not yet occurred and that must be either prevented (the threat against England must be warded off) or performed (the enemy must be given false information); they ask not who did it but what will happen. Because the event in a mystery has already occurred, the progress of its narrative is essentially a process of understanding, toward which the detective's actions are subordinated; because the event in a spy story has not yet happened, its hero must engage primarily in certain actions (to thwart or permit that event), and his gradually deepening understanding of the situation is valuable only insofar as it enables him to perform the decisive actions at the right moment. In a mystery, the culprit is identified only at the very end; in a spy story, the enemy can be known from the very beginning and the hero can be aware of his fiendish plan from a very early stage of the plot. Hence, the delay that is necessary, for a narrative must be generated in a mystery story by the successive creation and refutation of interpretative models, whereas that in a spy story tends to take the form of temporary obstructions to the hero's freedom of action; whether he is captured, pursued, or injured by the enemy, the crucial point is that he be made incapable of fulfilling his mission at once. Usually, the motives for at least the original murder in a mystery are separate from the hero's activity of investigation: the murderer acted, at least the first time, from greed or jealousy, anger or revenge. In the spy novel, on the other hand, the victims are those who know too much, who could prevent the enemy's fulfilling his plan, and the hero is in no less danger than they were. If the spy story belongs to the genre of the picaresque novel (where the end is known in advance and is delayed by episodes) and goes back ultimately to the *Odyssey* (in which Odysseus acts over and over again the rôle of a spy), the mystery might be correlated with the folk form of the riddle (which begins with a question and ends with its answer) and has its classical forerunner in *Oedipus the King* (in which Oedipus is not only detective and judge but also criminal and, ultimately, victim).

An example will help to make the differences clearer. In John Buchan's *The Thirty-Nine Steps*, Scudder recounts to the hero, Hannay, in the very first chapter the full details of the plot to murder Karolides in London on 15 July.[10] This same chapter ends with the murder of Scudder, but Hannay's reaction is revealing:

> Somehow or other the sight of Scudder's dead face had made me a passionate believer in his scheme. He was gone, but he had taken me into his confidence, and I was pretty well bound to carry on his work. . . . I hate to see a good man downed, and that long knife would not be the end of Scudder if I could play the game in his place. (pp. 36–7)

There is not a hint here of a desire to find the culprits and to bring them to justice; we have a murder, but not a mystery. To be sure, at the very end Hannay will confront the foreign agents with a warrant for their arrest for the murder of Scudder (p. 219), but we know that his intention is to prevent them from leaving the country with the details of the disposition of the British home fleet on mobilization and that this warrant is simply the most effective means available. Hannay knows from the beginning the enemy's intention to murder Karolides; the plot consists largely of a sequence of episodes entitled 'Adventure', of pursuits, captivities, and escapes, in which the Black Stone try to track Hannay down and prevent him from thwarting their plans while the police seek him in connection with Scudder's murder (this latter element is the only aspect of the novel in which it approaches a mystery, but it is narrated from the point of view of the putative murderer, is largely tangential, and is never treated with full seriousness). In the end, it turns out that Karolides cannot be saved, but we have already learned that his death is inevitable and that the real danger comes from the planned betrayal of the naval secrets (pp. 73ff). This is the danger toward which the plot as a whole is directed, and it is one that Hannay succeeds in averting at the last minute.

With this in mind, we can return to le Carré and see that his novels fall easily into three categories: spy stories, mysteries that often involve spies, and a third and most interesting group, in which the two modes are played off against one another. That some of his works are more or less straightforward tales of espionage no one will deny. The plot of *The Looking-Glass War* (1965), for example, is directed to the question of whether the East Germans are building a secret missile launching site. It turns out in the end that the indications that had seemed to point to this possibility had, in fact, been planted by Control in order to discredit a rival Ministry, and hence that the Head of the Circus is himself ultimately responsible for the murder of Taylor in the first chapter; but there is no murder investigation and no character who plays the rôle of the detective, and the question of who actually killed Taylor is barely raised and never answered. Again, *The Honourable Schoolboy* (1977) and *Smiley's People* (1979) are both directed toward bringing a foreign agent over into the West; though there are some extremely nasty murders, especially in the latter novel, those who die do so mostly because they knew too much, and the plots are aimed not toward the identification and punishment of the culprits but toward the final compromising and securing of the foreign agent; to this end the complex web of investigation, deception and extortion is woven.

In the present context, more interest attaches to le Carré's mystery stories. It is often forgotten that le Carré began his literary career with two quite short novels, *Call for the Dead* (1961) and *A Murder of Quality* (1962); though both feature Smiley, only the former involves any other spies and both are, in fact, best understood as detective novels. In *Call for the Dead*, Smiley investigates the apparent suicide of a member of the Foreign Office and discovers a series of anomalous circumstances that point unmistakably to murder. For the rest of the novel, Smiley tracks the murderers until, in a climactic confrontation, he himself kills the man who had ordered the diplomat slain. That this man was a foreign agent and that the diplomat had been killed because he had come to suspect that his wife was a spy are of little or no consequence for the plot of the novel (though they no doubt contribute to its success in other regards). We have here, in essence, a straightforward detective novel in the American tradition. Smiley has features in this first novel that he will retain throughout his literary career and that mark him as a familiar member of the ranks of literary detectives in general: his enigmatic nature (the novel introduces Smiley by dwelling upon the inexplicability for English society of Lady Ann's marriage to him); his marginality in matters personal (symbolized by his predilection for German literature, especially for the much-neglected Baroque period), marital (Lady Ann's separation from him is announced on the first page), and professional (in this, his first novel, he already retires from the Service); his co-operation with the authorized institutions of investigation (embodied, not for the last time, in Inspector Mendel) and his aloofness from them (indicated by his refusal to accept the Service's offer to decline his letter of resignation). These features would suffice to stamp Smiley as a detective, but others point no less clearly to the heritage of Hammett and Chandler rather than to that of Conan Doyle and Christie. Thus, Smiley becomes the victim of a physical assault to which he almost succumbs; conversely, at the end he does not arrest the criminal but instead slays him. Again, his participation in the case involves him personally in other ways than those connected immediately with the investigation; the head of the foreign agents had been Smiley's pupil before the war, and, although this gives Smiley the knowledge that enables him to lay a successful trap, it also means that, when Smiley kills him, he will be overwhelmed by remorse and self-loathing:

Dieter was dead, and he had killed him. The broken fingers of his right hand, the stiffness of his body and the sickening headache, the nausea of guilt, all testified to this. And Dieter had let him do it, had not fired the gun, had remembered their friendship when Smiley had not. . . . They had come from different hemispheres of the night, from different worlds of thought and conduct. Dieter, mercurial, absolute, had fought to build a civilization. Smiley, rationalistic, protective, had fought to prevent him. 'Oh God,' said Smiley aloud, 'who was then the gentleman. . . .'[11]

Such passages are characteristic of the American tradition, where in the end there may be little difference between detective and criminal beyond the fact that the former succeeds at the cost of the latter: is there any doubt at the end of a mystery by Christie or Sayers who the gentleman was? But the most telling evidence for assigning *Call for the Dead* to the American tradition of detective fiction derives from the structure of its plot. For Smiley is brought in, not after the murder, but before it, and the murder is a direct result of his introduction into the story. An anonymous letter had been received, denouncing the diplomat as a former communist, and Smiley had been ordered to interview him. One of the ironies of the plot is that the matter was thoroughly trivial, and Smiley saw no reason to pursue the investigation; but a foreign agent had observed the two walking in a park together, had concluded that the diplomat would betray them, and had decided he must be killed. Another irony becomes obvious at the end, when it turns out that the agent was right: the anonymous letter had been written by the diplomat himself, not in order to jeopardize his career but so as to establish a first contact with Smiley's Service.

To turn from *Call for the Dead* to *A Murder of Quality* is to move from the American to the English tradition of mystery stories. This is le Carré's purest detective novel: its plot could have come directly out of Agatha Christie. The case involves the murder of the wife of a faculty member at an exclusive boys' school; Smiley enters it only because she had written, expressing fears for her life, to a friend of his. The murder occurs before he arrives; he solves it with the help of the local police; at the end, the murderer is arrested. To be sure, le Carré uses the novel as a vehicle to explore the social and psychological tensions arising from contemporary changes in English life, and a kind of negative personal complicity on the part of Smiley in the case he is investigating is established by the repeated references to Lady Ann, who belongs to the social class of which the school is part in a way that Smiley never will; but, in terms of its plot, the novel is thoroughly conventional. It almost gives the impression that le Carré, at the beginning of his career, had deliberately chosen to apprentice himself first in the one tradition and then in the other before going on to more serious work.

The results are evident in le Carré's most interesting mystery novel, *Tinker Tailor Soldier Spy* (1974). Here the plot has the form of a murder mystery, although the victim, Jim Prideaux, did not die but was (only) shot, captured and tortured. There are four suspects, four highly placed officials in the Circus who could have been the Russian agent responsible for the betrayal of Prideaux's mission; and Smiley is brought out of retirement in order to determine which of the four is the guilty party by investigative procedures no different from those any traditional detective would use. Moreover, the clue that firmly establishes the guilt of Bill Haydon is of the most conventional sort:

> 'Sam, listen. Bill was making love to Ann that night. No, listen. You phoned her, she told you Bill wasn't there. As soon as she'd rung off, she pushed Bill out of bed and he turned up at the Circus an hour later knowing that there had been a shooting in Czecho. If you were giving me the story from the shoulder—on a postcard—that's what you'd say?'
> 'Broadly.'
> 'But you didn't tell Ann about Czecho when you phoned her—'
> 'He stopped at his club on the way to the Circus.'
> 'If it was open. Very well: then why didn't he know that Jim Prideaux had been shot?'[12]

This is only the slightest of variations upon the traditional scene in which the criminal, told the victim has been murdered, blurts out, 'My God, who shot him?' and the detective murmurs, 'Who said anything of his being shot?'

But this passage occurs only two-thirds of the way through the novel. Why, then, is Haydon not arrested at once? The reason casts light upon the way le Carré has modified the conventions of the mystery novel to suit his purposes. It will be recalled that the American tradition permits the detective's personal complicity in the case to become an important factor

162

in the plot; here le Carré develops this feature ingeniously by having Bill Haydon become notoriously adulterous with Lady Ann. It was no accident that Haydon had been in bed with Smiley's wife on the night Prideaux was shot. For if Smiley were to finger Haydon on the basis of the kind of evidence just cited, it would be thought he was acting out of jealousy: this had been part of Karla's design. Hence, Smiley must create a trap in which some new action of Haydon's will prove his guilt beyond any possible doubt, and the last part of the novel is devoted to his setting this trap.

Another problem remains, however. If *Tinker Tailor Soldier Spy* is, in fact, formally a murder mystery, why was Jim Prideaux not murdered? Why is the victim permitted to survive? Le Carré's innovation in this regard moves the detective novel beyond the realm of ordinary crime and inserts it into a specifically political context. For what is to be done with Haydon once he has been identified as the foreign agent? In the traditional criminal novel, the murderer's death or arrest provides an entirely satisfactory conclusion, but here both alternatives are quite problematic. For the English Service to kill Haydon would taint Smiley in a way le Carré is elsewhere at pains to avoid.[13] On the other hand, political considerations would require Haydon to be imprisoned and eventually sent to the East in exchange for some captured Western spy; yet, given the enormity of Haydon's betrayal, such an ending would violate the reader's sense of justice and seem intolerably weak. The demands of justice can only be satisfied if Haydon can be appropriately punished; and Prideaux's murder of Haydon, in spite of all of Smiley's precautionary measures, cleverly provides a satisfactory conclusion to the novel without implicating Smiley.

The last three novels we have considered can all be adequately interpreted in terms of their use of traditional mystery plots, but already in the third one we have seen how certain features point beyond the limits of that genre. In conclusion, I should like to turn to two other novels by le Carré in which the central categories of the mystery tradition are employed only so that they can be radically put into question.

*The Spy Who Came in from the Cold* (1963) begins with the death of an agent in Berlin. When Alec Leamas, his contact, returns to England, Control proposes to him a plan whereby the man responsible for the murder can be punished. Leamas accepts the plan because of his desire to avenge the agent's death upon the man who ordered it, the East German agent Mundt:

> 'That is, of course, if you're *sure you want* to . . . no mental fatigue or anything?'
> 'If it's a question of killing Mundt, I'm game.' (p. 17)

> 'He said there was a job he'd got to do. Someone to pay off for something they'd done to a friend of his.' (p. 99)

Leamas, like the reader, is convinced that he is involved in a typical mystery plot: the guilty will be brought to justice and the moral order will be restored. There is, to be sure, no detection (Mundt's guilt is clear from the beginning), and the plot is prospective insofar as it is directed toward the eventual compromising of the East German, yet reader and hero always look backward as they move forward and envision that ending as a satisfactory answer to the problem posed by the beginning. But, of course, it is revealed in the end that Leamas, and we with him, have been deceived: the object of Control's plot turns out to have been the death not of Mundt (who was, in fact, an English agent) but of his subordinate Fiedler (who had been on the point of discovering Mundt's treason and himself acts the rôle of the detective within Control's elaborate scheme). The conventions of the mystery story are used as a red herring to deceive the reader as well as the characters and they are exploded by the ending, in which the murderer is saved while the East German detective and the English avenger are killed. Le Carré takes considerable pains to establish Mundt's vile and vicious character—in contrast to him, not only Leamas but also Fiedler are thoroughly sympathetic figures—and the resulting jolt to the reader's sensibilities helps to make the novel's ending so fully and satisfactorily unsettling. But the contribution le Carré's inversion of the generic conventions of the mystery novel makes to achieving this effect ought not to be neglected; to discover that the search for truth and justice is not the real object but only a ruse to protect their opposites for reasons of national self-interest provides an ingenious surprise by purely formal means. To be sure, the traditional American mystery had allowed the possibility that society was so corrupt that the detective's uncovering of the truth could no longer save it;

Marlowe's Southern California is in many ways irredeemable, and, at the end of *The Big Sleep*, the small fry can be punished but Eddie Mars retains his nefarious power, and the murder of Rusty Regan may be brought to light but is immediately hushed up. Yet, by turning those who believe in the ideals of detection into naïve pawns in the hands of the cynical practitioners of *Realpolitik*, *The Spy Who Came in from the Cold* pushes Chandler's moral disillusionment an important step farther. Le Carré's novel implicitly asks the question whether English society has not reached the point at which the truth must be suppressed and justice thwarted if the society is to be preserved. In terms of literary genres, this can be translated into the question whether the mystery story is still possible in our time.

It is to this question that le Carré's *A Small Town in Germany* (1968) is most systematically addressed. The plot begins when Leo Harting, an employee at the British Embassy in Bonn, vanishes; he has taken sensitive files with him, and the suspicion of his defection is immediately invoked. Alan Turner is sent from England to track him down, and we seem to be confronted with a standard mystery in which the detective (Turner) pursues the criminal (Harting). But in the course of Turner's investigation a surprising truth emerges: Harting is evidently not a spy for the East but has himself been investigating the background of an important West German political figure, Karfeld. Eventually, it becomes clear that Karfeld had committed an atrocity during the Second World War and that Harting had come upon the traces of his crime. Instead of the detective (Turner) pursuing the criminal (Harting), we find one detective (Turner) pursuing another detective (Harting) who, in turn, is pursuing the real criminal (Karfeld). The differences between the two detectives are obvious. Harting, 'the memory man,'[14] is obsessed with discovering the truth about the past and with seeing justice done; no consideration of policy or of self-interest can prevent him from bending every effort to investigating the traces of a crime and to seeing to it that the man who bears the guilt for it is appropriately punished. In his moral rigour, unswerving determination, and investigative ingenuity, Harting is the perfect type of the classic literary detective. Turner, on the other hand, is bound by considerations of national policy, for the English have formed a secret alliance with Karfeld, based on mutual self-interest, and are desperately concerned that the German politician should not be discredited. Turner is himself too much a detective not to feel a powerful sympathy with Harting and to try his best not to obstruct him; but in the end he cannot prevent Harting from being killed and Karfeld from being saved. The war criminal can continue in his meteoric political career; the interests of England are protected; but the authentic detective is murdered and the inauthentic one is condemned to futility and self-hatred. Turner's last conversation with the diplomat Bradfield, who incarnates the cynicism of power in the novel, establishes its ultimate frame of reference:

> Turner searched frantically around him. 'It's not true! You *can't* be so tied to the surface of things.'
>
> 'What else is there when the underneath is rotten? Break the surface and we sink. That's what Harting has done. I am a hypocrite,' he continued simply. 'I'm a great believer in hypocrisy. It's the nearest we ever get to virtue. It's a statement of what we ought to be. Like religion, like art, like the law, like marriage. I serve the appearance of things. . . . He *has* offended,' he added casually, as if passing the topic once more in review. 'Yes. He has. Not as much against myself as you might suppose. But against the order that results from chaos; against the built-in moderation of an aimless society. He had no business to hate Karfeld and none to . . . He had no business to remember. If you and I have a purpose at all anymore, it is to save the world from such presumptions.'
>
> 'Of all of you—listen!—of all of you he's the only one who's real, the only one who believed, and acted! For you it's a sterile, rotten game, a family word game, that's all—just play. But Leo's *involved!* He knows what he wants and he's gone to get it!'
>
> 'Yes. That alone should be enough to condemn him.' (pp. 361–62)

If modern society is directed solely to the future rather than to the past, if the necessary and sufficient goal of national policy is survival, if the appearances must be preserved because there is nothing else besides them, what place can remain for the detective who seeks to decipher the enigma of the past, whatever the cost for the present? At the end of Chandler's novels, Marlowe may be condemned to futility; at the end of le Carré's novel, Harting is condemned to death. Marlowe may don the Hippocratic smile; Harting can no longer doff it. In the murder of Harting is figured the death of the traditional mystery novel. Authors may continue to write detective novels; le Carré himself has done so. But the insight to which le Carré has given voice in *A Small Town in Germany* may well anticipate the end of the genre. Future generations may no longer understand why the past century has been so obsessed with the discovery of truth and the punishment of crime. For them, the mystery novel may become mysterious in a way we would prefer not to envision.

## NOTES

1. Raymond Chandler, *The Little Sister* (Harmondsworth, Middx.: Penguin, 1977), p. 247.
2. What I have described in this paragraph are what seem to me the basic generic conventions of the literary detective. Of course, exceptions can be found for every one of these generalizations. There are mysteries without a murder (Chandler's *Playback*, an anomaly in many ways and evidently Chandler's farewell to the genre); mysteries in which the detective's love interest plays an important and constructive rôle (Sayers's *Gaudy Night*); mysteries in which the narrator is the murderer (Christie's *The Murder of Roger Ackroyd*) or the hero is (Highsmith's *The Talented Mr. Ripley*); mysteries that the detective does not solve (Bentley's *Trent's Last Case*) or that are solved without a detective (Christie's *And Then There Were None*). But all such cases are deformations of the expected conventions and must be understood as such; that is their point. Likewise, detective novels in which the detective is a member of the regular police force (such as those of McBain and Simenon) are not exceptions to the general outline sketched here, for in these novels the hero is always at odds with the police force as a whole and operates as an often insubordinate loner; the constitutive opposition between detective and police is simply transposed to the interior of the police, but is not thereby abolished.
3. Edgar Allan Poe, *The Complete Tales and Poems* (New York: Vintage, 1975), p. 141. Future references to this edition are indicated by page numbers in parentheses in the text.
4. Such tales as E. T. A. Hoffmann's 'Das Fräulein von Scuderi' (and even Poe's 'The Murders in the Rue Morgue') are transitional phenomena in this regard; here, although the crime itself does not directly concern the detective, his involvement in the case is due to his feeling of personal concern for an acquaintance who has been unjustly accused and to whom the detective feels obligations arising from an earlier connection. In both

cases, this excuse for the detective's participation has a very artificial air.

5. Walter Benjamin, *The Origin of German Tragic Drama*, translated by John Osborne (London: N.L.B., 1977), p. 166. I have revised the translation in a number of points to make it closer in meaning to the original.

6. So particularly in 'The Purloined Letter', where the laughter of the Prefect (p. 209) and of the narrator (p. 215) suffices to condemn them.

7. Sir Arthur Conan Doyle, *The Complete Sherlock Holmes* (Garden City, N.Y.: Garden City Books, n.d.), pp. 474, 488, 1323, 404.

8. Raymond Chandler, *The Big Sleep* (New York: Vintage, 1976), p. 168.

9. Even here, the contrast cannot be taken too strictly. A spy novel in which personal destinies were not at stake would be unreadable; and, in all mystery writers at some level and in certain ones (like Ross Macdonald) quite explicitly, the ultimate subject is the society in which such murders are performed.

10. John Buchan, *Adventures of Richard Hannay* (Boston: Houghton Mifflin, 1915), pp. 20, 31–2. Subsequent references are indicated in the text.

11. John le Carré, *Call for the Dead* (New York: Bantam, 1979), p. 137.

12. John le Carré, *Tinker Tailor Soldier Spy* (New York: Bantam, 1975), p. 238.

13. Elsewhere, Smiley is generally kept free from association with the more sordid activities of British Intelligence. In le Carré, the English tend (unrealistically perhaps) to torture and murder far less than their communist counterparts and to rely instead upon cunning and deception; what is more, Smiley in particular is usually spared direct involvement in those operations that would tend to cast doubt upon the morality of the Circus. The following exchange from *The Spy Who Came in from the Cold* (New York: Bantam, 1975), 49, is revealing:

> 'Why isn't Smiley here?' Leamas asked.
> 'He doesn't like the operation,' Control replied indifferently. 'He finds it distasteful. He sees the necessity but he wants no part in it. His fever,' Control added with a whimsical smile, 'is recurrent.'

Subsequent references are indicated in the text.

14. John le Carré, *A Small Town in Germany* (New York: Coward-McCann, 1968), p. 125. Subsequent references are indicated in the text.

# 8

# Le Carré:
# Faith and Dreams

## by PHILIP O'NEILL

The opening words of *Tinker Tailor Soldier Spy*, are 'The truth is . . .' and the novel eventually contradicts this philosophic certainty with its concluding three words, the sombre warning that it 'was after all a dream'. I think it is to exaggerate le Carré's intentions to read this novel as a philosophic quest after the nature of truth. To argue that le Carré has something to say about the condition of the European soul and is writing in a tradition going back to Schiller is in danger of overstating the case. However, le Carré is an important novelist whose interest for the contemporary reader lies elsewhere and whose popularity may be accounted for much more interestingly than by appeal to a little-known intellectual tradition. It is not the sophistication of his epistemological inquiry or his contribution to the essential nature of man that centres the le Carré *oeuvre* for the reader. Rather it is the political and ideological resonances in the novels, focusing in particular on Smiley, which make le Carré's protagonist a peculiar type of popular hero in late twentieth-century England. I feel the Smiley novels deserve to be unpacked to reveal the repertoire of uncertainties they contain which marks them as of particular interest to the contemporary reader. By concentrating on *Tinker Tailor* I hope to go some way in unwinding the subtleties in the novels.

Smiley in his various manifestations, particularly in the Karla trilogy, incorporates a plethora of values which mark him as a figure of special interest for a readership in a declining England. To emphasize this point, it is only necessary to recall some of the popular heroes from English thrillers earlier in the century. In contrast to either Bulldog Drummond, Richard Hannay or James Bond, to make a random sweep, Smiley is an odd type whose peculiarity is marked in both the public world and in the private world of personal relationships. The former diminution of influence in the public sphere is easily explained as a symptom of England's imperial decline, particularly post-Suez. However, after the sexual confidence of James Bond, particularly in the 1960s, Smiley's personal life is a sorry sequel. Smiley's far from satisfactory relationship with his wife Ann makes him a poor successor to Bond's sexual consumption, and there is little sexual display in the novels. The undoubted popularity of the television adaption of *Tinker Tailor* and *Smiley's People* certainly cannot be attributed to the public display of beautiful women who may be seen to compete with Ian Fleming's Pussy Galore and Honeychile Rider. Herr Kretzschmann's Blue Diamond club in Hamburg in *Smiley's People* is the only place where naked females are on display, but the attractions of this institution are hardly foregrounded. Pussy and Honeychile may have a more obvious successor in Lizzie Worthington in *The Honourable Schoolboy*, but while she is a definite sexual presence, Jerry Westerby's interest in her is definitely motivated by more than lust.

The whole question of le Carré's representation of female sexuality is fraught with problems. Pussy and Honeychile are the product of the 'sexually liberated' early 1960s, and while they are in the novel, and very definitely in the films, the precise object of the controlling male gaze, they are at best allowed to express, however mutedly and contradictorily, their sexuality. In some way at least this is a victory for women in that female sexuality is actually recognized. However, with the more finely tuned and cautious representation of sexuality in the 1970s, le Carré's treatment of women is both an advance and a retreat. It is an advance in that they are no longer sexually exploited to the extent that they are in the Bond novels and films. It is a retreat too for the women's movement however, in that, in these novels, Ann Smiley and indeed Lizzie Worthington are worthy creatures. They are no longer, to the same extent, the sexual chattels of the 1960s, but, by some process of back projection, they again have had to adopt the mantels of moral purity. Once again women become moral repositories where men measure the very definite inadequacies of a corrupt public world. By and large, le Carré returns us to this world where women are the moral arbiters and in them is enshrined the values found to be wanting in the world at large. This is a contradictory position for women, because it is just from such a moral entrapment that women had tried for so long to escape.

Smiley's world is altogether unpleasant and the contradictory nature of the representation of women is only one aspect of it. Le Carré may be writing in a world of slightly more enlightened sexual consciousness, but his is an attempt to deny female sexual choice rather than to accommodate it in a rational and even-handed way. Rather than portray positive female characters, in the Karla trilogy, whose sexuality is an aspect of their personality on a par with that of men, sexuality is circumvented whenever possible and the world is represented as motivated by other values. Throughout *Tinker Tailor* le Carré makes appeal to an older world, a very individual and self-conscious reference to the Pastoral myth, to a time when things were better than they are now. However, in the idiosyncratic expression given to this appeal in the novel, this older and, by implication, better world is most fully developed in that uniquely masculine institution, the public school. It is the values inscribed in the public school that condense and attempt to resolve many of the contradictions in the world at large.

*Tinker Tailor* draws a parallel between the public school, the Secret Service and the outside world. After betrayal and defeat in the public world, Jim Prideaux, a Circus agent, retreats into the shelter offered by Thursgood's school. The opening pages of *Tinker Tailor* describe life at the school, and when Smiley first appears in the novel he is measured by the terms and standards set by the school. Smiley is 'the final form for which Bill Roach was the prototype' (p. 21). Bill Roach is one of the less fortunate boys at Thursgood's, so Smiley is identified from the offset as an extrapolation and graduate of the public school. Some indication of the flavour of the education system available at Thursgood's is apparent in the opening chapter of the novel. It is no exaggeration to suggest that in this newly found sanctuary and retreat Jim Prideaux can express the values and beliefs which motivated him in the real world—values and beliefs, however, which served him ill and almost caused his death. The school boys quickly get Jim's number when trying to find a suitable nick-name for him.

> Yet Goulash did not satisfy them either. It lacked the hint of strength contained. It took no account of Jim's passionate Englishness, which was the only subject where he could be relied on to waste time. Toad Spikely had only to venture one disparaging comment on the monarchy, extol the joys of some foreign country, preferably a hot one, for Jim to colour sharply and snap out a good three minutes' worth on the privilege of being born an Englishman. . . .
> 'Best place in the whole damn world!' he bellowed once.
> 'Know why? Know why, toad?'
> Spikely did not, so Jim seized a crayon and draw a globe. To the west, America, he said, full of greedy fools fouling up their inheritance. To the east, China–Russia, he drew no distinction: boiler suits, prison camps and a damn long march to nowhere.
> In the middle . . . (pp. 16–17)

In the public sphere, in the real world, Jim's values have been found wanting. This is known even to his pupils; he had had 'a great attachment that had failed him' (p. 21). Yet the school is the place where Jim can recuperate and give voice to a vision of the world which, the implication is, is so obviously blinkered and inadequate. It is my intention, in this essay, to argue that le Carré does not value England as a middle road of moderation between competing monoliths. His intention is more radical and pessimistic than this. Jim's credo is a nationalism of despair, and there is little solace or consolation for him even in the Tory press.

> 'You can look at this one for nothing,' he bellowed as he sat down. And having hauled open his *Daily Telegraph* calmly gave himself over to the latest counsels of the juju men, which they understood to mean almost anyone with intellectual pretension, even if he wrote in the Queen's cause. (p. 18)

Thursgood's is the only space which can accommodate Jim Prideaux, the secret agent, whose blinding belief in England has almost cost him his life. Le Carré suggests that it is the public school, this very particular appropriation of childhood, with its definite inscription of gender, race and class, which establishes the values which govern the world-view of so many English men. However, as in Prideaux's case, it is also clear to le Carré that even if these values ever worked, they certainly do not give good service now. Le Carré simultaneously establishes them as values and distances himself from them.

Still, the schoolboy world is a condensed metaphor for a version of Pastoral, the idea that the past is better than the present. But this is obviously not a blind credo because Smiley is not a victim of this nostalgia. The past is not always an unqualified sphere of virtue as becomes clear when Smiley bumps into Roddy Martindale in the street. Martindale may be old Circus, but Smiley finds him distasteful. His triumphs, such as they were, were

> thirty years ago [and] Martindale spoke in a confiding upper-class bellow of the sort which, on foreign holidays, had more than once caused Smiley to sign out of his hotel and run for cover. (p. 23)

The acceptance of the past is not a general rule, a universal dictum. Martindale may be old Circus, but Smiley is intent to distance himself from his chance acquaintance. However, it is to a select range of these old values that, in part, Smiley appeals to counter Martindale's theory that Control is still alive: 'He died of a heart attack after a long illness. Besides he hated South Africa. He hated everywhere except Surrey, the Circus and Lord's Cricket Ground' (p. 25). England is collapsed into the Home Counties, Surrey and the Circus—the secret service continues the tradition of the school and cricket is, of course, the most English of games. Smiley is down-hearted by his inability to deal adequately with Martindale's brusque ways and manners and as a result sees himself as

> 'effeminate, non-productive . . .' He stepped widely to avoid an unseen obstacle. 'Weakness', he resumed, 'and an inability to live a self-sufficient life independent of institutions'—a puddle emptied itself neatly into his shoe—'and emotional attachments which have long outlived their purpose. *Viz* my wife, *viz* the Circus, *viz* living in London. Taxi!' (pp. 27–8)

Smiley's self-awareness is overwhelming at this point, and I argue that it is the project of the novel to measure the values of these institutions against the outside world. It should not go without comment either that Smiley, while in this mood of self-deprecation, sees himself as effeminate, a figure far removed from the masculine-heroic tradition of the man-of-action. However he also recognizes the crippling nature of an over-dependence on institutions both private and public. To be too much in thrall of the Circus is not, in Smiley's mind, necessarily a good thing. However it is his personal lack of sexual power which is emphasized when two girls out-distance him for the taxi he has just called.

Smiley does eventually make it home to Bywater Street where Peter Guillam is waiting to take him to see

> Mr. Oliver Lacon of the Cabinet Office, a senior adviser to various mixed committees and a watch-dog of intelligence affairs. Or, as Guillam had it less reverentially, Whitehall's head prefect. (p. 30)

Guillam's irreverence is not just accidental, as the fusion of school and the intelligence service is an articulation which pervades the novel. Just as the machinations of the Secret Service are an enigma to all concerned and one agent is constantly watching the other, so the running of the school is a secretive affair to the boys and it is also an institution where one watches the other. The school, too, is a place of legend and competing explanation. Prideaux had parked his Alvis in the Dip, 'a piece of Thursgood folklore'.

> To look at, it is no more than a depression in the ground, grass covered, with hummocks on the northern side, each about boy-height and covered in tufted thickets which in summer grow spongy. It is these hummocks that give the Dip its special virtue as a playground and also its reputation, which varies with the fantasy of each new generation of boys. They are the traces of an open-cast silver mine, says one year and digs enthusiastically for wealth. They are a Romano-British fort, says another, and stages battles with sticks and clay missiles. To others the Dip is a bomb-crater from the war and the hummocks are seated bodies buried in the blast. (p. 10)

In the school as microcosm the legends of the boys are the attempts to order an unknown world. In the macrocosm it soon becomes clear that it is Smiley's tragedy that his own legend involving his wife and the Circus are also inadequate to circumscribe reality. It is appropriate too that the truth about the Dip is so 'prosaic'. It was the beginnings of a swimming pool, 'But the money that came in was never quite enough to finance the ambition' (p. 11). Outside the school, the Circus really does not have the money to finance its ambitions on the stage of world politics. *Tinker Tailor* turns on the divergence of dreams and folklore from economic truth and prosaic fact.

It is in the language adopted by the Circus agents that provides the evidence to reinforce the impression of the school as a source of moral value. There is an implied opposition in the novel between the school and the world of politics, but as in all oppositions, the two worlds are not equally weighted. Rather the public school is valorized and privileged. It is given a positive valency which contrasts with the negative and degenerate adult world, and there is often something pathetic in the attempts of the Circus to present itself in the rhetoric of the public school. The public school argot becomes fused with the language of the Pastoral myth, of a vanquished past, a time which is regarded with great nostalgia. All this is seen in masculine-heroic terms, a period of chivalry and the knight-errant.

Guillam drives Smiley to a 'Berkshire Camelot . . . the ugliest home for miles around and Lacon had picked it up for a song' (p. 34). King Arthur's court is an appropriate name for the home of this contemporary mythologizer. It is his hope and that of the Circus to equate and demand that the values of the past are somehow made to accord with the present day. That the home was so cheap and outmoded is some indication of just how out-of-step and inappropriate are the values it represents. 'The same fire was burning there, too mean for the enormous grate' (p. 34). The present economic situation will not allow for the glory that once was. However, there is inscribed in the novel a certain self-consciousness involved in all this. It is a very studied nostalgia, a nostalgia that is aware of itself and of its own shortcomings. But it is also a nostalgia that countenances no reasonable alternative. The liberal imagination knows it is inadequate but simultaneously recognizes the necessity to muddle on. Lacon explains this to Smiley in his garden:

175

I realise that now. I didn't at the time. It's a little difficult to know when to trust you people and when not. You do live by rather different standards don't you? I accept that. I'm not being judgmental. (p. 65)

It is almost impossible to be judgmental in terms of the moral and political paradigms offered in the novel. Yet, as shall become clear, le Carré is judgmental. However the characters will certainly not accept the responsibility of their own failing. Even Smiley will let the buck pass. ' "I'm afraid you'll have to ask a woman that question, not us," said Smiley wondering again where Immingham was' (p. 66). A woman can answer Lacon's questions because they hold the moral purse-strings. To avoid the question, the men mythologize themselves endlessly. This is given its clearest statement in *The Looking-Glass War*:

> He noticed that they ascribed—it was a plot in which all but Haldane compounded—legendary qualities to one another. Leclerc, for instance, would seldom introduce Avery to a member of his parent Ministry without some catchword. 'Avery is the brightest of our new stars'—or, to more senior men, 'John is my memory. You must ask John.' For the same reason they lightly forgave one another their trespasses, because they dared not think, for their own sakes, that the Department had room for fools. He recognised that it provided shelter from the complexities of modern life, a place where frontiers still existed. . . . It was a scene in which Sarah played no part. (p. 66)

It is also clear from *The Looking-Glass War* that the world of heroic masculine legend is a world with no place for women. At times Smiley looks very uneasy with all this fabrication and seems to be aware of the futility of his efforts. 'It is sheer vanity to believe that one, fat, middle-aged spy is the only person capable of holding the world together' (p. 70). This self-knowledge nuances what are presented as Smiley's essentially 'good' qualities, but there is much masculine arrogance involved. Smiley, too, would rest easy with the 'facts', but his wife Ann is of a different opinion, and it seems that women are determined to shatter the masculine illusion in the effort to reach what can only be an irrational truth.

> Only Ann, though she could not read his workings, refused to accept his findings. She was quite passionate, in fact, as only

176

women can be on matters of business, really driving him to go
back, take up where he had left off, never to veer aside in favour
of the easy argument. Not of course that she knew anything, but
what woman was ever stopped by want of information? She felt.
And despised him for not acting in accordance with her feelings.
(p. 70)

Ann represents a certain sphere of influence and value even if
she had transgressed—she had broken one of her own rules.

> Bill was Circus and he was Set—her word for family and
> ramifications. On either count he would be out of bounds.
> Thirdly, she had received him at Bywater Street, an agreed
> violation of territorial decencies. (p. 143)

However, Ann is still a value to which Smiley will continue to
aspire. Hers is the feminine, irrational mode which can contain
contradiction, and the novel will endorse this view to some
extent. But, at this stage in the novel, Smiley has difficulty with
such obvious contradiction. He may tell himself that it is 'sheer
vanity' to believe he is the only person capable of holding the
world together, but then again, what if 'everything which he
had been calling vanity is truth?' (p. 71). To the masculine
mind this appears to be totally irrational, akin to Irma's choice
of Tarr as a father-confessor. Women are dangerous because
they will topple the castles-in-the-air, the Camelots and myths
of the men. The public world, like the public school, is a
masculine space.

The men must carry on. Peter Guillam is a 'chivalrous' fellow
(p. 72). He can be trusted to maintain the codes and uphold the
decencies. Yet even this contemporary knight in shining armour
is made uneasy. His equilibrium, his personal worth is dis-
turbed by a woman, Camilla, whose 'mysterious restraint'
unnerves him (p. 74). Guillam, indeed, is supersensitive to
women in the course of the novel. A chance encounter with
some secretaries around a new coffee machine sets him on edge
and reminds him of his threatened position.

> 'Good God, how long have you had that monster?' Guillam
> asked, slowing down before a shiny new coffee-machine.
>     A couple of girls, filling beakers, glanced around and said,
> 'Hullo, Lauder', looking at Guillam. The tall one reminded him
> of Camilla: the same slow burning eyes, censuring male
> insufficiency. (p. 78)

Women are allowed to censure in this novel, but they themselves are censured because, in their search for truth and in their disregard for propriety, they create anarchy. Life may be anarchic but even the most feeble of the masculine dreams is better than what women appear to offer. Women are a threat to order and order must be maintained. Consequently mythology and dream are necessary no matter how obviously contingent. There are women of course employed by the Circus but they are a breed apart—'groomed Circus brides whom no one ever marries' (p. 82).

Connie Sachs is the logical conclusion of this. Connie's sexual displacement, her lesbianism, removes her from the heterosexual mainstream in the novel and means that she wholeheartedly and enthusiastically adopts the masculine values of the Circus.

> 'Oh George', she kept saying. 'Do you know what she told me when they threw me out? That personnel cow?' She was holding one point of Smiley's collar, working it between her finger and thumb while she cheered up. 'You know what the cow said?' Her sergeant-major voice: ' "You're losing your sense of proportion, Connie. It's time you got out into the real world." I *hate* the real world, George. I like the Circus and all my lovely boys.' (p. 90)

Connie's masculinity—the 'sergeant-major's voice'—is emphasized as is her decided preference for the myths of the Circus as opposed to the real world, and it is decidedly appropriate that in her information to Smiley about Polyakov, she should begin her story 'like a fairy-tale' (p. 91). And in her fairy-tale of lovely boys the threat comes from women. An agent is compromised. ' "Some *girl* had made a fool of him," said Connie with great contempt. "The Dutch set him a honey-trap, my dear, and he barged in with his eyes wide shut" ' (p. 92). Connie does not just have one fairy-tale for Smiley but also tells him of Komarov, 'the hero of her second fairy-tale: not a defector but a soldier with the shoulder boards of the artillery' (p. 93). However, Polyakov is the villain of the piece—'Polyakov was not a fairy-tale hero' (p. 96). But Connie is so enchanted with Polyakov that, for her, 'he was her lover Aleks, though she had never spoken to him, probably never seen him in the flesh' (p. 96). For Connie, the fiction is all powerful. And it is a fiction or fabrication that is related like a fairy-tale. She completes one of her narratives in a way which recalls a children's fairy-tale or nursery-rhyme. 'Connie was sacked and Lapin went hippety-lippety home' (p. 100). Just to confirm the correspondence between the world of childhood and that of the intelligence services it is worth recalling that their training school, Sarratt, is referred to as the Nursery throughout the novel.

The encounter with Connie Sachs highlights many of the reasons for the necessity of myth. This retreat into a world of the masculine-heroic and/or childhood is a return to a less complicated time when such stories organized the confusion of life—they come from a time in the past 'before Empire became a dirty word' (p. 101). Once there had been the possibility that Haydon and Smiley would

> 'have brought back the old spirit. Instead of that Scottish twerp. Bill rebuilding Camelot'—her fairy-tale simile again—'and George—'
> 'George picking up the bits,' said Smiley, vamping for her, and they laughed, Smiley falsely. (pp. 101–2)

Connie Sachs condenses much of the matter of the novel, much of the tragedy as le Carré sees it. Whereas now 'All over the world beastly people are making our time into nothing', Connie Sachs identifies the past as 'A real time. Englishmen could be proud then. Let them be proud now' (p. 102). But Connie herself seems to recognize the futility of this clarion call, and she can only mourn the sad fate of her colleagues and successors.

> 'Poor loves.' She was breathing heavy not perhaps from any one emotion but from a whole mess of them, washed around in her like mixed drinks. 'Poor loves. Trained to Empire, trained to rule the waves. All gone. All taken away. Bye-bye world.' (p. 102)

Perhaps after this dirge for Empire, Connie's final words are anti-climatical as she identifies loss of Empire as all one with the destruction of Millponds, the house she grew up in as a child.

> 'You don't know Millponds, do you?' she was asking.
> 'What's Millponds?'
> 'My brother's place. Beautiful Palladian house, lovely grounds, near Newbury. One day a road came. Crash. Bang. Motorway. Took all the grounds away. I grew up there, you see.' (p. 102)

Like Evelyn Waugh's dread of suburbia in *Brideshead Revisited*, Connie sees the destruction of her childhood home, her past, by

179

a motorway as synonymous with all that is increasingly wrong with a more democratic England. England is now a place, as Prideaux explains, where his Alvis, the best of English cars, is 'Out of production, thanks to socialism' (p. 105).

To counter this situation, a myth, a strategic retreat from reality, is necessary so the Circus builds around itself a series of legends.

> 'It's the business of agent runners to turn themselves into legends,' Smiley began, rather as if he was delivering a trainee lecture at Nursery. 'They do this first to impress their agents. Later they try it out on their colleagues and in my personal experience make rare asses of themselves in consequence. A few go so far as to try it on themselves. Those are the charlatans and they must be got rid of quickly, there's no other way.' (p. 174)

To encapsulate and circumscribe reality a myth is necessary, but, in the particular situation that le Carré describes, to believe the myth is the way to tragedy. The myth is necessary but it is also imperative to be aware of its contingent and relative nature. This is how I read Haldane's advice to Avery in *The Looking-Glass War*.

> 'One more thing—this is most important—do not let him think we have changed since the war: that is an illusion you must foster even'—he did not smile—'even though you are too young to make the comparison.' (p. 130)

England's rôle in the world has changed since the war, yet the Circus must try to organize itself as if twenty years of history had no effect.

It is this relative mark of contingency that is unique to le Carré's thriller. In other works of the genre, what le Carré presents as legend is seen and accepted as fact. Le Carré does not like what he understands to be dogmatism, the positive faith of an older generation of agents. Then, at some time in the past, the ideology may have been fine, may have accorded with the facts, but now, while faith is still necessary, it must be recognized for what it is—faith as opposed to facts. Smiley explains this in conversation to Bland who learnt his trade-craft at Nursery, taught by a 'fanatic called Thatch' (p. 134):

> Nervous breakdowns or not Bland still bore the imprimatur of the Thatch philosophy for agents in the enemy camp: self-faith,

positive participation, Pied-Piper appeal, and all those other uncomfortable phrases which in the high day of the cold war culture had turned the Nursery into something close to a moral rearmament centre. (p. 135)

A 'moral rearmament centre' is not what is required now. Once, the philosophy may have accorded with the situation, but that is no longer the case. The present situation simply does not require a new philosophy but something much more complicated. Bland has now realized the fact, despite his education. ' "You're an educated sort of swine," he announced easily as he sat down again. "An artist is a bloke who can hold two fundamentally opposing views and still function" ' (p. 136). At this stage in the novel it is this form of double-think which Smiley finds distasteful. *Tinker Tailor* concludes with Smiley's recognition of the relative nature of all political systems but, at this point, he is fired by a quest for what he hopes to be the truth. Ultimately, Smiley will arrive at the conclusion that it is 'all a dream', an even more radical stance than Bland's double-think, but in this conversation he is troubled by what he sees as the radical nature of Bland's philosophy. Bland contradicts him. ' "That's not radical," Bland retorted, resenting any devaluation of his socialism, or of Haydon. "That's just looking out the bloody window. That's just England now, man" ' (p. 136). To counter this type of thought Smiley still has his standard, a basic belief that while the old values may not hold water, there are still principles to be upheld. As Smiley sifts through the evidence presented in the old Circus files and rehearses in his mind conversations of years ago, he is still motivated by a belief in the facts, the definitive word. 'Facts. What were the facts?' (p. 143). At the end of the novel, Smiley will have lost faith in all facts.

Smiley is not the only character who is lost in a labyrinth in the course of the novel. As a result of his searches through the Merlin files in the Circus library Guillam seems to echo Smiley's predicament. Just as Smiley finds himself thinking of Ann so Guillam has flashing thoughts about Camilla. Both men attempt to square the confusions in their professional lives by reference to their private relationships.

A sickening notion had struck him: it seemed so neat and so horribly obvious that he could only wonder why it had come to

181

him so late. Sand was Camilla's husband. She was living a
double life. Now whole vistas of deceit opened before him. His
friends, his loves, even the Circus itself, joined and re-formed in
endless patterns of intrigue. (p. 165)

The novel shows just how the public and private worlds are
connected despite many disclaimers to the contrary. The
intrigues and secrets of the Circus have Guillam doubt the basis
of his relationship with Camilla. It is Smiley's troubled relationship with Ann that is used to explain Smiley's lapse in his
interrogation of Gerstmann/Karla in the 1950s.

> Well, at first sight, he made little impression on me. I would have
> been hard put to it to recognise in the little fellow before me the
> master of cunning we have heard about in Irina's letter, poor
> woman. I suppose it's also true that my nerve-ends had been a
> good deal blunted by so many similar encounters in the last few
> months, by travel, and well by—well, by things at home. (p. 178)

Guillam's investigations in the library cause him to have even
more doubts about Camilla, and Smiley blames Ann and things
at home for the deterioration in his concentration. Women may
be moral custodians but they still interfere with the masculine
equilibrium. They call the men's bluff and ridicule the games
the men play with each other. Whether right or wrong, men still
want and need to uphold these proprieties and compete with
each other according to clearly defined rules. There is a struggle
between two philosophic and political systems and Smiley at
this stage explains how Gerstmann/Karla eludes him because 'I
felt I lacked philosophic repose. Lacked philosophy, if you like'
(p. 181).

Smiley's view of the world, with all its authorial endorsement
and authorization, is usually seen as the validation of an essential
individualism and the privileging of individualism over all forms
of collectivism whether they express themselves as Soviet communism or American technologism. This is true, but I believe
there is more involved. It is not just individualism versus
collectivism that is at loggerheads, but there is also a challenge
to the validity of philosophy itself. At the end of the novel
Smiley is a disillusioned man, and it is a disillusionment which
is all embracing and includes a dissatisfaction with both western
individualism and Soviet collectivism. One is seen as the

reflection of the other and it is now impossible to find 'philosophic repose' anywhere. This is hinted at in the interrogation of Gerstmann/Karla, as Smiley explains.

> I believed, you see, that I had seen something in his face that was superior to mere dogma; not realising that it was my own reflection. I had convinced myself that Gerstmann ultimately was accessible to ordinary human arguments coming from a man of his own age and profession and, well, durability. I didn't promise him wealth and women and Cadillacs and cheap butter, I accepted that he had no use for those things. I had the wit by then, at least, to steer clear of the topic of his wife. I didn't make speeches to him about freedom, whatever that means, or the essential good will of the West: besides, they were not favourable days for selling that story, and I was in no clear ideological state myself. I took the line of kinship. 'Look,' I said, 'we're getting to be old men, and we've spent our lives looking for the weaknesses in one another's systems. I can see through Eastern values just as you can through our Western ones. Both of us, I am sure, have experienced ad nauseam the technical satisfactions of this wretched war. But now your own side is going to shoot you. Don't you think it's time to recognise that there is as little worth on your side as there is on mine?' (p. 185)

Smiley is at his weakest at this point and is embarrassed to report this interview to Control. It is, however, still a very important passage as it anticipates the self-knowledge which Smiley gains at the end of the novel. *Tinker Tailor* does not just endorse individualism and warn of the dangers of collectivism. Rather it also recognizes the relative nature of all philosophy, all attempts to order the world. One may be just as successful as the other. Le Carré underscores the point that all philosophy is relative and contingent, but while the truth may constantly evade us, faith is still necessary. There is also the suggestion that in England's past, in the days of Empire there may indeed have been good and bad ideals but, unfortunately, the contemporary situation is a great deal more complicated. It involves now the self-conscious distrust of all philosophy but simultaneously recognizes that philosophy as faith is necessary. Smiley does not adopt this stance until the end of *Tinker Tailor* and still at this time in the novel believes that 'Karla is not fireproof because he's a fanatic. And one day, if I have anything to do

183

with it, that lack of moderation will be his downfall' (p. 188). However, while Karla is eventually defeated in *Smiley's People*, it is a Pyrrhic victory. Karla actually surrenders because of his love for his daughter. Smiley is the fanatic in this chase for Karla. Such is the relative nature of the values which the two men represent that, at the end of the Karla trilogy, the two men appear to be almost interchangeable. 'They exchanged one mere glance and perhaps each for that second did see in the other something of himself' (p. 334).

The difficulties confronted at this point in *Tinker Tailor*, the complex nature of understanding anything in such a contingent world, is emphasized for the readers by reference to Roach's problems in again coming to terms with Jim Prideaux. The school is again a metaphor for life. The schoolboy, Roach, sees Prideaux retrieve his revolver, but that his mentor-hero should have a gun in the first place, he finds hard to comprehend. So in dealing with this latest knowledge about Prideaux, Roach 'had tried mixing up reality with dreams in the hope that the event would be converted into something he had imagined' (p. 191). It is this conjuring with dreams and reality and Smiley's hope that the fact that there is a traitor in the Circus may in the end be all imagination, a dream, which is central to *Tinker Tailor* as a whole.

This theme, the confusion of dream and reality is apparent in the two interviews which Smiley has firstly with Max and then with Jerry Westerby, the honourable schoolboy himself. Appropriately enough, on his way to see Max, the retired Czech agent, Smiley passes a statue which only signifies to him a 'cosmic muddle' (p. 208). Max makes it all too clear that he will no longer allow the Circus to patronize him with stories of its genuine concern for his country.

> 'You want know some history? How you say "Märchen", please George?'
> 'Fairy-tale,' said Smiley.
> 'Okay, so don't tell me no more damn fairy-tale how English got to save Czecho no more!' (p. 216)

Unlike Max, Jerry Westerby seems to prefer a life of myth and fairy-tale. Made redundant from the Circus he indicates his predilection for mythologizing himself, however pathetically, by adopting a schoolboy version of Red Indian argot. ' "Too much wampum not good for braves", Jerry intoned solemnly' (p. 218). Westerby, like a schoolboy, sees the world in terms of cowboys and Indians, a too easy classification it is suggested. Jim Prideaux retreats into a school where he can regale his pupils with the stories of John Buchan and sing nursery rhymes to himself: 'he set course directly for the caravan, singing "Hey diddle diddle" as loud as his tuneless voice would carry' (p. 238). Both Prideaux's and Westerby's Manichean views of the world are unsatisfactory.

Prideaux has not really moved very far in switching from the Circus to the public school. The language he uses as he speaks to Smiley is a language which could serve in either sphere of life, and Prideaux even identifies Control and himself as a pair of schoolboys playing games with a nursery-rhyme.

> He gave me a drink and we sat there like a pair of schoolboys making up a code, me and Control. We used Tinker, Tailor. We sat there in the flat putting it together, drinking that cheap Cyprus sherry he always gave. If I couldn't get out, if there was any fumble after I'd met Stevcek, if I had to go underground, I must get one word to him even if I had to go to Prague and chalk it on the Embassy door or ring the Prague resident and yell at him down the phone. Tinker, Tailor, Soldier, Sailor. (p. 245)

Fairy-tale and legend are common to both schoolboy and agent. Both appropriate the world too easily in terms of right and wrong, good and bad. At the end of *Tinker Tailor* the reader is made to see that this is all a dream.

This knowledge does not come easy however and Guillam is one of the first characters who has to deal with the situation when all his previous beliefs are shown as facile. When Haydon is eventually uncovered as the mole, Guillam is greatly disappointed.

> Haydon was more than his model, he was his inspiration, the torch-bearer of a certain kind of antiquated romanticism, a notion of English calling which—for the very reason that it was vague and understated and elusive—had made sense of Guillam's life till now. In that moment Guillam felt not merely betrayed; but orphaned. His suspicions, his resentments for so long turned outwards on the real world—on his women, his attempted loves—now swung upon the Circus and the failed magic which had formed his faith. (p. 299)

With the recognition of Haydon's treachery, Guillam feels 'orphaned' and the 'magic' of the Circus no longer offers him a secure position from which he is able to organize and order his life. After his sexual failings, his inability to relate fully to women and his dissatisfaction with life in general, this is another great disappointment. Again it is clear that the Circus operates as a microcosm, a substitute family for its members.

It is Smiley, however, who articulates most vividly the sense of disappointment and betrayal. The reader is not allowed to forget that this is a most difficult situation for Smiley; 'All these events and cameos unrolled with a theatrical unreality', we are told (p. 300). (Smiley's reaction is very similar to Roach's attitude to Prideaux's revolver.) Haydon's transgression is large, but Smiley's essential humanism still tries to forgive the man.

> Somewhere the path of pain and betrayal must end. Until that happened, there was no future: there was only a continual slide into still more terrifying versions of the present. This man was my friend and Ann's lover, Jim's friend and for all I know Jim's lover too; it was the treason not the man that belonged to the public domain. (p. 297)

It is necessary to concentrate on just what is meant by this reference to 'still more terrifying versions of the present'. Empire may have fixed philosophy so that there was a version of reality that accorded with the facts as understood by the English ruling-class at least. In his attempt to redeem Haydon or at least think less badly of him, Smiley can see how England's decline as a world power may be seen as a betrayal to Haydon.

> He saw with perfect clarity an ambitious man born to the big canvas, brought up to rule, divide and conquer, whose visions and vanities all were fixed, like Percy's, upon the world's game; for whom the reality was a poor island with scarcely a voice that would carry across the water. Thus Smiley felt not only disgust; but, despite all that the moment meant to him, a surge of resentment against the institutions he was supposed to be protecting. (p. 297)

I do not accept that this may be explained sufficiently as only a valorization of individual values and a critique of collectivism. It is that too, but the 'terrifying visions of the present' also render individualism untenable. Smiley, the popular hero of our

England in decline, is completely disillusioned. No values whatsoever are now tenable; there are only those terrifying versions of the present, one merely shadowing the other, expedients in a contingent world. In *Tinker Tailor* le Carré is writing about a chaotic post-modern England without value. The old values of Empire, such as they were, are antiquated now; contemporary society has no absolutes but merely competing, relative-value systems.

England has lost its voice on the political platform of world politics, and le Carré refuses to endorse either America or the Soviet Union. Hence the recourse to dreams.

> Smiley shrugged it all aside, distrustful as ever of the standard shapes of human motive, and settled instead for a picture of one of those wooden Russian dolls that open up, revealing one person inside the other, and another inside him. (p. 316)

Smiley is describing a world where there is no hierarchy of discourse, no final word. This can hardly be seen as a statement of individual humanism but more a statement of post-modern cynicism. And while there is the suggestion that Karla had 'seen the last doll inside Bill Haydon', this surely goes against the entire project of the novel. Karla had seen the last doll only up to that point in time but could not really predict Haydon's future behaviour. There is now no grammar to history or laws which might attempt to predict the future. It is fitting then that the novel should end with the words 'all a dream'. These are Roach's words and refer to Thursgood's. However, as so often before, Roach's comments also may be read as a reference to Smiley. At this point Smiley is travelling to Immingham in yet another attempt to reconcile himself with Ann. This is a hopeless task as the final description of Ann makes clear—'tall and puckish, extra-ordinarily beautiful, essentially another man's woman' (p. 317)—but le Carré applauds Smiley's effort. Smiley is doomed to failure but his blind faith and conviction is to be congratulated.

## NOTE

Page references are to the British paperback editions published by Pan: *The Looking-Glass War* in 1966, *Tinker Tailor Soldier Spy* in 1975, *Smiley's People* in 1980.

# 9

# The Writing on the Igloo Walls: Narrative Technique in *The Spy Who Came in from the Cold*

by ROBERT GIDDINGS

> Nothing amuses the Eskimo more than for the white man to crane his neck to see the magazine pictures stuck on the igloo walls. For the Eskimo no more needs to look at a picture right side up than does a child before he has learned his letters *on a line*. . . . The extreme bias and distortion of our sense-lives by our technology would seem to be a fact that we prefer to ignore in our daily lives.
> —Marshall McLuhan, *Understanding Media* (1964)[1]

One major result of the impact of French structuralism on English and American literary criticism has been the energy expended in deconstructing the rôle of the 'author'. This has been a long time in coming. Susan Sontag claims the movement has been going for a century.[2] Be that as it may, the movement is in full cry now:

> Inevitably, disestablishing the 'author' brings about a redefinition of 'writing'. Once writing no longer *defines* itself as responsible, the seemingly common-sense distinction between the work and the person who produces it, between public and private utterance, becomes void. All pre-modern literature evolves from the classical

188

conception of writing as an impersonal, self-sufficient, free-standing achievement. Modern literature projects a quite different idea: the romantic conception of writing as a medium in which a singular personality heroically exposes itself. This ultimately private reference of public, literary discourse does not require that the reader actually know a great deal about the author. . . .[3]

Thus (and more) Susan Sontag. Many issues come into play in the discussion of authorship and the rôle of the reader, and, as Susan Sontag is generously the very first to admit, consciousness as given can never wholly constitute itself in art but must always strain to transform its own boundaries and to condition the boundaries of art. Within these boundaries the reader needs to know why, and how, so many of John le Carré's effects can be rendered cinematically with such apparent ease. Le Carré's pictorial imagination can be *placed*.

Between the 'author' and the 'reader'—the creator and the consumer, as it were—the shape, texture and condition of form, which is the result of the technology of production and distribution, intrudes itself. The means of production will have an immense, immediate and obvious impact on the nature of the art produced in any culture. Artists work within the technical limitations of their day. Geniuses transcend them. Whether Homer existed as an identifiable unique individual is not the issue here; the important fact is that 'Homer' produced the unique and overwhelming masterpieces the world now knows as the *Iliad* and the *Odyssey* in the way that he did because the existing mode of literary production of the day favoured the telling of long stories rhapsodically.[4] Oral culture reached the mind through the ear; its culture had to be memorable.

The advent of printing seriously eroded the necessity of patterned language, as literary works no longer required memory and recitation for their production and consumption. As prose narrative began to replace epic a noticeable exactitude of geography and chronology became a feature of what we now recognize as 'the novel'—although its beginnings are clearly to be seen in much Elizabethan prose. John Lyly goes to some trouble to create a believable sense of time, smattering the narrative with times and days and months, in *Euphues: The Anatomy of Wit* (1578) and *Euphues and his England* (1580):

189

'Euphues, having gotten all things necessary for his voyage into *England* . . . tooke shipping the first of December, by our English Computation. . . .'[5] In sixteenth- and early seventeenth-century drama, location is not always very important. If the audience need to know where the action is taking place, they will be told ('Ay, now am I in Arden: the more fool I . . .'), but otherwise the action could be located generally in a forest, in a street, a palace, a hovel, a coastline or a battlefield. But at the same time we begin to notice that the writers of narrative prose fiction are starting to particularize time and place. Miguel de Cervantes went to considerable trouble to get time and place correctly ascribed in his *Exemplary Novels*, which were published in 1613. Samuel Putnam comments on the exact topography of *Rinconete and Cortadillo*:

> The Molinillo inn at which the two lads meet was situated on the road from Toledo to Cordova; it was two leagues from Tartanedo and four leagues from Almodovar del Campo; and the Alcade inn, as stated, was half a league distant. . . . The allusions to sites in and about Seville are similarly accurate. . . .[6]

Similar comments could be directed at the realistic elements in le Carré's beloved *Simplicissimus* (think of Smiley, in *Tinker Tailor*, contemplating the sale of an early edition of Grimmelshausen).

Hearing, rather than sight, had dominated the more ancient poetic world which preceded writing, and even those societies which experienced the revolution of writing and became manuscript cultures were still oral–aural. Texts could be written down and preserved, but a large part of what we would recognize as 'literature' was still committed to memory. The reasons are obvious—manuscripts were expensive and not in very wide circulation, they were often not easy to read and a high proportion of the population were not literate. The coming of print revolutionized the way we wrote about the world and the way we perceived the world. In the words of Walter Ong:

> . . . print replaced the lingering hearing-dominence in the world of thought and expression with the sight-dominence which had its beginnings with writing but could not flourish with the support of writing alone. Print situates words in space more relentlessly than writing ever did. . . .
>
> Most readers are of course not consciously aware of all this

locomotion that has produced the printed text confronting them. Nevertheless, from the appearance of the printed text they pick up a sense of the word-in-space quite different from that conveyed by writing. Printed texts look machine-made, as they are. Chirographic control of space tends to be ornamental, ornate, as in calligraphy. Typographic control typically impresses more by its tidiness and inevitability: the lines perfectly regular, all justified on the right side, everything coming out even visually. . . . This is an insistent world of cold, non-human, facts. . . .[7]

As the means of literary production seemed to emphasize this sense of reality as a result of the very shape and texture of their product, so the creative imaginations of writers inclined, during the centuries which succeeded the invention and development of printing and paper manufacture, to concentrate on an output which attempted credible reality. Sometimes the technology gave rise to an almost immediate reaction in literature. Clearly the modern novel is the child of the printing revolution. Samuel Richardson's creation of a new literary genre, the epistolary novel—which plays so significant a part in the course of Leavis's Great Tradition and led directly to the rich psychological novels of George Eliot and Henry James—was the direct result of technical developments in the industry which employed him.

Richardson was born the son of a London joiner but was apprenticed to the printer John Wilde at Aldersgate when he was 17 years old. He became compositor, proof-reader and later printer on his own account. He published newspapers and books, printed the Journals of the House of Commons and as Master of the Stationers' Company and Law-Printer to the King was a solid citizen. His contribution to literature had been minor. He compiled a few indexes and wrote a few dedications, but that was that. But he was approached by two successful booksellers, Charles Rivington of St. Paul's Churchyard and Thomas Osborne of Paternoster Row, who asked him to write a model letter-writer for such 'country readers' as 'were unable to indite for themselves'. Richardson compiled a book which they published, *Letters written to and for Particular Friends, on the most Important Occasions*. But Richardson also realized that a story could be told as a series of letters and that telling a story in this

191

way would have several significant advantages. Letters are human documents. They are personal to those who write them and to those for whom they are intended. In reading letters the consumer of a novel so constructed would believe they were overhearing an unfolding series of real events involving real people. Point of view could be exploited. Motives could be explored. All this could be done in ways which were new to the novel and which would in turn be absorbed into the way succeeding novelists created novels. The publication of Richardson's *Pamela; or Virtue Rewarded* in November 1740 ensured that the novel would never be the same again. The following February a second edition had appeared; a third appeared in March and a fourth in May. Ladies held up copies of the book at public gardens to show that they had got it, and Dr. Benjamin Slocock of Southwark commended it from his pulpit.

Impressive though its immediate vogue obviously was, the importance of Richardson's *Pamela* is deeper than that, and for all the mockery of Henry Fielding and the author of *An Apology for the Life of Mrs. Shamela Andrews* (1741)—they may have been one and the same person—the novel had made a leap forward and there would be no retreating, although masked for a while by the triumph of *Tom Jones* and the earlier novels of Smollett whose great strength was in narrative synthesis, Richardson had definitively pointed the way forward to the novel of analysis.

The application of steam power to printing and the development of the railway complex throughout Britain were changes which brought great opportunities not only to periodic journalism but to novel 'authorship' in the widest sense. William Nicholson took out a patent for a cylinder press in 1790, but it was Frederick Koenig in Germany who constructed the first power-driven press in 1811. His pioneering work was built on by Andrew Bauer who made a flat-bed printing machine with a continually revolving cylinder. The issue of *The Times* for 29 November 1814 proclaimed that it 'was printed by steam power'. This machine could produce 1,100 impressions an hour, and by 1827 these machines could print on both sides of the sheet. Applegarth and Cowper produced a machine for *The Times* before 1830 which could print 4,000 impressions an hour.

The age of popular publishing, much of it financed by serial publication, had dawned.[8] An essential aspect of Dickens's genius lay in its ability to adapt itself to the new developments in literary production and distribution. Serial publication was a good way for a story-teller to earn a living, but a narrative extended over eighteen months—and most of Dickens's novels were serialized in monthly parts over a year and a half—required the ability to handle a vast canvas with complex plots and numerous characters,[9] but he was influenced significantly by other technological developments in the arts in the early nineteenth century, notably melodrama.[10] There are numerous passages in Dickens's novels which are obviously influenced by the craze for melodrama, where we can see the novelist deliberately and often painstakingly seeking to reproduce on the printed page some of the gaslit and—to modern tastes—garish and crude excitement of the stage:

> 'I have learnt it!' cried the old man. 'From the creature dearest to my heart! O, save her, save her!' He could wind his fingers in her dress; could hold it! As the words escaped his lips, he felt his sense of touch return, and knew that he detained her.
> The figures looked down steadfastly upon him.
> 'I have learnt it!' cried the old man. 'O, have mercy on me in this hour, if, in my love for her, so young and good, I slandered Nature in the breasts of mothers rendered desperate! Pity my presumption, wickedness, and ignorance, and save her.'

This is Dickens writing under the power of a good head of steam in the *Fourth Quarter* of *The Chimes*, published by Chapman and Hall in December 1844, and even allowing for the fact that it is the narrative of a series of dreams experienced by Toby Veck who falls asleep on New Year's Eve while reading a newspaper, it must be admitted that the language is hardly what we would expect from a London ticket-porter in reduced circumstances. But the language of melodrama becomes absorbed into the general apparatus of the novelist's craft, as Edith Granger's rejection of the advances of Mr. Carker in *Dombey and Son* (1846–48) will testify. The requirements of the lending library also had an impact on the novelist's art. As an undergraduate I remember being constantly reminded by my mentors of the brilliant compression of Henry James's imagination and the deep, rich, vast, bottomless hugeness of his mind as it expressed itself in slender volume form. Many years later I was to learn that by the time Henry James came upon the scene considerable changes in the material mode of literary production had meant a shift from what Terry Eagleton has described as 'the densely populated "three-decker" novel, with its diffuse, multiple plots', to the 'more "organic" single volume'.[11]

In the early cinema we see film working on the basic assumptions of narrative prose fiction and drama and basing its grammar and syntax initially on the existing literary traditions. This early literary allegiance is well demonstrated in examples which enshrine a profound contradiction in terms—silent versions of Shakespeare, such as Emil Jannings's *Othello* (1922), Johnston Forbes Robertson's *Hamlet* (1913) and Herbert Beerbohm Tree's *Macbeth* (1916, directed by D. W. Griffith). Moving film was able to exploit the innate authority of photography, which—as Marshall McLuhan has argued—extends and multiplies the human image to the proportions of mass-produced merchandise, yet, by drawing on the western European experience of print and painting, creates a false world which we fully believe in; characteristically he coined a pun for it—the reel world.

The cinema was originally called 'The Bioscope' because it was claimed that it could present the actual forms of life, in the form of a public spectacle. Moving film, McLuhan claims, is a spectacular wedding of the old mechanical technology and the new electric world. In a brilliant minor masterpiece, only a few pages in length, McLuhan likened the cinema spectator to Don Quixote. Like Cervantes' hero the viewer of film is wholly and completely transferred from one world—his own—to another, that world created by typography and film:

> That is so obvious, and happens so completely, that those undergoing the experience accept it subliminally and without critical awareness. Cervantes lived in a world in which print was as new as movies are in the West, and it seemed obvious to him that print, like the images now on the screen, had usurped the real world. The reader or spectator had become a dreamer under their spell. . . .[12]

McLuhan goes on to elaborate his argument that moving film as a non-verbal experience may be compared with photography, as a form of statement without syntax. Like print and photography, moving film assumes a very high-level literacy in those who use film. Film is baffling to the non-literate. Although film is an imitation of life, it has to be read, and we have to learn to read it. Film does have some kind of powerful impact on those who have not seen it before. McLuhan quotes the celebrated examples of the African natives who wanted to know where characters went when they went off screen as evidence of the case that the linear logic and grammar of film has to be learned; nevertheless the surface quality of film itself, even in its black and white form and with no sound track, does show a world of movement which looks like life. It is an historically attested fact, and a fact of considerable significance, that on 10 March 1895 when the first celluloid film was projected to an audience by Louis Lumière, the viewers left their seats in fright when they saw film of a train arriving in a station.[13] The point appears to need some emphasis; film is its own language, with its own way of telling things. The full cultural apprehension of film may not come until we have learned the grammar and syntax of the new language—let us go that far with McLuhan as the argument seems on the whole to be a sound one—*but* the initial, immediate impact of film seems charged with innate information. After all, the Lumière film of the train was totally silent,[14] and yet it carried enough information to convince its audience that what they were seeing was 'real'. It is a strong part of McLuhan's argument that a literate audience, used to following printed imagery line by line without questioning the logicality of lineality, will be more ready to accept film sequence. It seems, then, that when film appears in our culture at the turn of the nineteenth and twentieth centuries, it is able to build on the very sturdy foundations laid in western European culture by our long experience of writing and printing and reading. In other words, cinematography was an extension of literacy.

As McLuhan points out, it was René Clair—whose early professional experience was literary (he was a journalist) but who went into films from beginning as an actor and wrote and directed many films, including *A Nous la Liberté, Quatorze Juillet, Le Dernier Milliardaire, Les Belles de Nuit, Les Grandes Manoeuvres*— who observed that if three characters bore on stage, the dramatist ceaselessly has to strive to explain or motivate their

being there, whereas a film audience will simply accept mere
sequence as rational. Whatever the moving camera shows us,
we accept as part of what the film-maker wants to tell us. We
are transported to another world:

> The close relation, then, between the reel world of film and the
> private fantasy experience of the printed word is indispensable to
> our Western acceptance of the film form. Even the film industry
> regards all of its greatest achievements as derived from novels,
> nor is this unreasonable. Film, both in its reel form and in its
> scenario or script form, is completely involved with book culture.[15]

The emphasis on associating literature and film owes a great
deal for its surviving success in film theory to the imprimatur of
almost classical authority granted it by Sergei Eisenstein. It was
Eisenstein who located the primal springs of Griffith's genius as
a film-maker in the novels of Dickens.[16] A theorist who comes to
the matter from the other direction is Siegfried Kracauer.
Kracauer has a great deal to say about the surface quality of
film, about matters of style and the flexibility of film as a
language which, he believes, are the result of its ultimate
derivation from photography:

> Like the embryo in the womb, photographic film developed from
> distinctly separate components. Its birth came about from a
> combination of instantaneous photography. . . . with the older
> devices of the magic lantern and the phenakistoscope. Added to
> this later were the contributions of other nonphotographic
> elements, such as editing and sound. Nevertheless, photography,
> especially instantaneous photography, has a legitimate claim to
> top priority among these elements, for it undeniably is and
> remains the decisive factor in establishing film content. The
> nature of photography survives in that of film.[17]

The craze for structuralist analysis of texts has tended to
emphasize the importance of deep structural meanings, hidden
agendas, and mythic structures of narrative meaning based on
the relationship between characters. This has often been
extremely valuable, but the work of Propp and Eco has tended,
in the main, to divert attention from the surface structure of
works which attempt something in the narrative mode.[18]
Kracauer's words bring us back to focus our attention on those
qualities we immediately perceive, that we perceive with such

immediacy that we do not notice them: the photographic quality of moving film, its ability to be stuck together as a raw material by a film-maker of genius and turned into an artwork; the latent charge in film which can be so edited in montage that new meanings can be constructed in a process which cinematographically parallels dialectic materialism—thesis/antithesis/synthesis[19]; the manner in which film enables us to concentrate on reaction as much as on action; and on all the tricks of the trade in terms of sound and vision. Kracauer is correct to assert that it is the very nature of photography which survives in film and which establishes film *content*.

The argument that film is a degenerate art and that to adapt classic novels for films is to corrupt sacred texts is a familiar one in British culture. (Its leading exponent is Dr. Jonathan Miller.) It is impossible literally to translate a novel into film terms. Certain things possible in literature (which are among the things which make literature the great high cultural commodity which it is assumed to be) are not possible in film. For example, in *Great Expectations* Dickens likens Wemmick to a post-box. He does more than this, of course, being the great poet that he is; he says that Wemmick does not so much eat his food as post it. Now, how can we show that in film? We can show Wemmick eating and then cut in (or even fade up) a post-box. But what will that do? It will make viewers think that Wemmick is thinking about posting a letter as he is eating. Or it may suggest that Wemmick works for the Post Office. But it cannot convey what Dickens wants to convey.

Much as we may respect the argument that the way we read film owes much to our experience of reading written or printed words, there are numerous ways in which the language of film must be seen as unique to itself and not just an extension of literature.

Moving film can show a whole scene, a room full of people, a landscape, a street—all in one moving shot—so that a great deal of information can be delivered in one go. This is beyond literature. It has enormous powers, then, of exposition—and it is significant that exposition is one of the most difficult things convincingly to bring off in literature. The fact that film can be shot in pieces then stuck together at will in the editing process gives film a whole battery of effects not available in literature:

fading, dissolving, cutting. An effect such as the scream of the landlady suddenly cutting to the shriek of express train bound for Scotland in Hitchcock's *The Thirty-Nine Steps* (1935) would not be possible in literature.[20] The multiplicity of angles and points of view which can be brought together all in the same moment—such as the murder of Marion in *Psycho* (1960)—can only be constructed in film. It is tribute to film, and of course to the genius of Hitchcock, that many people who have seen *Psycho* believe the murder-in-the-shower scene to be in colour and that they have seen the knife enter Marion Crane's bare body. This amazing sequence is a superb example of the film-makers' art. It is a combination of photography (it needed a week of filming, and seventy-eight set-ups), editing (it lasts only a minute on screen) and sound (the music by Bernard Herrmann adds to visual effects rather than simply supporting them).[21]

In film it is possible much more easily than in drama or narrative prose to concentrate on reaction. For example, we can see the face and changing reactions of a person as we hear the voice and sounds proving the information which prompts those reactions. Our response to what we see can be conditioned by the angle and distance of camera shots selected by the director and editor of film. This is not possible in drama. This quality in film is repeatedly exploited by Eisenstein. Flashback is extremely effective in film but very difficult indeed in drama or narrative prose, as film is very strong at creating the idea of 'present' time—the time that you are actually watching the action—and then reverting easily into a sequence clearly signalled as the 'past'. Orson Welles constantly exploits this in *Citizen Kane* (1940).[22] The endless tricks possible with the camera—deep focus, multiple image, mixing, fading, filtering, point-of-view, zooming and tracking—add a whole new vocabulary to narrative which does not exist elsewhere.[23] To dismiss film as degenerate and of lower intrinsic aesthetic merit than drama or the novel is to be a cultural Luddite. But the mythology is very strong.

Film and television are media with their own languages— languages no less worthy of respect than the printed text. But it is in the nature of the production and consumption of 'high culture' in our society that there is an in-built snobbery about print. Bernard Levin commented, in a book review in the *Sunday*

*Times* in September 1983, that a particular author's technique 'of undercutting . . . has a cinematic gloss but also a cinematic superficiality.' So there you have it, stated for all it is worth—literature is *ipso facto* a higher art than film.

Cultural snobbery has always demonstrated itself by its allegiance to the immediately preceding mode of production. We have all heard it: 'Have you seen X?' 'No. But I have read the book. . . .' To have read the book is better than to have seen the film. It is significant that to have heard the radio version of something on the B.B.C. is slightly better than having seen the film of the same thing. This is an essential part of the grammar of culture. It is the argument of fashion and anti-fashion. The trick is to resist change, which is always perceived as a sign of degeneracy. The classics are relics from previous modes of production.

The ability to adapt to change, Charles Darwin believed, was one of the things which enabled life to survive. But we still resist new forms of cultural production and distribution. The classics are good for you. It is as simple as that. They are to the soul what a high-fibre diet is to the body. It is vastly more upmarket to consume the wholemeal of 'literature' and 'the theatre' (e.g. the West End theatre) than to consume the junk food of the mass media.

Very recent cultural history will show how this grammar actually works. Hollywood musicals of the '30s and '40s were originally regarded as shallow, cheap, ephemeral entertainment. The next stage was the development of a camp interest in the genre. Today, the 'best' of them are regarded as classics, worthy of being shown on B.B.C. 2, the channel of opera, Jane Austen and documentaries about Evelyn Waugh. The consequences of this are considerable. It means that the more what is seen on television, for example, is 'like' literature, the 'better' it is. That is to say *Barchester Chronicles, Brideshead Revisited, Kilvert's Diary, Mansfield Park, The Jewel in the Crown, Tender is the Night, Hotel du Lac*—O.K. But *Minder, Rumpole, The Likely Lads, Auf Wiedersehen Pet* and other popular favourites are hardly acceptable. It means that a lacklustre, overdressed movie such as *A Room with a View*, in which a team of well-intentioned British thespians seem to be enunciating their lines as if fearful that the actual words might come to some harm as they leave their lips, was hailed as a great film in 1986.

But there have now been several generations of writers who lost their innocence by being exposed to the cinema. It could be argued that the cinema has influenced developments in modern narrative prose fiction. It is well-documented fact that Evelyn Waugh loved going to the pictures. No one would claim that Waugh was, by any stretch of critical generosity, a 'novelist's novelist'. His novels are markedly free from literary associations. Poor Tony Last is condemned to reading the novels of Dickens to the end of his life. The narrative sequence of *Brideshead Revisited* is constructed as one vast flashback. Len Deighton is another interesting example. He was educated at art school and has always admitted his admiration for the movies, especially espionage movies. The narrative infrastructure of his novels owes much to his experiences at the cinema and indeed, unlike the heavyweights of the British literary establishment (that is to say, those who are more likely to win the Booker Prize than Len Deighton is), he was never exposed to an Eng. Lit. education. In his creation of his working-class hero—Harry Palmer—and the series of adventures in which he is usually placed (*The Ipcress File* (1962), *Horse Under Water* (1963), and *Funeral in Berlin* (1964)) he seems to have created a kind of novel whose genre really belongs, root and branch, to the cinema. Alistair MacLean is another novelist whose espionage/adventure novels seem naturally made for the cinema—in particular *Puppet on a Chain*, *Where Eagles Dare* and *Bear Island*. Interestingly enough, when the considerable literary abilities of Graham Greene (novel) and Tom Stoppard (screenplay) were combined in *The Human Factor* (1979) the results were emphatically not good cinema. John le Carré has achieved a considerable feat in combining some very characteristic elements of the cinema with the requirements of prose narrative. He has created a *genre* unmistakably his own: the espionage story in the form of a novel with 'class'. He has his entry in Margaret Drabble's edition of *The Oxford Companion to English Literature* (1985)[24] and his novels have been serialized on B.B.C. 2 as starring vehicles for Sir Alec Guinness. The similarity with Graham Greene is worth recalling for several reasons. Like Greene, le Carré had a public school and Oxford education, and worked for the British Foreign Office. Both authors share an interest in the seedy and the ambiguous as qualities of life in the modern world, both in terms of private and public life.

Graham Greene spent four-and-a-half years immediately before the outbreak of war in 1939 as a film reviewer, and we therefore have some very useful insight as to his views and opinions of numerous films. Interestingly enough, he did not like Hitchcock, who had—it seemed to Greene—an 'inadequate sense of reality'. He had a low opinion of *The Thirty-Nine Steps*. The oft-praised details of Hitchcock's films, Greene claimed, added up to nothing:

> His films consist of a series of small 'amusing' melodramatic situations: the murderer's button dropped on the baccarat board; the strangled organist's hands prolonging the notes in an empty church . . . very perfunctorily he builds up to these tricky situations (paying no attention on the way to inconsistencies, loose ends, psychological absurdities) and then drops them: they mean nothing: they lead to nothing.[25]

Greene himself divided his fictions into two categories: entertainments and novels, and in this respect he seems aware of the entertainment value of films. Of course, many of his fictions have been turned into films, and he has written screenplays.[26] He notes with obvious relish the cinema's ability to construct and to project atmosphere, particularly (in those monocrome days) the atmosphere of decay, fear, treachery and things falling apart in general. Writing of the 1935 remake of Liam O'Flaherty's novel, *The Informer*, directed by John Ford and starring Victor McLaglen, Greene said:

> It is superb material for the screen: very few words are needed for this drama; terror is not a subtle sensation: it can be conveyed very much easier by images alone than scruples, guilt, tenderness. You only need the Black and Tan patrols through the Liffey fogs, the watching secretive figures outside the saloons as the drunken informer drifts deeper and deeper with his cronies into the seedy night life of Dublin. Mr. Victor MacLaglen has never given an abler performance, and the film, even if it sometimes underlines its points rather crudely, is a memorable picture of a pitiless war waged without honour on either side in doorways and cellars and gin-shops. (*Spectator*, 11 October 1935)[27]

Graham Greene highlights several qualities which are highly relevant when considering the fiction of John le Carré. One is the generation of atmosphere—the fog which is also emblematic of moral ambiguity. The endless, meaningless conflict (The Troubles in this case, but in le Carré's case, the Cold War) within which human beings and their torments and tensions get drawn into and the way human beings devalue their own high moral conception of themselves and the motives behind their high-principled actions by selling each other. As is so often the case in *film noir* as a genre, the story is difficult to follow (cf. *The Big Sleep*), but the incomprehensibility of what is going on is part of the sophistication itself as well as being emblematic of the confusions and contradictions of modern life itself.

It seems to me that one of the permanent fascinations of John le Carré's art is the way he has inverted the usual practice, and instead of adapting fiction to film, he has adapted film to fiction. *The Spy Who Came in from the Cold* was published in 1963, a year after Ian Fleming's *Dr. No* had been filmed. There was a spate of espionage movies, mostly with a Cold War backdrop, during the 1960s, which was the decade when John le Carré's fiction began to make its unmistakable mark. Among the titles which come most easily to mind are *The Manchurian Candidate* (1962), *From Russia With Love* (1963), *Hot Enough for June* (1963), *Licensed to Kill* (1965), *Goldfinger* (1964), *Charade* (1964), *Thunderball* (1965), *Operation Crossbow* (1965), *Where the Spies Are* (1965), *The Liquidator* (1965), *Our Mr. Flint* (1965)—(*The Spy Who Came in from the Cold* was released in 1966)—*Torn Curtain* (1966), *Arabesque* (1966), *Funeral in Berlin* (1967), *The Naked Runner* (1967), *Double Man* (1967), *Assignment K* (1968) and *On Her Majesty's Secret Service* (1969). Between 1964 and 1967 our television screens regularly gave us *The Man From U.N.C.L.E.* John le Carré's fiction, then, offered the literary equivalent to the genre of espionage thriller which was very much in vogue. His genius lies in adding ingredients of his own, and working the mixture up in terms of narrative prose fiction which passes muster as 'literature'. That entry in *The Oxford Companion* must not be ignored.

Le Carré imports much from the language and style of popular film in *The Spy Who Came in from the Cold*. It is located in a situation which does not seem to need any explication—the Cold War is simply *there* (like The Troubles in *The Informer* and in much modern television drama set in Ireland) as a backdrop for the melodrama of the foreground. The basic plot mechanism

concerns a British professional spy of considerable expertise; he
is set up in a situation so that it seems he is finished, then fired
and dismissed from the service. This is done to make him an
obvious target for recruitment by 'the enemy'. This in turn has
been planned so that he may be used to destroy his great
opponent and opposite number behind the Iron Curtain, Hans-
Dieter Mundt. The narrative tricks are all familiar ones, and
they are familiar because we have all seen them many times
before in the movies. As Leslie Halliwell tersely observes, it is
no more and no less than 'The old undercover yarn with trimmings . . .'.[28] But when examined it is clear that many, if not
all, the worthwhile qualities (or trimmings, if one insists on
Halliwell's phrase) are there on the pages of le Carré's novel. It
reads like a film. The exposition in the opening pages is
astonishingly cinematic. Le Carré's imagination seems to present
itself on the page in the manner of a film; his story unfolds like a
movie. It is monochrome. Not much seems to happen. The
dialogue is laconic. Details of landscape and location and of
character are sparse:

> The American handed Leamas another cup of coffee and said,
> 'Why don't you go back and sleep? We can ring you if he shows
> up.'
> Leamas said nothing, just stared through the window of the
> checkpoint, along the empty street.[29]

Unlike that familiar sense in an English novel that you are at
the beginning of something, which will have a middle and,
eventually, an end, you seem at the opening of *The Spy Who Came
in from the Cold*, suddenly to be *there*, in the middle of things.
Films do not open, as novels do. You enter them. You sit in the
dark. The credits roll by *and you are there in the action*:

> 'You can't wait for ever . . . he's nine hours over schedule.'
> 'If you want to go, go. You've been very good,' Leamas added.
> 'I'll tell Kramer you've been damn good.'
> 'But how long will you wait?'
> 'Until he comes.' Leamas walked to the observation window
> and stood between the two motionless policemen. Their binocu-
> lars were trained on the Eastern checkpoint.
> 'He's waiting for the dark,' Leamas muttered, 'I know he is.'
> 'This morning you said he'd come across with the workmen.'
> Leamas turned on him.

'Agents aren't aeroplanes. They don't have schedules. He's blown, he's on the run, he frightened. Mundt's after him, now, at this moment. He's only got one chance. Let him choose his time.'[30]

The detail is very sparse as we come into the midst of the action. The dialogue is very curt, cinematic. The action is present and continuous. The difficulty we have in attempting to understand what is going on is all part of the sophisticated incomprehensibility of the genre, which contributes to its hardboiled and cynical nature. It must have been simple to translate this to the screen. It was not 'written for' the cinema, but it is in the style of a series of films immediately recognizable to the generation which would have seen any of that series of gunmen/spy melodramas directed by Carol Reed in the late 1940s and early 1950s: *Odd Man Out* (1946), *The Third Man* (1949) and *The Man Between* (1953).

The ingredients are immediately recognizable. There is a grainy black-and-white realism, bordering on the harsh and inhuman. The setting is invariably a large urban area—Dublin, Berlin, Vienna, it does not really matter—which is torn apart by some vast inexplicable international or internecine conflict which divides people into goodies and baddies. Moral values are reduced to black-and-white terms. And yet the entire moral ambience is ambiguous. Who is really virtuous? Who is really guilty? Who really wins, in the end? The conflicts and tensions within which the human beings we watch have to play out their pitiful destinies are confusing to those caught within them. We who are watching do not need even to know the whys and wherefores of them. It is enough that we acknowledge that they are there. What made these movies so intoxicating was their atmospheric intrigue, and it is this which John le Carré has so brilliantly transported to the printed page:

> Pushing up the collar of his jacket, Leamas stepped outside into the icy October wind. He remembered the crowd then. It was something you forgot inside the hut, this group of puzzled faces. The people changed but the expressions were the same. It was like the helpless crowd that gathers round a traffic accident, no one knowing how it happened, whether you should move the body. Smoke or dust rose through the beam of the arc-lamps, a constant shifting pall between the margins of light.[31]

Le Carré is at his most efficient and sparkling at this kind of thing, because it is intensely visual. He has certain images and effects of light in his imagination as he writes, and it his gift to be able to translate these visual impressions into words. It is not simply a matter of landscape and description, though, for he is equally brilliant in evoking action. The scene where Karl finally appears riding his bicycle and is shot before Leamas's eyes contains some of le Carré's finest writing, because he makes you see exactly what Leamas sees, as he sees it. You are there, as it happens:

> The East German fired, quite carefully, away from them, into his own sector. The first shot seemed to thrust Karl forward, the second to pull him back. Somehow he was still moving, still on the bicycle, passing the sentry, and the sentry was still shooting at him. Then he sagged, rolled to the ground, and they heard quite clearly the clatter of the bike as it fell. . . .[32]

He is at his weakest at those very moments at which novelists are supposed to shine. Le Carré is not convincing when he tries to convey what his characters are thinking. His prose then becomes laboured and we sense a straining after the right images and metaphors. The result is a rather turgid literariness:

> Leamas was not a reflective man and not a particularly philosophical one. He knew he was written off—it was a fact of life which he would henceforth live with, as a man must live with cancer or imprisonment. He knew there was no kind of preparation which could have bridged the gap between then and now. He met failure as one day he would probably meet death, with cynical resentment and the courage of the solitary. He'd lasted longer than most; now he was beaten. It is said a dog lives as long as its teeth; metaphorically, Leamas's teeth had been drawn; and it was Mundt who had drawn them.[33]

This is not good writing. It is inelegant and unsure of itself. It lacks clarity and the syntax betrays its basic lack of purpose. It is unmistakably what it is—an Englishman trying to write as Hemingway and not making a very good job of it. Yet the moment le Carré writes visually his prose comes to life in his hands in a way which is almost electrical:

> They walked to her flat through the rain and they might have been anywhere—Berlin, London, any town where paving stones

turn to lakes of light in the evening rain, and the traffic shuffles despondently through wet streets.[34]

This is the writing of a mind fully and congenially engaged in its subject-matter. The sentences read well because the ideas and images are clear in the writer's mind; le Carré knows what he wants his readers to see and he can reproduce it easefully on the page before you. The whole of his early relationship with Liz is handled with equal brilliance, right up to the moment she leaves him:

> 'Good-bye, Liz,' he said. 'Good-bye,' and then: 'Don't follow me. Not again.'
> Liz nodded and muttered: 'Like we said.' She was thankful for the biting cold of the street and for the dark which hid her tears.[35]

This is supremely confident prose which knows where it is going. One notices time and again that when le Carré presents action, it is always seen externally, in cinematic terms. This is true even where the real nature of the action is necessarily ambiguous, such as the scene in the grocer's shop when Leamas assaults the shopkeeper. We see what happens as the camera would see it. We hear what is said, we see people's reactions, we seem to see Leamas strike the grocer, but we are not exactly sure what happens. We do not learn the real professional details until we hear what was said in court about the fractured cheek bone and the dislocated jaw. At moments such as these, le Carré's prose leaps into life. It always weakens when he is trying to show what is in a character's mind. It is then the syntax faulters and similes and metaphors become leaden:

> Christ, they're rushing their fences, Leamas thought; it's indecent. He remembered some silly music hall joke—'This is an offer no respectable girl could accept—and besides, I don't know what it's worth.' Tactically, he reflected, they're right to rush it. I'm on my uppers, prison experience still fresh, social resentment strong. I'm an old horse, I don't need breaking in; I don't have to pretend they've offended my honour as an English gentleman. On the other hand they would expect *practical* objections. They would expect him to be afraid; for his Service pursued traitors as the eye of God followed Cain across the desert.[36]

The plot structure of *The Spy Who Came in from the Cold* is one that would be familiar to those with a wide experience of movie dramas of the '40s and '50s: good guy set up as bait by dismissal and criminal conviction so as to be snaffled up by the bad guys, thus providing the entrance to the labyrinth where the answer to the problem may be found. But it is also put before us cinematically: the lengthy section which details the steady establishment of the relationship between Leamas and Peters not only looks and reads like cinematic material, but le Carré uses this opportunity for lengthy flashbacks which fill in all kinds of details we need to know about Leamas's past and the espionage operations.[37]

The narrative techniques are all strongly reminiscent of the movies. There is the cross-cutting between what is happening to Liz in London and what happens to Alec Leamas in East Germany. He signs letters he does not fully understand. He begins to fear the whole thing is going wrong. Then he is arrested and comes face to face with Mundt:

> Above him shone the light, large, clinical and fierce. No furniture, just whitewashed walls, quite close all round, and the grey steel door, a smart charcoal grey, the colour you see on clever London houses. There was nothing else. Nothing at all. Nothing to think about, just the savage pain.
>
> He must have lain there hours before they came. It grew hot from the light, he was thirsty but he refused to call out. At last the door opened and Mundt stood there. He knew it was Mundt from the eyes. Smiley had told him about them.[38]

The climax of *The Spy Who Came in from the Cold*, which covers the tribunal, is written in a magnetic style. I do not think le Carré ever surpasses it in any of his other novels. It is entirely gripping from beginning to end. But it is based on a model which the cinema very early in its history found was wholly appropriate to the kind of narrative it could cope with—the trial. The gradual unravelling of the truth of a matter, through the presentation of the case by opposing advocates, the interrogation of witnesses, the presentation of witnesses—all this has become an area of dramatic technique wholly suitable to cinema with its effective use of cross-cutting, reactions shots and unique ability denied to stage drama of focusing attention entirely and directly at its own will. What better witness could we call than Leslie Halliwell, who deposed in the *Filmgoer's Companion*: 'Courtroom scenes have been the suspenseful saving grace of more films than can be counted; and they also figure in some of the best films ever made.'[39]

The deception and exploitation of Alec Leamas does not dawn on him; it strikes him 'with the terrible clarity of a man too long deceived . . .'.[40] At the same moment we too become aware of the whole plot mechanism. All the pieces suddenly make sense, just as in *Citizen Kane* the riddle of 'Rosebud' is resolved in a flash. And once again we must acknowledge the mastery with which the basic lessons and principles of film narrative have been fully absorbed—albeit unconsciously in all probability—by John le Carré, and carried over into narrative prose. Technology and science made new things possible and in turn some of these new and exciting possibilities have been carried over into the craft of the novel. Graham Greene has publicly opined that *The Spy Who Came in from the Cold* is the best spy story he has ever read—and this comment is printed on the back cover of the paperback edition. It is not hyperbole to claim that it is also the best spy story ever written, but it must be acknowledged that the art of the cinema made it possible. It was John le Carré who had the sense to exploit those possibilities. The last fourteen pages of the novel, the chapters 'The Wall' and 'In from the Cold', comprise almost entirely dialogue and visual descriptions of the very bleak location where the final catastrophes occur. Their impact on the imagination, stark and powerful as they are, is entirely the result of their cinematic quality.

John le Carré is the master of this particular genre. We need not seek for those qualities of moral awareness and deep psychological probing, combined with irony and compassion which Dr. F. R. Leavis and his followers have taught us to expect from the novel. If every picture tells a story, not all stories can be told in pictures.

## NOTES

1. Marshall McLuhan, 'The Photograph—Brothel Without Walls' in *Understanding Media* (Routledge & Kegan Paul, 1964), p. 204.
2. Susan Sontag, *Under the Sign of Capricorn* (Writers and Readers, 1980), p. 13.

3. Sontag, op. cit., p. 15.
4. Walter Ong, *Orality and Literacy: The Technologising of the World* (Methuen, 1982), pp. 17ff.
5. John Lyly, *Euphues and his England* (1580; London, Arber Reprints, 1910), p. 225.
6. Miguel Cervantes, *Three Exemplary Novels*, translated by Samuel Putnam (Cassell, 1952), pp. 221–22.
7. Walter Ong, *Rhetoric, Romance and Technology* (Ithaca and London: Cornell University Press, 1971), pp. 284–303. See Keith Selby, *Time and the Novel*, unpublished M.A. dissertation, University of Wales, 1981. *The Rambler*, 31 March 1750. Cf Robert Giddings, *The Tradition of Smollett* (Methuen, 1967), pp. 46ff.
8. See Louis James, *Fiction for the Working Man 1830–1850* (Oxford University Press, 1963), pp. 32ff.
9. See Robert Giddings (ed.), *The Changing World of Charles Dickens* (Vision Press, Barnes & Noble, 1983), pp. 10–16, and John Butt and Kathleen Tillotson, *Dickens at Work* (Methuen, 1970).
10. Louis James, *Print and the People 1819–1851* (Allen Lane, 1976), pp. 83–7.
11. Terry Eagleton, *Criticism and Ideology* (New Left Books, 1976), p. 104.
12. Marshall McLuhan, 'Movies: The Reel World' in *Understanding Media* (Routledge & Kegan Paul, 1964), p. 304.
13. Keith Reader, *The Cinema: A History* (Hodder & Stoughton, 1979), pp. 4–5.
14. See Peter Wollen, 'Cinema and Semiology: Some Points of Contact' in *Readings and Writings: Semiotics and Counter Strategies* (New Left Books, 1982), pp. 3–17.
15. McLuhan, op. cit., p. 305.
16. See Gerald Mast and Marshall Cohen, (eds.), *Film Theory and Criticism* (Oxford University Press, 1979), pp. 394ff.
17. Quoted from Siegfried Kracauer, 'Theory of Film: The Redemption of Physical Reality' (1960) in Mast and Cohen, op. cit., p. 7. Cf. J. Dudley Andrew, *The Major Film Theories* (Oxford University Press, 1976), pp. 106ff.
18. See especially 'Narrative Structures in Fleming' in Umberto Eco, *The Role of the Reader: Explorations in the Semiotics of Texts* (Hutchinson, 1981), pp. 144–72, and Terence Hawkes *Structuralism and Semiotics* (Methuen, 1977). A useful starting point might be the essay on the 'Structural Analysis of Narratives' by Roland Barthes, reprinted in *Barthes: Selected Writings*, edited by Susan Sontag (Fontana, 1980), pp. 251–95.
19. This is the basis of *montage* as evolved by Eisenstein. See Reader, op. cit., pp. 18–22, and *The Complete Films of Eisenstein*, translated by John Hetherington (Weidenfeld & Nicolson, 1974).
20. For an excellent brief analysis of Hitchcock's *The Thirty Nine Steps* (1935) see Donald Spoto, *The Art of Alfred Hitchcock* (W. H. Allen, 1977), pp. 37–43.
21. See John Russell Taylor, *Hitch: The Life and Work of Alfred Hitchcock* (Faber, 1978), pp. 256, and Spoto, op. cit., pp. 371–75, and Robert Giddings: 'Sound and Vision' in the *Listener*, 17 May 1984.
22. See Pauline Kael, *The Citizen Kane Book* (Boston: Little Brown, 1972), and

Ronald Gottesman (ed.), *Focus on 'Citizen Kane'* (Englewood Cliffs, New Jersey: Prentice Hall, 1971).

23. See James Monaco, *How to Read a Film* (Oxford University Press, 1981), pp. 140–91, and *The Moving Picture Book*, op. cit., pp. 46–74.
24. Significantly enough, neither Alistair MacLean nor Len Deighton merit a place in *The Oxford Companion to English Literature*.
25. Graham Greene, *The Pleasure Dome: The Collected Film Criticism 1935–1940*, edited by John Russell Taylor (Oxford University Press, 1980), p. 2.
26. *Stamboul Train* (1934); *This Gun for Hire* (1942); *The Ministry of Fear* (1943); *Confidential Agent* (1945); *The Man Within* (1946); *Brighton Rock* (1947); *The Fugitive* (1948); *Fallen Idol* (1948); *The Third Man* (1949); *The Heart of the Matter* (1953); *The End of the Affair* (1955); *The Quiet American* (1958); *Our Man in Havana* (1959); *The Comedians* (1967); *Travels with my Aunt* (1973).
27. Graham Greene, *The Pleasure Dome*, op. cit., p. 26.
28. Leslie Halliwell, *Film and Video Guide*, 5th edn. (Granada, 1985), p. 916.
29. John le Carré, *The Spy Who Came in from the Cold* (1963; Pan Books, 1987), p. 1.
30. Ibid., p. 1.
31. Ibid., p. 7.
32. Ibid., p. 12.
33. Ibid., p. 13.
34. Ibid., p. 35.
35. Ibid., p. 44.
36. Ibid., p. 67.
37. See pp. 74–91.
38. Ibid., p. 163.
39. Leslie Halliwell, *Halliwell's Filmgoer's Companion* (Granada, 1980), p. 159.
40. *The Spy Who Came in from the Cold*, op. cit., p. 217.

# Notes on Contributors

ALAN BOLD was born in 1943 in Edinburgh where he attended university and trained as a journalist. Since 1966 he has been a full-time writer and visual artist, and since 1975 he has lived in rural Fife writing books and contributing features regularly to the *Scotsman* and occasionally to the *New Statesman, T.L.S.* and *Glasgow Herald.* He has published many books of poetry including *To Find the New, The State of the Nation,* a selection in *Penguin Modern Poets 15* and *In this Corner: Selected Poems 1963–83.* With the artist John Bellany he has collaborated on *A Celtic Quintet, Haven* and *Homage to MacDiarmid.* He has edited many anthologies including *The Penguin Book of Socialist Verse, The Martial Muse, The Cambridge Book of English Verse 1939–75, Making Love, The Bawdy Beautiful, Mounts of Venus, Drink to Me Only, The Poetry of Motion.* He has also written critical books on *Thom Gunn and Ted Hughes, George Mackay Brown, The Ballad, Modern Scottish Literature, MacDiarmid: The Terrible Crystal* and *Muriel Spark.* He has exhibited his Illuminated Poems (pictures combining an original poetic manuscript with an illustrative composition) in venues as varied as Boston University and the National Library of Scotland.

MELVYN BRAGG was born in Wigton, Cumberland, in 1939. He was educated locally and at Oxford, where he read Modern History. Since then he has made his living as a novelist and broadcaster. His novels include: *For want of a Nail, The Second Inheritance, Without a City Wall, The Hired Man, A Place in England, The Nerve, Josh Lawton, The Silken Net, Autumn Manoeuvres, Kingdom Come,* and *Love and Glory.* He is also the author of *Speak for England,* an oral history of England since 1900 through the people of a Cumbrian town, and *Land of the Lakes,* a comprehensive survey of the Lake District, and *Laurence Olivier,* an essay. His latest book, *The Maid of Buttermere,* reached the bestseller list for a number of weeks. He is currently working on the biography of Richard Burton. In October 1984, *The Hired Man,* with lyrics and music by Howard Goodall, opened in the West End. Melvyn Bragg is also the Editor and Presenter of television Arts programmes. He began in the B.B.C. on *Monitor.* At present he is Head of the Arts Department at London Weekend Television where he edits and presents the *South Bank Show*—I.T.V.'s networked Arts programme. He writes a weekly column on the Arts in *Punch*. He is a Fellow of the Royal Society of Literature.

STEWART CREHAN Senior Lecturer in the Department of Literature and Languages, University of Zambia, was born in 1942. He graduated from Newcastle University in 1964 and took a Ph.D. at Edinburgh University in 1970. His publications include: *William Blake: Selected Poetry and Letters* (1976), *Blake in Context* (1984) and, with Charles Sarvan, *Readings in Poetry* (1984). He has published articles on eighteenth-century, nineteenth-century and modern African literature. He is currently writing a book on African fiction.

OWEN DUDLEY EDWARDS is Reader in Commonwealth and American History in the University of Edinburgh. He was born in Dublin in 1938, studied in the Johns Hopkins University and taught at the University of Oregon (1959–65), reached Scotland in 1966 and after two years teaching history at the University of Aberdeen came to Edinburgh. He is the author of *P. G. Wodehouse* (1976), *The Quest for Sherlock Holmes: A Biographical Study of Arthur Conan Doyle* (1982), and various other works including essays in the volumes in this series dealing with Scott, Fitzgerald and Matthew Arnold. He is also a broadcaster and journalist, is married with three children, is a Roman Catholic, and has never to his knowledge met or witnessed David John Moore Cornwell.

ROBERT GIDDINGS was born in Worcester in 1935 and educated at the universities of Bristol and Keele. He was Lecturer in English and Communication Studies at Bath Technical College 1964–82, Fulbright Exchange Professor, St. Louis, Missouri 1975–76, and Tutor, The Open University 1971–81. Since 1982 he has been Senior Lecturer in English and Media at the Dorest Institute of Higher Education. His publications include *The Tradition of Smollett* (1967), *You Should See Me in Pyjamas* (1981), *True Characters: Real People in Fiction*, with Alan Bold (1984), *Musical Quotes and Anecdotes* (1984) and several titles in the Critical Studies Series, including *The Changing World of Charles Dickens*, *Mark Twain: A Sumptuous Variety* and *J. R. R. Tolkien: This Far Land*. He has contributed to the *Sunday Times*, the *Guardian*, *Tribune*, *New Society*, *Music and Letters*, *New Statesman*, *Music and Musicians*, *British Bandsman* and the *Listener*, as well as to the Critical Studies volumes on Smollett, Johnson, Scott and Auden.

## Notes on Contributors

VIVIAN GREEN has been fellow and tutor of Lincoln College, Oxford, since 1951, and Rector of the college since 1982. He is the author of some sixteen books mainly historical in character and including *The Young Mr. Wesley* (1961), *Martin Luther and the German Reformation* (1964), *Religion at Oxford and Cambridge, c. 1160–1960* (1964); his most recent work is *Love in a Cool Climate: The Letters of Meta Bradley and Mark Pattison 1879–84*. He has been identified as one of the ingredients in the character of le Carré's George Smiley. Interviewed on the subject of Smiley, le Carré mentioned 'my mentor at Oxford' (Green, as senior tutor, admitted le Carré to Lincoln College when he went to read Modern Languages at Oxford) and in a letter of 24 January 1983 named the Revd. Dr. V. H. H. Green: 'It was Green's quiet, and shrewdness, which I liked.' When not resident at Oxford, Dr. Green lives at Burford in the Cotswolds.

GLENN W. MOST was born in 1952 in Miami, Florida. He studied at Harvard, Oxford, Yale, and Tübingen Universities, receiving a Ph.D. in Comparative Literature from Yale and a D.Phil. in Classics from Tübingen, both in 1980. He has taught Classics and Comparative Literature at the Universities of Yale, Heidelberg, Princeton, Siena, and Michigan; starting in September 1987 he is Full Professor of Classical Philology at the University of Innsbruck. He has published books and articles on Greek and Latin poetry, history of classical scholarship, Romanticism, ancient and modern philosophy, literary theory, and the detective novel.

PHILIP O'NEILL has tutored for the Open University and is now a lecturer in English at Crewe and Alsager College of Higher Education. He is the author of *Wilkie Collins: Women, Property and Propriety*.

MARGARET MOAN ROWE was born in Glasgow, Scotland, in 1941. She grew up in Philadelphia, Pennsylvania, where she received a B.A. from Holy Family College and M.A. and Ph.D. degrees from Temple University. She is an Associate Professor of English at Purdue University in Indiana and has published critical essays on Charlotte Brontë, W. H. Auden, L. P. Hartley, Virginia Woolf and Muriel Spark.

TREVOR ROYLE was born in Mysore, India, in 1945 and his childhood was spent in Malaya and Scotland. He was educated in St. Andrews and Aberdeen, and between 1971 and 1979 he was Literature Director of the Scottish Arts Council. A full-time writer, journalist and broadcaster, his previous books have ranged over football, military history and Scottish literature. His most recent publications are: *Death Before Dishonour: The True Story of Fighting Mac*; *James and Jim: A Biography of James Kennaway*; *The Macmillan Companion to Scottish Literature*; *The Kitchener Enigma*; and *The Best Years of their Lives*.

# Index

Ackerley, J. R., 28
Allenby, Lord, 92
Ambler, Eric, 63, 64
Arafat, Yassir, 131, 132
Atwood, Margaret, 69, 80

Balfour, A. J., 92
Barley, Tony, 104
Barrie, James, 65
Barthes, Roland, 115
Begin, M., 137, 142
Benjamin, Walter, 153–54
Bingham, John, 99
Birley, Robert, 38
Blackwood, John, 90
Blunt, Anthony, 11, 13, 100
Boswell, James, 51
Boyle, Andrew, 11
Buchan, John, 53, 63, 64, 92–5, 101, 158
Bunyan, John, 53
Burgess, Guy, 11, 12, 100

Campion, Susan, 28
Carr, John Dickson, 95
Carson, Sir Edward, 93
Cervantes, 42, 51, 194
Chandler, Raymond, 148, 155–57, 160, 166
Childers, Erskine, 63, 64, 91
Christie, Agatha, 57, 58, 115, 148, 160
Clair, Rene, 195
Cockburn, Claud, 99
Conrad, Joseph, 55, 63, 105, 107
Cornwell, Charlotte, 18, 130, 135–36
Cornwell, Ronnie, 12, 18, 26–39
Crowley, Aleister, 100

Dacre, Lord, see Trevor-Roper, Hugh
Deighton, Len, 200
Demosthenes, 42
Dickens, Charles, 20, 310, 193, 195–96
Doyle, Sir Arthur Conan, 41–53, 57, 148, 160
Driberg, Tom, 99
Du Maurier, Guy, 91

Eagleton, Terry, 194
Eisenstein, S., 196, 198
Eliot, George, 191
Eliot, T. S., 54
Euripedes, 95

Eustace, Jane, 15

Fielding, Henry, 192
Fitzgerald, F. Scott, 15
Fleming, Ian, 22, 63, 98, 99, 103, 156, 170, 202
Flower, Newman, 95
Forsyth, Frederick, 106
French, Sir John, 92

Genette, Gerard, 114
Gosse, Edmund, 27
Greene, Graham, 9, 52, 55, 61, 200–1
Grey, Sir Edward, 92
Griffith, D. W., 196
Grimmelshausen, H. J. C. von, 20, 34, 190
Guinness, Sir Alec, 200

Haig, Earl, 92, 93
Hall, Sir Reginald, 93
Halliwell, Leslie, 203, 207
Hammett, Dashiell, 148, 155, 160
Hay, Ian, 99
Hitchcock, Alfred, 198, 201
Hollis, Sir Roger, 13
Homberger, Eric, 67
Homer, 189

Iser, Wolfgang, 104, 110

James, Henry, 54, 55, 191, 193
Joyce, James, 16

Kennaway, James, 13–16, 18, 97–8
Kennaway, Susan, 14, 15, 97
Klauer, Wilhelm, 100
Knight, Maxwell, 13, 99–100
Knightley, Philip, 62
Koenig, Frederick, 192
Kracauer, Siegfried, 196

Leavis, F. R., 191, 208
le Carré, John, Works by: *Call for the Dead*, 10, 13, 38, 43–7, 54, 55, 69, 70–1, 74, 111, 160–61; *The Honourable Schoolboy*, 16, 27, 49, 52, 74, 75, 77–9, 110–14, 123–25, 159, 170; *The Little Drummer Girl*, 9, 10, 18, 19, 20, 22, 49, 58, 61, 63, 65, 79–81, 110, 129–43; *The Looking-Glass War*, 10, 16, 49, 60, 69, 70, 73, 89, 98, 159, 176, 180; *A Murder of Quality*, 9, 16, 22, 25, 58, 69, 70, 82,

215

# Index

161–62; *The Naïve and Sentimental Lover*, 9, 15–
16, 26, 41, 64–8, 137; *A Perfect Spy*, 18, 19, 22,
25–39, 49, 78, 81–4, 87–9, 98, 111; *A Small
Town in Germany*, 15, 20, 53, 69, 73–4, 106,
117–19, 121, 165–67; *Smiley's People*, 10, 16, 54,
56, 61, 74, 76, 101, 107, 108, 111–13, 119–22,
156, 159, 170, 184; *The Spy Who Came in From the
Cold*, 9, 10, 13, 17, 38, 41, 48, 49, 51, 58, 69,
71–3, 87, 88, 105–19, 115–17, 163–64, 202–8;
*Tinker Tailor Soldier Spy*, 10, 11, 16, 17, 21, 54,
74, 75, 107, 111, 114, 118, 119, 125, 134,
162–63, 169–87, 190
Leitch, David, 62
Le Queux, William, 91
Lewis, Peter, 48, 71, 72
Lyly, John, 189

Macauley, T. B., 42
Macdonald, Ross, 148, 155
Mackenzie, Sir Compton, 95–6, 101
Maclean, Donald, 11, 12, 100
McLuhan, Marshall, 194–95
Mann,Thomas, 20
Maugham, Somerset, 9, 63, 64, 95–101
Mauriac, Francois, 64
Merry, Bruce, 106, 111
Miller, Jonathan, 197
Monaghan, David, 55, 69, 73, 74, 81
Murray, Gilbert, 95
Murray, Keith, 32, 38

Nicholson, William, 192
Neuse, S. M., 120
Northcliffe, Lord, 92

Oakeshott, Sir Walter, 38
O'Flaherty, Liam, 201
Ong, Walter, 190
Oppenheim, E. P., 66, 91, 94
Orwell, George, 42

Page, Bruce, 62
Philby, Kim, 11, 13, 100

Plato, 42
Poe, Edgar Allan, 51, 146–48, 154

Reed, Carol, 204
Reisz, Karel, 14
Richardson, Samuel, 191, 192
Rohmer, Sax, 43
Rutherford, Andrew, 52, 64

Sandford, Folliot, 32
Sauerberg, Lars Ole, 72
Sayers, Dorothy L., 57
Sayce, Richard, 33
Schiller, J. C. F. von, 169
Scott, Sir Walter, 51
Sharp, Ann, 13, 15, 31, 61
Sillitoe, Sir Percy, 96
Slocock, Benjamin, 192
Smollett, Tobias, 192
Sontag, Susan, 188–89
Spark, Muriel, 74
Spillane, Mickey, 103
Stevenson, R. L., 51, 512
Stoppard, Tom, 10
Symons, Julian, 53

Tennyson, Alfred Lord, 56
Tey, Josephine, 62
Thatcher, Margaret, 10, 11
Todorov, Tzvetan, 106, 114
Trevor-Roper, Hugh, 62

Voinov, V., 103

Waugh, Evelyn, 99, 199, 200
Welles, Orson, 198
West, Nigel, 90
Wheatley, Denis, 99
Wilson, Edmund, 43
Wodehouse, P. G., 41–3, 56–62
Woolf, Virginia, 80
Wright, Peter, 11